# Sexual Fields

# Sexual Fields

*Toward a Sociology of
Collective Sexual Life*

EDITED BY ADAM ISAIAH GREEN

THE UNIVERSITY OF CHICAGO PRESS     CHICAGO AND LONDON

ADAM ISAIAH GREEN is associate professor of sociology at the University of Toronto.

The University of Chicago Press, Chicago 60637
The University of Chicago Press, Ltd., London
© 2014 by The University of Chicago
All rights reserved. Published 2014.
Printed in the United States of America
23 22 21 20 19 18 17 16 15 14      1 2 3 4 5

ISBN-13: 978-0-226-08485-5 (cloth)
ISBN-13: 978-0-226-08499-2 (paper)
ISBN-13: 978-0-226-08504-3 (e-book)
DOI: 10.7208/chicago/9780226085043.001.0001

Library of Congress Cataloging-in-publication Data

Sexual fields : toward a sociology of collective sexual life / edited by Adam Isaiah Green.
    pages    cm
    Includes bibliographical references and index.
    ISBN 978-0-226-08485-5 (hardcover : alkaline paper)—ISBN 978-0-226-08499-2
(paperback : alkaline paper)—ISBN 978-0-226-08504-3 (e-book)   1. Sex—Social
aspects.   2. Social structure.   3. Sex customs.   I. Green, Adam Isaiah, editor.
HQ16.S472 2014
306.7—dc23

2013025189

♾ This paper meets the requirements of ANSI/NISO z39.48-1992 (Permanence of Paper).

# Contents

Foreword by Omar Lizardo   vii      Preface by Verta Taylor   xiii
Acknowledgments   xvii

INTRODUCTION    Toward a Sociology of Collective Sexual Life   1
                *Adam Isaiah Green*

CHAPTER 1.    The Sexual Fields Framework   25
              *Adam Isaiah Green*

CHAPTER 2.    Sexual Field, Erotic Habitus, and Embodiment at
              a Transgender Bar   57
              *Martin S. Weinberg and Colin J. Williams*

CHAPTER 3.    Sexual Field Theory: Some Theoretical Questions
              and Empirical Complications   71
              *Peter Hennen*

CHAPTER 4.    Rejecting the Specifically Sexual: Locating the Sexual
              Field in the Work of Pierre Bourdieu   101
              *Matt George*

CHAPTER 5.    Circuits and the Social Organization of Sexual Fields   123
              *Barry D. Adam and Adam Isaiah Green*

CHAPTER 6.    Sexless in Shanghai: Gendered Mobility Strategies in a
              Transnational Sexual Field   143
              *James Farrer and Sonja Dale*

CHAPTER 7.    The Crucial Place of Sexual Judgment for Field Theoretic
              Inquiries   171
              *John Levi Martin*

References   189      Author Index   203      Subject Index   207

# Foreword

The book that you hold in your hands is presumably about sex and sexuality. However, to read this book as one that is exclusively about sex, narrowly conceived as a subject matter of social scientific investigation, would be a grave mistake. For in many ways this book is about sexuality only insofar as the social organization of sexual desire provides a strategic microcosm within which to address some of the most fundamental questions in social theory. In the parlance of "ethnomethodology," in what follows sexuality and sexual desire are not only a *topic for* analysis but also a *resource through which* the various contributors attempt to address (and maybe provide a resolution to) some of the central problems in the theory of action today. Therefore, yes, this *is* a book about the "social organization of sexual fields" precisely because the social organization of sexual fields allows us to begin to conceptualize in the most fruitful way possible the organization of action and motivation across all fields of action. This statement acquires more significance when we remind ourselves that if we are to develop a coherent approach to the explanation of social action, that approach must perforce take the form of a *field theory* (Martin 2011). If social theory is to make progress in explaining why persons are *motivated* to do what they do, then we must come to terms with *desire*. Sexual fields are the sites where we can find the nonrandom organization of desire.

There are some eerie parallels between theoretical developments in sexuality studies and the theory of action since the 1970s. The key challenge has always been to provide a coherent explanation to what is an obdurate observation: sexual desire and even sexual "behavior" are patterned and regular; the issue is to attempt to account for the origins of this regularity. We may call this *the problem of sexual order* (or, maybe even more accurately, the *sexual* problem of order). Social learning models attempted to shed light on the problem of sexual order by proposing the (fantastic) hypothesis that this order could be explained by building this model *into* the actor. Via a massive learning process, actors could be molded into desiring subjects; sexual styles and modes of self-presentation acquire regularity via processes of identification with and imitation of available, culturally sanctioned role models. This approach domesticates desire by making it a pliable product of institutionalized cultural scripts. This contrasts with the decided nondomestication of desire in the body of scholarship that came to be known as *queer theory* (Green 2007). Here, rather than being a product of social conditioning, desire (especially non-heteronormative desire) is that which destabilizes any attempt to create order via the imposition of a set of authoritative discourses. Yet, precisely because of the fact that desire is recovered as a subversive, destabilizing force, we lose the capacity to properly theorize it (because it becomes a veritable deus ex machina). If in standard approaches in the sociology and psychology of sexuality desire is *caused* by some sort of social process, the deconstructive penchant of queer theory questions the very capacity to engage in this sort of explanation in the first place, without reifying the very same categories that are supposedly doing the explanation.

At the level of epistemological challenges in the explanation of social action, this impasse feels a lot like déjà vu. In fact, it seems to recapitulate a rather familiar story. This is the story of how, after more than a hundred years of trying to produce "scientific" accounts of human action, social scientists have instead left in their wake accounts that, when they sound scientific, fail miserably at explaining anybody's action (and fail in equal fashion at convincing any real person that that's an account of their own or *anyone's* action) and, when they actually succeed in explaining action, do not end up sounding very scientific (they essentially reproduce the very explanations that people give for why they do the things that they do). While this story seems unrelated to the contents of the book that you are about to read, it is actually a prelude to my main point—namely, that a field theory is our best bet at developing an account of action that actually *explains* why people do the things they do (or why they want the things they want, which in some cases—the successful ones—amounts to the same thing) in a way that does not ultimately amount to a paraphrase of their own explanations with long

Latinate words and that is actually recognizable as an account of some-body's action for everybody, expert or layperson alike.

The contours of the problem are now well known, but solutions continue to be elusive. In their attempt to explain why people (or "the folk," as distinct from expert scientists) do the things that they do, social scientists rely on a fairly well-established model of how beliefs and wants combine to produce action. It has long been noted—sometimes with glee, at other times with embarrassment and chagrin—that there is nothing particularly special (or even scientific) about this particular account of action, for it happens to be indistinguishable from that which the folk (whose action the social scientist is putatively trying to make sense of) use to account for their *own* and *each other's* actions (Heritage 1984). The recipe goes like this: if you want to explain why people do what they do, all you have to do is link what people *want* to what they *believe* in order to derive some sort of plausible story (e.g., one that preserves the "rationality" of the actions that "follow") for why persons *do* one thing and *not* the other in some sort of setting or situation (generic or specific) (Parsons 1937).

In this respect, the fundamental model of the explanation of action that continues to dominate the social sciences is, as our colleagues in the philosophy of mind and the philosophy of action would be quick to point out, a form of "belief-*desire* psychology." Here, the desires provide the motivation or the "force" that *impels* actors to act, and the "norms" provide the grooves that canalize that action and make it regular and predictable. It is a rather unremarked fact in the philosophy of action that *desire* stands at the center of any coherent attempt to explain social action, but so little has been done to theorize the nature and provenance of this desire.

Just as in philosophy, there have been various (failed) attempts in the social and human sciences to wiggle out of the strictures of belief-desire talk. The desire (pun intended) on the part of social scientists and philosophers to find an explanatory vocabulary of action that is *not* shared by the folk is actually perfectly understandable, for, if the language that we (as social scientists) use to explain action is the same as that used by the very people whose action we want to explain when they account for their own activity, then it seems like the job of the social scientist (as an expert endowed with some sort of specific explanatory authority) in this whole thing is quite superfluous. In fact, taking this insight to its ultimate conclusion leads to a dissolution of (or the imposition of a symmetry between) the social scientist/folk distinction so that social science discourse merges into folk discourse as just another, not more scientific and certainly not more authoritative, way of making sense of one another's actions. Note that this "ethnomethodological" (or "populist") diagnosis of traditional action theory functions as a "deconstruction" of the very explanatory project of establishment sociology.

In between the epistemological bumbling of those who think that action is an effect of (sociological?) causes and the enlightened deconstructionism of those who revel in controverting the experts and joining the folk as just another producer of accounts about action without claiming any special epistemological or authoritative validity, there lies field theory. Like the standard explanatory model, field theory keeps all the folk vocabulary around, including talk of beliefs and desires, norms and valuations. Unlike the folk, however, who can do very well in accounting for their action by pointing to the unproblematic (taken-for-granted) qualities of those beliefs and wants, a field theory is not content with remaining at the level of phenomenology. Instead, acknowledging the unquestionably local validity of the "felt" qualities of both objects and situations as sufficient for the "motivation" of action, a field theory attempts to disaggregate qualitative judgments predicated on objects as "glosses" that point to the bundle of *relations* within a "space" of position takings. This space is never exhausted by the local phenomenology of any one actor; instead, all actors experience the qualitative impact of objects *from* their position without making this judgment necessarily invalid (each judgment is perspectival, but the global organization of perspectives can be reconstructed by the analyst).

A field emerges when the qualities imputed to a given set of objects by the relevant set of actors align themselves nonrandomly along some intuitively graspable dimension of valuation and evaluation. These qualities thus come to be dually constituted by the bundle of relations that specify the positions that each actor occupies in that arena. Fields unite the relevant qualities, which are retrieved from *objects*, by *actors*, endowed with the relevant *capacities*, who, because of their sensitivity to these qualities, come to be organized in a *positional space*. The act of quality retrieval and perception ("that's ugly"; "that's sexy") is a *judgment*.

As shown in the various contributions that follow, qualities specify the relation that an actor, endowed with a set of a capacities built via a specific history of acquisition, has in relation to a given object the qualities of which she is sensitive to; in retrieving a quality *the actor directly perceives her relation to the object.* Through this mechanism, actors, qualities, objects, and judgments come to be mutually specified: thus, the positions of the various actors are specified by their distribution of judgments across the relevant objects; the position of the objects in the field is specified in the same way (an object's position is given by the distribution of judgments across the actors). Fields can develop across a very diverse set of judgments all tied to some sort of defining quality. Here, the desire for the object is endogenously organized via routine experience in the field, experience that results in the honing and refining of an "erotic habitus" (Green 2008a). No longer do we need to presuppose that desire is some amorphous energy waiting for exogenous cultural scripts to give it organization. In fields, desire is endogenously organized, and action is immanently ordered.

A field theory is thus *primarily* a theory of *desire*—what people want. In that respect, it reverses the perennial concern (in action theory) with beliefs and the relegation of wants to some sort of exogenous process. Because fields are essentially constituted by the nonrandom organization of desire and the desires are directed at persons who are *simultaneously objects of desire and desirers of other persons/objects*, sexual fields are (to borrow a phrase from the French literary theorist Roland Barthes) *the field degree zero* and, thus, the privileged case from which to empirically investigate how action is ordered within fields.

This is important because a lot of the empirical development of field theory has been done in settings in which desire for objects (paintings, books, scientific articles) or products mediates between actors. In sexual fields, no such external objects are required to mediate between persons. Sexual fields represent the limiting case in which persons encounter one another in their dual role as both contributors to the organization of the field via their own classifying judgments and objects of classification open and vulnerable to the judgments of desire and quality of the other players. Sexual fields thus induce a purely endogenous dual ordering of persons and objects in which the persons (and those persons' qualities) are the objects. Objects are arranged in an order according to the rank of the persons who choose them, and persons are arranged in an order according to the rank of the objects that they choose. Sexual fields are unlike other fields in that we encounter persons on both sides of the ledger.

In this respect, it is important to not underestimate one important feature of sexual fields: the fact that their foundation in *desire* is impossible to ignore. All fields are, of course, founded in desire; insofar as to desire an object is to *recognize* in that object the qualities that allow us to enter into an appropriate relation with it (and by implication with other persons who also align their desire toward the object in similar or opposed ways), this cannot be any other way. However, in most other fields, these fundamentally erotic foundations of "social integration" are euphemized away, even "sublimated," so what was initially desire is "misrecognized" as something else. In sexual fields, desire is out in the open for all to see, as is the "negative" of desire: rejection. It is precisely because the pattern of acceptances and refusals is so apparent and the ordering of actors within these sets of relations so stark that sexual fields reveal the fundamental dynamics of fields in such a strategic way.

It is no wonder that, when trying to characterize that which energizes actors to engage in action within a field by competing for that "which is at stake," Bourdieu resorts to the Freudian term *libido* (1997b, 167). The contributions that follow show how, in mutually constituting one another as both subjects and objects of desire, field actors effectively *invest themselves* (and their bodies) in "games" of mutual cognition and recognition from which the deepest foundations of social order are revealed in seemingly mundane acts of erotic judgment.

*Omar Lizardo*
*University of Notre Dame, 2012*

# Preface

Verta Taylor, University of California, Santa Barbara

This book illuminates the concept of sexual fields, one of the most important developments in contemporary sexual theory. Until recently, sociologists viewed sexuality as part of a natural order in which biological sex, gender, and sexuality are closely linked and relatively immutable. *Sexual Fields: Toward a Sociology of Collective Sexual Life* moves the study of sexualities to the mainstream of sociological analysis by proposing a distinctively social framework for understanding the various types of collective erotic life—singles' bars, gay male leather communities, heterosexual dating Web sites, gay bathhouses, women's coffeehouses, sex/circuit parties, erotic chat rooms, drag bars, S/M clubs, swingers' resorts, trans bars, college hookup cultures, et cetera—that cater to a plurality of desires, practices, and bodies found throughout Western societies. Drawing on Bourdieu's theory of practice and his concept of the *sexual field*, Adam Isaiah Green and the contributors to this volume illuminate the power of the sexual fields approach to shed light on the social organization of erotic life in the variety of specialized sexual subcultures that have developed in modern societies. The concept of sexual fields refers to the institutionalized matrix of erotic relations and preferences within particular social spaces that links social structure to individuals' sexual desires, practices, and identities. It is a pathbreaking approach that allows us to understand the social structure of the multiple and distinct erotic worlds that constitute the complex sociosexual landscape of a given neighborhood or community and, thus, understand how individuals' erotic choices and sexual scripts are structured by social factors, including race, class, gender, age, ability, and ethnicity, as well as how different kinds of sexual fields are connected to the political, social, cultural, and commercial conditions of neighborhoods and communities.

In the past three decades, sociologists have proposed various frameworks for analyzing sexuality. Social constructionism, which dominated the study of sexuality in the 1980s, represented the first theoretical attempt to denaturalize sexuality by calling attention to the social basis of sexual desire and identity. Because the social constructionist tradition grew out of social problems theory, early research on sexual subcultures in sociology concentrated on the study of "deviant" sexualities, such as prostitution, pornography, and especially homosexuality. The essays in this collection represent the work of a new generation of scholars who understand that sexual life is not monolithic; rather, it resides in semiautonomous erotic worlds or "specialized sexual milieus" with distinctive preference structures, sexual and otherwise, that shape individuals' choice of partners, sexual practices, sexual scenes, and even sexual identities. Whereas research in the social constructionist tradition treated sex and sexuality as properties of individuals, the sexual fields approach emphasizes the "social" or collective aspects of sexual desires, practices, and identities, accentuating the relationship between sexuality, social structure, culture, and politics.

If social constructionism failed to address the structural and institutional basis of sexuality, it took queer theory, which originated in the humanities, for scholars to recognize the significance of the heterosexual/ homosexual binary as the structural foundation of a modern regime of sexuality that regulates and disciplines individual identities by excluding and devaluing other ways to frame the self, the body, and sexual desire. In the 1990s, queer theory burst on the scene to challenge essentialist constructions of sexuality and gender and to interrogate how sexual subjectivity is constructed and regulated through discursive practices and gender and sexual performances that reinforce heteronormativity. Heteronormativity, according to Schilt and Westbrook (2009, 441), is "the suite of cultural, legal, and institutional practices that maintain normative assumptions that there are two and only two genders, that gender reflects biological sex, and that only sexual attraction between these 'opposite' genders is natural or acceptable." Queer theory advanced the study of sexuality by introducing the idea of a "sexual system"—or a matrix of sexual meanings, discourses, and practices embedded in social institutions—that had been absent in social constructionist perspectives on sexuality. The hallmark of queer theory has been its emphasis on the identity performances and narratives people use to resist, challenge, and subvert the regimes of normality that bear on the sexual and gender status quo. But, because of its origins in the humanities and literary studies, queer theory has been biased toward cultural analyses, ignoring sociology's tradition of social structural and institutional analysis that foregrounds the role of institutions and socialization in shaping the sexual.

The sexual fields approach represents a tremendous advance in the sociology of sexuality by viewing sexual subcultures in their own terms, rather than through the lens of deviance, as was the case with social constructionism. The study of sexual fields embraces the agenda of queer theorists by turning its gaze on and making visible *the queer*, which, by definition, is whatever is at odds with the normal, the legitimate, the dominant (Halperin 1997, 62). The sexual fields framework also provides a theoretical bridge that connects the social structure of a sexual field to individuals' sexual scripts, the sexual script being, heretofore, the primary conceptual lens used by social constructionism for understanding the imprint of the social on sexual desires, behaviors, and identities. This is a book that every scholar of sexuality should own. The sexual fields approach likely will set the research agenda for the sociological study of sexuality over the next several decades. The contributors to *Sexual Fields* are creating a new and distinctively sociological theory of sexuality, and this book represents the state of the art as far as the sexual fields approach is concerned.

# Acknowledgments

The completion of this book is a milestone in a long journey across two countries and multiple institutions of higher education. Its ideas emerged in the presence of a few very special mentors, a few very special friends, a few terrific colleagues and students, a few doubters, and one very important convert.

Of course I have to start at my roots: My dad is a man of tremendous generosity and heart and made the journey imaginable and believable. My mom passed to me the gift of writing and issued the call to develop a voice. Viola gave me unconditional love. And Nick, "the pup," kept me glued together after I had shattered into a thousand pieces of despair.

At college I was first found by Margaret Hofeller, a social psychologist who taught me about attribution processes, probability curves, and the possibility of a career in the social sciences. Warren Mintz brought the human experience to sociology. And, when a few years after graduation I showed up lost at the office door of Linda Longmire, I was welcomed back into the academy with open arms, good humor, and an abundance of opportunities to make something of my life. Thank you, Linda.

In graduate school I had the good fortune to receive the meticulous and steadfast mentorship of David Greenberg. By dint of their genius, Jeff Goodwin and Robert Max Jackson dazzled and inspired. Kathleen Gerson was a first-rate mentor, a brilliant big-picture thinker, and now a dear friend.

I owe every success following graduate school to Brian Powell, who plucked me out of NYU, supervised my work as a postdoctoral fellow at Indiana University, and offered unwavering good spirits and an occasional, much-deserved slap on the snout. "B," as I call him, is nothing short of an angel in my life. Jane McLeod generously delivered me to medical sociology, patiently read my stuff with razor-sharp analytic acumen and blunt, no-bullshit assessments, and helped me become a better thinker than I was when I had entered the program. Finally, Tim Hallett was the earliest supporter of bringing Bourdieu to sexual life, and I am especially thankful to have fortuitously crossed paths with him at this vulnerable time in my intellectual development.

I have been blessed with a few very dear friends. Doron, my "fairy godmother," has spent nearly two decades now protecting me from the world and perhaps most from myself. My roommate and friend Norm—an acquired taste—has been an unexpected source of gravity and peace of mind. Liena Gurevich's smart comments on my job talk were pivotal in my hiring at the University of Toronto, and I am always grateful for her companionship. Jormah has been an emotional rock and an extraordinary champion of mine.

The book itself is a product of the intelligence and creative energy of a handful of scholars who took a chance to think outside the box. John, Matt, James and Sonja, Marty and Colin, Peter and Barry, I am eternally indebted. Thank you!

I must also thank Brigid Burke and Rachael Carson, talented graduate students, both of whom took great care in the preparation of the manuscript.

To Doug, well, what can I say? Thank you for listening and, eventually, believing! No one loves your rhetorical efflorescence more than I.

Finally, I have to thank Karrie Ann Snyder, who first came into my life at the start of graduate school in a flower dress, a fluffy perm, and an odd rambling bit about car noises and finger dances. Karrie held my hand through a three-semester statistics sequence and showed me how to turn a fraction into a percentage on a calculator. No one on the planet knows me so deeply or has witnessed so patiently the vicissitudes of my life. I literally don't know who I'd be without her.

# Toward a Sociology of Collective Sexual Life

Adam Isaiah Green, University of Toronto

As a doctoral student in New York City, I read social theory and searched for a life partner at the same time, which meant, in practical terms, that my intimate life became an object of study. As well, I bartended and worked as a bouncer at gay bars and nightclubs to cover the exorbitant rent of my Manhattan studio, my jobs affording me first-hand observations of sexual social life even when I was not myself an active participant. Hence I was both a "player" in and an observer of "the game" throughout my graduate career, until a move to the Midwest for a postdoctoral fellowship. And there, in a small, quiet office at Indiana University, far removed from the *Sturm und Drang* of sex and New York City, I had time to reflect on my experiences with a new set of eyes. Indeed, there was no question that I had been embedded in a very particular youth-oriented, middle-class, white-dominated, urban gay milieu while living in Manhattan, variations of which had been described in outstanding accounts such as Martin Levine's *Gay Macho* (1998), Francis Fitzgerald's "The Castro" (Fitzgerald 1986, 25–120), and Martin Weinberg and Colin William's "Gay Baths and the Social Organization of Impersonal Sex" (1975a), to name only a few. But, as insightful and provocative as they were, these accounts produced less a general framework for thinking about contemporary sexual social life than an account of the institutions and practices of a particular class of urban, gay male erotic worlds in the 1970s and 1980s. And, perhaps precisely because the fieldwork of these ethnographies was of such high quality, the data tended to exceed their explanatory frameworks, generating more questions than they answered. In fact, this literature had brilliantly captured forms of sexual stratification whereby the struggle for partnership and social esteem was highly explicit and institutionalized in the very fabric of social life. Yet, because this generation of research was the first of its kind to investigate gay sexual community from outside the framework of deviance and social control (Seidman 1996), it typically approached its subject with a kind of anthropological curiosity that led to two unintended but related effects. First, while the erotic worlds of large urban gay centers such as those in San Francisco and New York City were no longer cast in the terms of degeneracy, they nevertheless maintained a degree of exoticism relative to collective sexual life elsewhere. Second, the phenomenon of sexual stratification was descriptively rich in its narration but restricted in terms of its conceptual elaboration, short-circuiting a consideration of how sexual status orders work more generally. Consequently, analysis rarely moved beyond the sociogeographic borders of the locations in which the fieldwork was conducted, and little developed by way of extrapolation from these particular cases of life in the gay ghetto to the structure of erotic worlds more generally. In short, while my experiences in Chelsea were probably not particularly unique, to my mind they posed lines of inquiry that the extant literature had yet to sufficiently address.

This brought me to the work of Pierre Bourdieu. For, when I walked from Chelsea to the West Village and bartended in these distinct locales, I had the strong impression of crossing from one "field" to another, each field characterized by distinct sets of actors, internal logics, institutionalized modes of interaction and self-management, and positions in social space that conferred advantage on some and disadvantage on others. For instance, in Chelsea, land of the "Chelsea boy," I was just one of many white, gay-identified, middle-class, twenty-something men of that era. In this neighborhood, I developed a deep, intuitive sense of the game, including knowledge of the logic of sexual status and my own position within that system of sexual stratification. There, the men wore short haircuts, baseball hats, strategically tight T-shirts with random team emblems, two- and three-day-old stubble on their artificially tanned faces, tribal tattoos, and an armor of beefy muscles from their abdomens to their collar bones. Congregating in groups on the street, the Chelsea boys appeared relaxed and sociable even as they vigilantly monitored the pedestrian traffic. Surveying the men around them, both on the streets and in a network of bars and clubs, they were careful to retain their cool, no matter how attractive the men in their sights, so as never to appear too eager and thereby relinquish field position. In these settings, I grew keenly, often painfully aware of my body and its bearing, the fit of my clothing, the affect of my gait, the pump (or lack thereof) of my muscles, the expression on my face. Indeed, in the context of the dominant structure of desire within gay Chelsea, I knew precisely what Henning Bech (1997) aptly called *the gay gaze*. This probing, scrutinizing gaze was trained on a highly eroticized set of physical and affective characteristics and, like the effects of panoptic surveillance (Foucault 1975), came to impose itself from within my mind as a measure of my social worth. Put differently, when I entered Chelsea, I traversed a range of local physical *sites* that were populated by a more or less steady flux of gay men whose collective erotic dispositions, projected into social space, established a palpable system of sexual stratification that amplified and institutionalized their individual desires to constitute the parameters of a *sexual* field.

Walking south, below Fourteenth Street, I entered the West Village, and the change from one sexual field to another was abrupt and palpable, as if I had crossed into an entirely new geography. The similarities between the two spaces ended at a strong gay presence. The faces were less often white, the bodies less uniformly gym trained, the affect less controlled and more colorful, the clothing more varied, and the men typically older than I by at least a decade, often two. There, the glances men gave one another were less cautious, heavier, and more persistent, and it was not uncommon to be approached directly on one corner or another for sex or catcalled on Christopher Street and Seventh Avenue. Because I was less intimately aware of and connected to the gay structure of desire in the Village, I was in somewhat foreign terrain and experienced a sense of otherness that was at once strange and psychically lighter than my experience of Chelsea. Here, I could walk down the street without having the kind of epic, inner consideration that arose in Chelsea, as I was traversing a sexual status order of which I was less intuitively aware and in which I had little to lose. In short, Chelsea and the Village housed distinct sexual sites mapped onto the territories of distinct Manhattan neighborhoods, but they were also distinct social arenas in the Bourdieusian sense, each with their own particular internally generated logics of status and practice.

At the same time as I was immersed in graduate school and roaming the streets of New York City, I watched as my own mother and father reentered the dating market as middle-aged divorcees. Over the course of a decade, and for many years after, I observed the trials and tribulations that came with their pursuits of intimate partnership, and I grew keenly aware of the marked differences in their experiences, which I believe came less as a function of their personality differences than from the fact of their different genders. Whereas my father had few problems meeting and dating women while his weight fluctuated and his youthful appearance waned, my mother encountered much less forgiving conditions wherein her age and the appearance of her face, hair, and body were directly correlated with the interest of men, both in real time and online, where she had set up a personals profile. And, whereas my father, a successful middle-class entrepreneur, had an abundant supply of available women to date, including women decades younger than he was, my mother—an accomplished, attractive, financially independent academic—faced a much more restricted dating pool, one composed mostly of men a decade or more older than she. While the structure of this age-graded system of stratification would have had little consequence in her twenties and thirties, in her fifties and sixties she paid a heavy age penalty.

Taken together, these biographical features of my life and those of my parents led me to consider the diverse structural conditions each of us faced on account of our sexual orientation, age, and gender differences. And so in Bloomington, Indiana, I took stock of all these data and began to conceive of sexual social life in terms of structures and processes that were shaped by but far exceeded the concept of subculture. Indeed, we were all immersed in the struggles of a kind of Bourdieusian field that located each of us in social space, shaping possibilities for partnership and, ultimately, our respective life paths.

Nevertheless, as I sought to make sense of sexual social life in these terms, I found that the Bourdieusian approach to routine practice was a promising but incomplete analytic for capturing sexual stratification and the sexual field. For the sexual field is a different breed of field from the political field, the economic field, or the field of cultural production, in part because the traditional field resources of cultural, economic, and social capital are not necessarily the most significant sources of power, but also, and even more importantly, because sexual fields lack formal structures that confer symbolic power through credentialing and review, such as those found in political fields or fields of elite cultural production. In fact, for a sexual field to both coordinate and socialize desires and practices, to serve both as a "field of force" that organizes taste and as a "field of struggle" within which actors vie for dominance (Martin 2003), one needed to look to Bourdieu and then beyond him. Thence the birth of the *sexual fields framework* (Green 2008a, 2008c, 2011) and the inspiration for this volume.

But, before turning to a discussion of the content of the present volume, I first consider the broader historical context in which a sexual fields analysis becomes necessary and, arguably, conceivable. Toward this end, I offer a brief orienting discussion that contextualizes the object of study in this volume and specifies the conditions under which it emerged.

## Collective Sexual Life in the Late Modern Period

Today, just outside the bedroom of the monogamous couple, there lies a terrain of erotic worlds, each one organized by the pursuit of intimate partnership and sexual pleasure yet with its own particular institutional and subcultural character. Such erotic worlds constitute what we may think of as *collective sexual life* insofar as they bring together individuals in search of partnership, from sex on premise to a prospective marital partner. Anchored to friendship and family networks, bars, coffeeshops, nightclubs, college dorms, fitness centers, speed-dating events, bathhouses, swingers' resorts, private parties, and the online worlds of cyberspace among still others, collective sexual life takes shape in physical and virtual sites that organize the otherwise diffuse sexual desires of the population at large in specialized arenas of interaction and meaning making. For instance, compare the sociosexual specificity of the heterosexual, white, middle- and upper-middle-class twenty and thirty somethings of Manhattan's Upper West Side, where Jewish men and women meet one another in coffeeshops, local restaurants, and a Jewish speed-dating group, to the raunchy gay leather scene of San Francisco's Tenderloin district or the small, relatively hidden social life of the lesbian community in Salt Lake City, the hedonistic swingers' resorts of Jamaica and Mexico, the swanky, art deco hotel bars of Miami's South Beach, the postfeminist women at the Grove, Fire Island, who summer on its shores to meet other like-minded women, the late-twenty- to forty-something techies of San Francisco's Silicon Valley who venture downtown in between software programming and market analysis, the coed keg parties at large state universities in the South and the Midwest, the edgy, largely black hip-hop nightclubs of Atlanta, or the now ubiquitous Internet chat rooms and dating sites linked to nearly every major city in the Western world. These distinct arenas constitute highly specific kinds of collective sexual life that bring together members of a given sociodemographic within particular "scenes" that articulate a given aesthetic code and a "style of life . . . spirit . . . meaning . . . mood" (Silver, in press).

These obvious examples aside, it is crucial to underscore the point that sexual fields are not limited to bars, nightclubs, or vacation resorts, though indeed these are particularly amenable to a sexual field analysis since much of the action is explicit, publicly accessible, and, as John Levi Martin notes in chapter 7 of this volume, realized in the simple terms of one individual's movement toward or away from another. Nevertheless, sexual fields arise just as readily in the form of dating networks among friends and coworkers because these operate with a semblance of positionality whereby any given player's value as a prospective date is relative to other players within the bounded context of a social space. Here, sexual fields affect actors because individuals will imagine their own value and the value of their prospective partners relative to the sexual status of others within the social networks in which they circulate. Moreover, as Barry Adam and I discuss in chapter 5 of this volume, such networks need not be those characterized by traditional ties of dependence, such as those obtaining between family, friends, and coworkers, but may take much looser forms of association, such as that found in a *circuit* whereby actors merely rub elbows together in shared spaces of sociality. In fact, some of the more powerful effects of a sexual field occur less from the real-time action of sexual sociality than from the social psychological work of positioning oneself within a field's tiers of desirability—an issue I explore in greater detail in chapter 1 of this volume. In short, once an individual actor enters the domain of sexual social life, she enters the gravitational pull of a sexual field in which her location in social space, including her social esteem and significance, her sense of self, and opportunities to engage with desirable others, is conditioned therein.

While such semiautonomous erotic worlds are not the invention of our era, they are surely uniquely organized by the conditions of the modern West. For, as many scholars have observed, in the last two centuries, broad structural shifts related to the growth of capitalist markets, urbanization, and the changing socioeconomic status of women have co-incided with technological and cultural developments—including the advent of the birth control pill, the popularity of the Internet, the waning influence of religion, and the rise of sex-positive norms—to produce a domain of sexual life ever more free from traditional institutions of control, such as the family and the church (Adam 1985; D'Emilio 1983; Giddens 1992; Halperin 1989; Padgug 1989). Yet such freedom can be overstated, not the least because the sexual domain is itself organized by status hierarchies that stratify actors, enabling and constraining the kinds of partnerships one may obtain.

For all these reasons, when studying sexual life outside the context of the monogamous dyad, scholars have begun to think of sexual sociality as a *kind* of social life in its own right, with its own particular social organization, status hierarchy, and regulative principles (Farrer 2010a; Green 2008a, 2008b, 2011; Laumann, Ellingston, Mahay, Palk, and Youm 2004; Martin and George 2006; Weinberg and Williams 2009). Put differently, the analytic focus in this body of work has shifted from the substance of any particular desiring subject or sexual community to a consideration of the broader social architecture of collective sexual life.

Without question, some of the most developed erotic worlds have emerged in gay male enclaves in Western cities over the past century (Fitzgerald 1986; Hennen 2008; Herdt and Boxer 1992; Levine 1979). Nevertheless, even a cursory glance at the sexual landscape makes clear that erotic worlds are hardly the terrain of male homosexuals alone. For instance, following World War I, a precocious milieu of unmarried, sexually active adolescents materialized in locales throughout North America, prompting a robust virginity pledge movement in the United States and decades of public and government concern over the prevalence of adolescent pregnancy and sexually transmitted infections. And, in a related vein, owing in part to the sexual revolution of the 1960s, heterosexual college students have forged a no-holds-barred "party scene" (Armstrong, Hamilton, and Sweeney 2006; Sanday 1990) wherein "hooking up" (Kalish and Kimmel 2011) is a commonplace, normative practice carrying little expectation of enduring commitment. In fact, to the extent that today's college students can expect to forestall marriage until their late twenties and beyond, this form of impersonal sexual sociality may continue for many years after college and well past young adulthood (Kimmel 2008).

Once married, heterosexual adults may subscribe to norms of marital fidelity (Laumann, Gagnon, Michael, and Michaels 1994), maintaining monogamy or cheating, but some pursue alternative sexual arrangements in the context of swingers' clubs and resorts, private parties, and Internet Web sites designed exclusively for sexual exploration and partnership outside the dyadic marital unit (Gould 1998). Moreover, high divorce rates ensure that a significant proportion of middle-aged men and women will reenter collective sexual life in search of casual dating and new relationship partners. And longer life spans coupled with the popularity of erectile dysfunction drugs make sexual sociality relevant well beyond midlife and sometimes into old age (Lindau et al. 2007; Waite, Laumann, and Das 2009).

In cases of divorce or the death of a spouse, actors who return to sexual social life—be it in search of a long-term relationship or a short-term sexual encounter—will find themselves obliged to play the field once again, largely irrespective of the medium through which they seek partners. For instance, when searching for a long-term partner following a divorce, middle-aged heterosexual men and women are likely to rely on interpersonal and work-related networks rather than the singles' bar or nightclub. While some of the substance of what is considered desirable may change—for instance, economic and cultural capital may hold increased importance in partner selection—the fact of the unequal distribution of these capitals has the effect of producing yet again a system of stratification that advantages some actors while disadvantaging others. As well, though sexual attractiveness may be less important in midlife for determining partnership selection, sexual desirability still matters in the form of preference structures that typically disadvantage middle-aged women relative to their younger female counterparts. As Sontag (1979) notes, on account of "the double-standard of aging," middle-aged, middle-class women have more difficulty securing a new partner than do men of this demographic and are typically restricted to men close in age or older than themselves. Compared to men over forty, women over forty are both less likely to remarry following a divorce and, when they do remarry, are more likely to marry older mates (England and McClintock 2009). In fact, research demonstrates that, in every age category from thirty-five years on, women are more likely to be single than are their same-age male counterparts. Moreover, by the time men reach their sixties, they tend to marry down nine to twelve years in age (England and McClintock 2009). In this sense, my own parents' experiences with dating

in midlife were not just artifacts of their personal, idiosyncratic dispositions but, rather, emblematic of broader patterns of sexual stratification.

Collective sexual life is consequential for those who actively participate in it but also for those who do not. That is, even when one is "out of
the game," as when one is monogamously coupled, sexual fields remain
relevant. First, the notion that one is partnered and thereby "out of the
game" is itself a testament to the historical centrality of being "in the
game" and, perhaps, the loss one may feel by conceiving oneself as situated on the sidelines. Second, though one may not be an active player
within a sexual field, social life is rarely sequestered entirely from sexual life. As a quick example, the heterosexual husband who hangs out
with friends on guys' night at a local bar will, whether he likes it or not,
be situated within a domain of social relations likely populated by both
men and women. Should he find himself desirable (or undesirable!) to
the women he encounters, the field will affect his perception of self and
his perception of possibilities beyond the marital dyad, perhaps precipi-
tating a reevaluation of the quality of his own marriage. In sum, the potential effects of sexual social life on nonactive field players must not be
assumed to be negligible but, rather, must be taken up as an empirical
question.

But, perhaps as much or more than any other historical factor, communication technologies have shaped contemporary collective sexual
life, bringing awareness of and ease of access to potential partners and
sexual scenes across a diverse and ever-widening expanse of social and
physical geography. Match.com and eHarmony, for example, are now
staple Web sites catering to heterosexuals across North America in
search of long-term partnership. eHarmony, in fact, makes the astound-
ing claim that its Web site produces an average of 542 marriages *every
day*![1] Alternatively, AdultFriendFinder.com—a Web site designed primarily for shorter-term heterosexual liaisons—claims forty million subscribers worldwide looking for sex and casual dating. Members may use
the site to locate local sex partners, to arrange sexual liaisons on future
travels across the country or overseas, or to browse the range of offer-
ings for a "virtual" affair. Other sites, such as SeekingArrangement
.com, pair seekers with "sugar daddies" or "sugar mommas" and provide
well-off, high-profile members the ability to select younger partners for
sex and companionship. AshleyMadison.com, which boasts over five million subscribers, is designed explicitly for married individuals looking
to have a "discreet" tryst with other married partners. With the tagline,

"Life is short, have an affair!" this Web site facilitates sexual encounters that might otherwise be difficult to arrange and risky to manage. For those with a more traditional orientation to coupling and strong religious affiliations, Web sites such as JDate and ChristianSingles.com facilitate faith-based relationships. Senior citizens, too, while the slowest demographic to make use of the Internet, are not unrepresented in the menu of choices for online sex and dating. SeniorMatch.com, for example, promises to connect members with "50+ young and passionate singles!" And iPhone applications such as Scruff and Grindr use GPS technology so that gay and bisexual men can locate one another in real time for sex and dating. Providing the precise geographic coordinates of all gay and bisexual men who use the application, these technologies give "pictures, stats and map locations at a tap."[2]

In a related vein, the pronounced autonomy of the modern sexual field coupled with the Internet has produced a degree of field specialization perhaps never seen before. Online, actors are encouraged to exercise sexual preference structures around a highly particular set of desired characteristics and erotic themes, including demographic characteristics such as age, race, class, religion, and marital status, physical characteristics such as height, weight, body shape, and hair color, and, of course, sexual interests, from an attraction to people dressed as teddy bears (i.e., the Furry Fandom) to an attraction to people who sit on or pop balloons (i.e., balloon fetishists). Today, for instance, middle-aged men can exercise preferences for younger partners by systematically limiting the search criteria on dating Web sites that give them access to literally thousands of female singles. Conversely, older women on Cougarlife.com have access to men in their twenties and thirties who are attracted to women decades older than themselves. And gay male Web sites, such as BigMuscle.com or BigMuscleBear.com, provide gay and bisexual members the ability to search the sites' databases for partners on the basis of not only age, height, weight, and sexual orientation but also the size of body parts, including biceps, quadriceps, and even calves. As well, both sites host real-time social events, including dance parties and charity walks. In total, these examples illustrate the extent to which the autonomy of the sexual field coupled with the computer age has facilitated meeting partners within and across geographic areas but also the growth of increasingly specialized sexual milieus around ever more narrow preference structures.

In sum, sexuality in the contemporary West can be characterized by at least two core features. First, relative to other historical periods, collective sexual life is decoupled from broader institutions of social control to constitute a domain of social life in its own right. En masse, individuals have the freedom to pursue a sexual life relatively unencumbered by the constraints of a reproductive imperative, the problem of serial pregnancy, the crushing guilt of sex-negative legal and moral codes, arranged marriage, and the proscriptions of custom that dictate when and with whom one might have sex (Giddens 1992; Halperin 1993). Second, in a related vein, contemporary actors have access to diverse sexual milieu such that they may choose individual partners and sexual scenes on the basis of remarkably rarified preference structures, sexual and otherwise. Beyond the obvious formation of highly specialized erotic worlds, the implication is that the information age permits actors more precision in choice of partners and sexual scenes and that this added capacity for selectivity will bear on long-term partner choice, too.

But how to propose a general framework with sensitizing concepts that can make sense of this broad expanse of contemporary sexual social life and the multitude of ways that individuals can seek out partnership? And how to formulate a systematic, sociological approach to collective sexual desires and desirability in a manner that moves beyond local description? These questions have inspired scholars to consider collective sexual life through the lens of field theory, opening up new lines of sociological analysis of intimate life.

## Field Theory and the Sexual Fields Framework

This volume represents a collective effort to approach sexual life outside the predominant subcultural and historical accounts that characterize sociological and anthropological literatures. This effort began as an international conference that I organized in 2010 at that University of Toronto that brought together scholars across the globe, from Tokyo and London to Chicago and Honolulu, in order to consider how Bourdieu and field theory might be put to use in the study of contemporary sexual life. The conference spilled over into the twilight hours of two heady evenings as participants cut their teeth on the prospects of a field theoretical framework applied to sexual life. In total, the weekend proved to be so fruitful and stimulating that I proposed to its participants a volume on the topic. Toward this end, the present volume identifies a set of em-

pirical and theoretical issues related to collective sexual life and draws
from field theory and the sexual fields framework to bring focused attention to the topic. In this effort, a synergistic dialogue between me,
the contributors, and the voluminous work of Bourdieu emerges. In this
sense, the scholarship in this volume is best read as multiple points of arrival into a field-inspired study of contemporary sexuality. It is not the
last word but the beginning articulation of a sociological perspective devoted to thinking through the social organization of sexual life from the
vantage point of field theory.

Because not all readers of this volume will be familiar with field theory and the sexual fields framework, I provide a brief outline here of
their core features as developed in the sociological literature.

*Field theory*

In sociology, field theory has had perhaps its greatest impact via Bourdieu's (1977, 1979/1984, 1990c) formulation of the routine practices of social life—an approach picked up and extended in a broad spectrum of
empirical and theoretical work (DiMaggio 1987; Emirbayer and Johnson 2008; Ferguson 1998; Fligstein 2001; Lizardo 2004; Wacquant 2004;
Widick 2003). In this approach, the core concepts of *field*, *capital*, and
*habitus* are brought together to frame action as a form of "practice," in
contrast to the individual-level "behaviors" proposed by psychological
theories, the scripted, rule-following actions proposed by social learning theories, or the calculated, rational actions proposed by rational action theory.

In field theory, practice is situated in the context of interrelated yet
semiautonomous arenas of contention, or *fields*, each with their own particular logic and regulative principles (Bourdieu 1977, 1979/1984; Bourdieu and Wacquant 1992). In the Bourdieusian rendering of field theory, a field is a socially structured arena composed of situated agents,
institutionalized practices, and an overarching logic or regulative principle (Bourdieu 1977; Bourdieu and Wacquant 1992). Fields acquire their
structural characteristics insofar as they are composed of distinct positions in social space, each of which exists in relation to the others and to
the distribution of field-specific resources, or what Bourdieu refers to as
*capital*.

For Bourdieu, capital takes three major forms: economic, social, and
cultural (Bourdieu 1977). Capital confers systematic advantage to those

who possess it by providing the capacity to obtain the field's rewards. In principle, capitals are interconvertible with one another so that the acquisition of one form of capital in any given field has the capacity to be converted to another form of capital in a second field (Brubaker 1985). The classic instance of this interconvertibility is found in the study of education and class reproduction (Bernstein 1971; Bourdieu 1990c; Willis 1977). For example, on account of the resources that accrue from family background, including dispositions related to cognition, the use of language, and relations to authority, middle-class students acquire a form of cultural capital that is rewarded by and consolidated within primary and secondary educational systems and, later, institutions of higher learning (Bernstein 1971; Bourdieu 1977, 1990c; Nash 2010; Willis 1977). In turn, this cultural capital is converted to economic capital as middle-class graduates acquire access to positions of power, authority, and esteem in the labor market on account of their cultural capacities and sensibilities. Those who lack cultural capital—that is, generally the working class and the poor—are hard-pressed to compete with their middle-class counterparts because they lack the sensibilities and know-how rewarded by the gatekeepers of the professions. Thence the reproduction of class inequality. One important implication of this example is that, while fields are autonomous social configurations, they are at the same time structurally interconnected as agents parlay their capital from one field to another.

Nevertheless, field and capital are insufficient by themselves to explain how an actor arrives at a given practice, no less to explain variations in practices between them. For this latter task, Bourdieu suggests, one must enlist the habitus, a cognitive structure composed of "durable and transposable dispositions" produced by the objectification of social structure at the level of the subconscious (Bourdieu 1977, 72; also Bourdieu and Wacquant 1992, 13, 126). The habitus organizes practice insofar as it provides the "strategy-generating-principle(s)" of action but, importantly, without the usual, rule-following or end-seeking properties of rational, conscious striving (Bourdieu 1977, 72). Rather, through perceptual and classificatory schemas that organize an otherwise chaotic universe of inputs, on the one hand, and through the generation of practical actions derived from these schemas, on the other, the habitus orients actors to the social world in a manner such that individuals are themselves unaware (Bourdieu 1977, 1979/1984). Accordingly, in the Bourdieusian formulation, practice emerges at the point of intersection between two objective structural orders: the internal cognitive structure that is the habitus and the external configuration of relations with its uneven distribution of capital—that is, the field (Lizardo 2004).

## The sexual fields framework

While Bourdieu's groundbreaking work on field theory—from cultural production and education to the problem of class reproduction—extends only minimally to the domain of sexual life, there are reasons to believe that such an extension is both consistent with and analytically productive for field theory more generally (for more on this point, see George [chapter 4 in this volume]). In fact, a careful examination of the social organization of collective sexual life reveals at least two interconnected characteristics that make it, as Martin (chapter 7 in this volume) suggests, perhaps its most important case.

First, as I note above, sexual life brings actors into specialized arenas of "organized striving" (Martin 2003, 20) that establish collectively held definitions of desirability. This makes the question of desirability itself amenable to field theoretical analysis and *a problem to be explained* (Martin and George 2006). Whereas desire and desirability are themselves enormously complex matters that sociology has, traditionally, few tools to understand (Epstein 1991; Green 2008b; Stein 1989), field theory and the sexual fields framework, by contrast, provide an account of the sociological components of both at the level of collective life. As I and others show throughout this volume, sexual desire and desirability in the context of a sexual field are much more than merely a collection of individual desires; they are, in significant measure, *field effects* that represent the transformation of individual desires into "hegemonic systems of judgment" (Martin and George 2006, 126), or, in the language of the sexual fields framework, *structures of desire* (Green 2008c).

Structures of desire are site-specific, transpersonal valuations of attractiveness that coordinate desirability in a manner that recalls the twin metaphors of a field as both a *field of force* and a *field of struggle*. For instance, in a bar, structures of desire materialize in the talk about who is attractive among patrons and in a given site's representations of desirability, including advertisements, videos playing in the venue, the bar's atmosphere, the appearance of bartenders and popular participants, and patterns in deference and demeanor whereby those deemed attractive breeze through waiting lines, get offered drinks, command the attention of onlookers, (or, on the Internet, become featured profiles on a given Web site), and enjoy overall high status (Green 2008c, 2011). In this sense, structures of desire represent both the collectivization of desires of field participants and what participants *believe* is desired by others (Green 2008a, 2011). Two immediate points follow, both with respect to the socialization of desire (and desirability). First, sexual field scholars reframe the analysis of desire and desirability from questions concerning *individual* desires to questions about *collective* desire. This means that sexual fields scholars are less concerned with the idiosyncratic desires of any particular individual than with the patterned valuations of attractiveness that obtain statistical regularity within a given sexual field. Second, by focusing on the collectivization of attitudes and desires, sexual fields scholars attend to the process of aggregation itself, whereby individual constructions of desirability are transformed into structures of desire that are irreducible to the attitudes and desires of individuals alone. Not unlike processes of intensification highlighted by urban sociologists (e.g., Fischer 1975), the collective nature of interaction in the sexual field transforms attitudes, desires, and practices into new normative forms, in terms of both what we desire and what we *think* others find desirable—such as proper comportment, attractive appearance, and desirable status markers, including socioeconomic background. Put differently, it is impossible to understand sexual social life, including interaction, partnership choice, and sexual practice, without an analysis of field properties that socialize the very things we want, do, and desire. This is perhaps the key insight of sexual field scholarship.

Second, because individual actors are differentially valued in collective sexual life, their social fate emerges in the context of status structures that operate much the same as any field of distinction. Hence, the core concepts of field theory—field, capital, and habitus—are particularly instructive as analysts observe how individuals and groups move through and adapt to sexual stratification. For the rewards of the sexual field—including both partnership choice and social significance—are in large measure dependent on the degree to which actors possess resources that articulate with the structure of desire of the sexual field in which they have a stake. While some of these resources may include social, economic, and cultural capital, depending on the arena, they also include *sexual capital* (Green 2008c; Martin and George 2006)—a species of capital irreducible to but interconvertible with other capitals.[3] To the extent that sexual capital is not evenly distributed within a given sexual field but, rather, keyed to the particular characteristics of individual players, actors are stratified in a manner that conditions their experiences and subsequent strategies of action (Green 2008b, 2008c, 2011). This means that sexual capital is *at once* both a resource embodied by individual actors and a property of the field itself. Here, outward comportment (i.e., "front") and even embodied dispositions (i.e., "hexis") emerge and change in the context of the field as actors become oriented to and socialized by the field's particular structure of desire. In effect, players of the sexual field are disposed to develop a reflexive relationship to their bodies, affect, and style in a manner that makes sexual capital part of the struggle itself. By attending to the complex relationships of field, capital, and habitus, a field theoretic framework, and the sexual fields framework more specifically, puts in high relief the phenomenon of sexual stratification and the ways in which actors both shape and are shaped by the field.

To the extent that the sexual fields framework takes as its focal point sexual stratification, one of the chief questions the approach raises concerns the relationship of sexual desire to power. Of course, there is a very broad and rich body of research and analysis, from radical feminism to queer theory, that suggests that power and desire are rarely separable. But the question itself is confused if *desire* and *power* are not properly specified from the outset with respect to the unit of analysis the analyst wishes to consider.[4] In a sexual fields approach, to the extent that the analyst is primarily interested in *collective*, as opposed to *individual*, desires, power is potentially in play in a variety of forms, including power in the Foucauldian (subjectification), Bourdieusian (capital), and even Weberian (coercion) variants. For instance, George (chapter 4 in this volume) argues that "metasexual authority" as seen in sexology but also in lesbian and gay and feminist discourses has operated in the twentieth century to organize sexuality along lines of a bourgeois, object-choice paradigm that constituted sexual subjectivities in a manner commensurate with the field of power in which it emerged. Here, power in the Foucauldian sense of subjectification and expertise ("power-knowledge") is wound so tightly to identity, and, in turn, desire, that the two are rendered inextricable. In the Bourdieusian sense of power as capital, Farrer and Dale (chapter 6 in this volume) focus on how race, national identity, and gender work together to configure relations of desire between Western men, Western women, and Asian men and women in Shanghai. To borrow elsewhere from Martin's (2005) work, power itself may be sexy insofar as Asian women come to desire well-off, worldly Western men, but it is perhaps not so for Asian men, who may find Western women's socioeconomic status off-putting. And Green (chapter 1 in this volume) and Martin (chapter 7 in this volume) reflect on the popularity tournament—a phenomenon that relates one's social standing within a field to the reproduction and consolidation of one's desirability, or lack thereof. Here, desirability is not only the function of the possession of a given set of individual attributes; it is also a subconscious response to an individual's or a group's *perceived* desirability to others.

Alternatively, Hennen (chapter 3 in this volume) argues that not all sexual fields are configured so neatly along axes of power and that, even when power itself is eroticized, it may not operate quite in the manner one would expect. On the first point, he notes that the formation of the bear community was built on a decidedly democratic, nonlooksist ethos that located desirability across a wide range of otherwise devalued body types. And, with respect to sexuality and power, he notes that both the bears and the leathermen institutionalized sexual practices that were not penetration centered, thereby divesting gay male sexuality of its usual alignments with power and the "active/passive" binary.

In short, how and whether power and sexual desire are related in *collective* sexual life are not so much answered resolutely by the sexual fields framework but, more accurately, put into question across contexts and along multiple lines of theoretical inquiry.

## Contemporary Research on Sexuality and the Sexual Field

Having sketched an introductory backdrop against which to consider the topic of this volume, I now turn to the ways in which its contributors have appropriated and extended field theory to make sense of a diverse array of empirical and theoretical issues in contemporary sexual life.

In chapter 1, I revisit the sexual fields framework as it has evolved since 2008, both in my own thinking and in conversation with the contributors to this volume. This is to suggest, not that the ideas I set forth here represent a final theoretical consensus regarding the state of and future directions in sexual field theory, but, rather, that my own work has been profoundly informed by the research of my peers in a way that incorporates insights from all the authors contributing to this volume. For instance, while I have always regarded the sexual fields framework, above all, as a productive heuristic for the study of collective sexual life,

I am also persuaded by Martin's strong argument (chapter 7) that the key analytic turn in a sexual field analysis is to show how attraction is it-self an outcome of field processes or, put more simply, a *field effect*. To-ward that end, beyond returning to and developing further the core con-cepts of the framework in chapter 1, I am especially concerned to specify a range of ways through which the aggregated judgments and apprecia-tions of participants in a given field come to bear on the perceived de-sirability of any given actor or class of actors, thereby offering a socio-logical account of that part of desiring that may be attributed to the fact of collective sexual life.[5] Here, I consider how the "popularity tourna-ment," along with subcultural processes associated with the socialization of desire and the aggregation and intensification of norms of attractive-ness, constitute three central ways by which fields "act back" on, consti-tute, and transform desire and desirability.

Similarly, picking up on Weinberg and William's provocative essay (chapter 2) on the interplay between subjective (habitus) and objective (field) elements in the formation of desire and Hennen's intriguing work (chapter 3) on the historical trajectory of change in erotic habitus and the sexual field, I also consider at length the thorny relationship of the objective elements of a sexual status order with the subjective elements involved in the perception of that status order. The objective sexual sta-tus order and the subjective elements of apprehending that status order, in fact, cannot be assumed to follow one another in a one-to-one cor-respondence; rather, they constitute a relationship for which "pluralis-tic ignorance" is possible—i.e., desirability amounts to what others think others find attractive. For instance, as Armstrong (2010a) makes clear, one cannot assume that sexual capital is itself a function of desirabil-ity as a first-order phenomenon. Rather, under some conditions, it may arise out of the aggregation of individual *attitudes* about a particular so-cial type, such as the impact of being labeled a "slut" on the subsequent diminishing desirability of those American co-eds associated with this stigmatizing status (for more, see Hamilton and Armstrong 2009). In to-tal, by analytically separating out (and then putting back together again) the objective and subjective elements of a sexual field, I draw attention both to the complexities of position taking there and, more importantly, to the process by which desire and desirability enter into and are trans-formed by the gravitational pull of the sexual field.

In chapter 2, Weinberg and Williams offer the case of a sexual field inhabited by trans women and their admirers as a means to flesh out and deepen the conceptual relationship between a field's structure of desire and the erotic habitus. Conducting extensive ethnographic research at "Mabel's" bar in San Francisco, Weinberg and Williams build on the work of Jackson and Scott (2007) to outline three processes of "embodiment" through which interaction in a sexual field can extend the parameters of desirability *to incorporate what might otherwise be undesirable.* That is, in this extraordinary analysis, they show how the particular structure of desire at Mabel's facilitates an intersubjective rapport between the trans women and their male audience that works to minimize and suspend the disjunct between the biological sex of the trans women and the men's sexual desire for feminine women. Ethnographically rich, elegant, and conceptually sophisticated, Weinberg and Williams's analysis moves sexual field theory forward by illustrating the interactional underpinnings of sexual desire and desirability as these shape embodiment and, in turn, sexual capital.

In chapter 3, Hennen pulls our attention away from the microlevel, interactional dynamics that organize desire in the sexual field and toward a consideration of the development and transformation of sexual fields over time. Offering a fresh look at the fieldwork he conducted on gay bears and leathermen (see Hennen 2008), he makes the provocative argument that sexual fields have historical trajectories whereby the logic of desire and desirability of one field metamorphoses to shape the logic and organization of a second, "splinter" field. Historicizing sexual fields and structures of desire in this way, Hennen positions himself to propose a *field-capital-desire complex* whereby each element conditions the other and, in total, creates the possibility not only of reproduction of the sexual field but also of its transformation. Moreover, in his careful analysis of the development of bear subculture, Hennen pushes sexual field theory forward by suggesting that, in some instances, the Bourdieusian metaphor of a field of struggle may not be analytically productive, as it rests on the axiom that fields are always arenas of battle and social stratification. In early instantiations of the bear subculture, for instance, Hennen finds a sexual field that acts like a gravitational field or a field of force, but far less by way of an institutionalized status order. This pathbreaking analysis lends sexual field theory a critical concept of historicity but, even more, a breathtaking theoretical statement about the sociohistorical formation of fields of collective desire and sexual subculture.

It also paves the way for an innovation on Bourdieu's conceptualization of a field insofar as such social spaces may and may not function as organized structures of competition.

In chapter 4, George tackles the thorny question of why Bourdieu failed to develop the concept of a sexual field even when so much of his analysis of modern sexual life implied it. In a bold and ironic methodological maneuver, he engages in a reflexive sociological praxis by locating Bourdieu in the broader context of a field of power whereby nineteenth- and twentieth-century experts, activists, and their interlocutors—from Freud to Kinsey to gay liberation—were struggling to define their own field positions by articulating a model of sexuality as "sex-itself," that is, a sexuality fully autonomous from the larger structures and processes that mark the modern and late modern period. Because Bourdieu abhorred what he regarded as the "pseudoscience" of sexology and psychoanalysis and their mythic construction of a libido that inhered in the physical rather than the social body, and because his own academic capital was at stake in the construction of field theory and its fully socialized libido, he turned a blind eye to the sexual field, choosing not just to ignore it but to build a theory of fields that all but categorically denied its possibility. Thus George writes: "With only slight exaggeration, we can say that his biographical trajectory and the particular contours of the theories he was developing were largely reactions to the autonomization of the sexual field" (p. 108).

In chapter 5, Adam and I consider how one kind of network structure—what we call sexual *circuits*—operates to shape both the character of any given sexual field and the reference groups through which intersubjective assessments of sexual capital are conceived. Circuits represent associations of field actors that arise through participation in collective sexual life whereby actors become familiar with one another on the basis of the simple fact of rubbing elbows together within physical or virtual space over time. We argue that collective sexual life is composed of this special kind of network formation that meets the traditional definition of neither weak nor strong ties but is, nevertheless, consequential for the phenomenology of inhabiting a position within the sexual field. Moreover, by drawing on data from Adam, Husbands, Murray, and Maxwell's (2008a) earlier survey work on sexual circuits and sexual health in Toronto, we present an oblimin factor analysis that demonstrates the broad outlines of precisely this kind of network configuration as collectivities of men cohere around particular sexual sites, ranging from the men's restrooms of local universities to the main street of the LGBTQ community in downtown Toronto. Hence we show the sociospatial dimensions of a *sexual district*, composed of a range of sexual fields, each with more and less overlapping circuits of participants—that is, what we might think of as the social anatomy of the sexual field.

One key implication of the data is that the character of sexual circuits can vary in terms of heterogeneity, configured more and less differentially by age and ethnicity depending on the particular sexual site in question. This of course raises further questions regarding how and why a given sexual field is configured more or less heterogeneously and with what status effects on its participants. In chapter 6, Farrer and Dale speak more directly to how sex, class, race, and nationality are configured in a heterosexual field in Shanghai—what they refer to as an *ethnosexual contact zone*, a phenomenon made increasingly common by the interpenetration of national markets around the world. Whereas Western- and European-born men typically hold a high degree of sexual capital among local, Chinese-born women in Shanghai, the same cannot be said for their counterparts—Western, European women. In fact, quite the contrary, Western men typically experience a marked sense of *increasing* sexual status when arriving from the West in Shanghai, while Western women experience a marked *decrease* in sexual status and, moreover, can feel marginalized from the field entirely. This raises a critical paradox because, generally, global standards of attractiveness circulating in reform-era China in everything from advertisements for makeup and fashion to skin-lightening creams represent white women as the ideal. Under these curious distressed field conditions, Western women are thus forced to adapt to their newly disadvantaged field positions— positions that often include a kind of masculinization by and in relation to Chinese-born men. Farrer and Dale's fascinating analysis makes clear the critical point that sexual capital is not an individual, "portable portfolio" of personal assets (contra Hakim 2011) but contextually constituted in ways that are reducible to neither global standards of attractiveness nor national or racial status. They also brilliantly distill how sexual desire and desirability in a sexual field may reflect less the essentialized desires of a given group, including those configured by racialized colonial categories, than the historical structure of opportunities for interaction afforded by collective sexual life.

Finally, if the contributors to this volume implicitly ask what field theory can do for our study of contemporary sexual life, they also pose the converse question: What can collective sexual life tell us about field theory? And it is precisely on this turn that Martin (chapter 7) suggests that sexual attraction is not only relevant to field theory but may also constitute the "*ur-phenomenon* for a field phenomenology" (Martin 2010). This is so by virtue of the fact that desiring in a sexual field constitutes the simplest form of valuation whereby an agent either moves toward or away from another on the basis of attraction. If it can be shown that sexual fields affect perceptions of attractiveness and, in turn, partnership choices, we have perhaps the ideal case for understanding how the objective structures of a given field materialize at the individual level in the form of new cognitive and somatic dispositions and, in turn, new strategies of action. One of the most rudimentary sexual field effects, Martin tells us, is via what Waller (1937) called the "rating and dating system," by which the latter referred to the popularity tournament on college campuses whereby the attraction of one student to another was, in part, a function of how popular the other was deemed to be. In Waller's work, those deemed popular became more attractive dates. In short, the fact of the field produced "aggregated and organized perceptions" (Martin 2010) of desirability above and beyond preexisting individual preferences. As Martin so eloquently writes: "Like the Churinga discussed by Durkheim (1912/1954) in the *Elementary Forms*, the object glows with borrowed magic because it incarnates social relations. And *this* is the core phenomenological experience from which a field effect stems" (pp. 181–82). Accordingly, Martin proposes a set of methodological imperatives moving forward to capture the phenomenology of attraction as this emerges in the context of the social relations of the sexual field.

\*   \*   \*

In total, this volume represents a pioneering set of empirical and theoretical chapters that use field theory and the sexual fields framework to deepen a sociological understanding of intimate life. It establishes the relevance of a Bourdieusian field theoretic to the sexual domain and at the same time moves considerably beyond Bourdieu to capture the particular structures and processes attendant to collective sexual life, not the least of which includes an explicit articulation of the sexual field. In this way, the scholars whose work is included in this collection highlight the sociological underpinnings of desire and desirability and their historical transformations while providing a striking range of innovative conceptual tools along the way.

Still, this collection is only the beginning of what we hope will be a sustained and growing dialogue among scholars of sexuality to think through how our sexual lives—that is, what often appear to be the most enigmatic features of human life—are organized in ways that bear the unmistakable imprint of the social. Among other features of this imprint, those structures and processes of sexual life that align and transform the otherwise diverse desires of individuals, conferring status and desirability unequally on individuals and groups, are perhaps some of the most subtle, insidious ways that the thing we call *society* translates to and is objectified in the life of the individual. The present volume establishes the foundation of a field-informed analysis for distilling this relationship and, we hope, inspiration for future scholars of contemporary sexual life.

## Notes

1. http://www.eharmony.com/about/eharmony.

2. http://www.grindr.com.

3. The terms *sexual capital* and *erotic capital* are interchangeable in this literature. However, for a very different concept of erotic capital, see Hakim (2010, 2011). And for a field theoretic criticism of Hakim's concept, see Green (2013).

4. For a sociological approach to the question of *individual* desire, see Green (2008a).

5. I am not suggesting that sexual desiring is only a function of field processes or only a function of the social more broadly conceived. Rather, my intent here is to isolate that part of desiring and desirability that can be attributed to sexual sociality.

# CHAPTER ONE

# The Sexual Fields Framework

Adam Isaiah Green, University of Toronto

Individual attraction is a messy affair for the social scientist, both hard to predict and subject to nearly limitless variation. Yet, at the level of *collective* life, attributions of attractiveness are not randomly distributed but, rather, reveal a systematicity that both reflects and produces the desires and attitudes of specialized publics. And this is perhaps what makes collective sexual life so compelling as a sociological phenomenon: it is not just that the social worlds in which we seek partnership establish the terrain in which "the game" is played but, more, that the very process of bringing actors together in social space has an *independent* effect on those desires such that sexual likes and dislikes, partnership preferences and sexual practice, are transformed. Put differently, the erotic worlds in which we find sex and partnership establish the conditions of possibility for intimate life but also socialize the very things we want and come to desire.

Late modernity is a particularly good time to conceive of the social organization of intimate life in this way because, as many scholars point out, sexual life has perhaps unprecedented independence from traditional institutions of control to constitute a domain of social life in its own right (D'Emilio 1983; Giddens 1992; Halperin 1993). Beyond the influence of macrolevel historical shifts related to the development of industrial capitalism and the dominance of an independent wage labor system, a host of more recent factors have facilitated the autonomization and specialization of collective sexual life. These include the rise of information and communication technologies, advances in methods of birth control, women's increasing financial independence, the waning influence of religious norms, delayed marriage, and significant rates of divorce. In the context of these factors, collective sexual life has developed as a kind of social order in its own right, but one for which the sociological literature has yet to develop sufficient theoretical tools to understand (Martin and George 2006).

In what follows, I build on my earlier work and the work of others to deepen "the sexual fields framework" (Green 2008a, 2008c, 2011) and provide a more extensive theoretical examination of collective sexual life. My intended unit of analysis, *collective sexual life*, is that domain of social life that exists outside the parameters of the monogamous dyad, including those interactions and spaces, in real time and cyberspace, that facilitate intimate partnership, be it a dating Web site catering to those in search of a serious, long-term relationship or marriage or a public restroom where men look for sex on premise.[1] Implicitly, this means that the analysis of collective sexual life includes its participants, along with those sites, networks, institutions, and subcultures within which intimate partnerships are forged.

In this chapter, I focus in three ways on the analysis of collective sexual life. First, I reflect on and deepen key sensitizing concepts that orient the approach, including the concepts of the *sexual field*, *sexual capital*, and *structures of desire*. Second, within this discussion, I illuminate some complexities associated with theorizing a *sexual* field and the ways in which a field theoretic can add to our understanding of collective sexual life. Here, I am especially concerned with both the microlevel, subjective process by which individual actors imagine sexual status orders and the processes by which fields themselves socialize desire and desirability. Third, I reflect on how we might consider sexual fields in the context of structures and processes that are both macro and micro in relation to the field. In this regard, I conclude with a set of empirical and theoretical considerations awaiting development in the future study of collective sexual life.

## Collective Sexual Life

A macrolevel examination of collective sexual life reveals a mosaic of sexual milieus organized loosely by the social cleavages of race, ethnicity, class, and sexual orientation (Laumann, Gagnon, Michael, and Michaels 1994; Laumann, Ellingston, Mahay, Palk, and Youm 2004). Closer still, we find these cleavages parsed into sexual niches, each niche anchored to a particular set of networks, physical and virtual sites, with particular subcultural forms. To the extent that these sexual niches orient individuals around a shared logic of desirability whereby actors seek out and vie for sexual partnership, social significance, and esteem, we have a sexual field (Farrer 2010a; Green 2008b, 2008c, 2011; Martin and George 2006; Weinberg and Williams 2009).

The approach I develop here draws from a Bourdieusian field theoretic and extrapolates from its core concepts—field, capital, and habitus—to capture the structural and processual features of collective sexual life (Green 2008c). This approach—what I call the *sexual fields framework*—has been picked up, elaborated on, and complicated by scholars of sexuality (Farrer 2010a; Paul, Ayayla, and Choi 2010; Weinberg and Williams 2009; Wilton 2009). In the years following the original formulation of the sexual fields framework, I have had the opportunity to reflect on it, including a more extensive consideration of its core concepts: sexual field, sexual capital, structure of desire, and erotic habitus. What is more, in editing this volume, I have dialogued with all the contributors and have discovered the ways in which their interpretations of the framework have extended but also challenged my own. Below, I sketch out the sexual fields framework in light of my own ongoing reflections and those of my colleagues.

## The Sexual Fields Framework: Core Concepts

A *sexual field* emerges when a subset of actors with potential romantic or sexual interest orient themselves toward one another according to a logic of desirability imminent to their collective relations and this logic produces, to greater and lesser degrees, a system of stratification.

Collective sexual life is often anchored to physical and virtual nodes, or *sites*,[2] the most commonplace of which include nightclubs, bars, fitness facilities, dorms, workplaces, coffeeshops, house parties, and dating Web sites, among many others. To the extent that sites are inhabited by actors who come to the field with overlapping sensibilities and tastes—that is, overlapping *erotic habitus*—their preferences aggregate to take the form of collective systems of valuation and judgment. These collective valuations constitute a *structure of desire* as they articulate desire and desirability in a manner that exceeds the purview of any single actor but for which all actors are obliged to consider should they wish to play the game (Green 2011). Hence, collective sexual life may be captured by the twin metaphors of a field—both in the sense of a "force field" that orients desire, like a field of gravity, and a "battlefield" of organized struggle (Martin 2003) (but see Hennen, chapter 3 in this volume).

Structures of desire eroticize and assign value to certain bodies, affects, and practices while rending others neuter or undesirable. In turn, structures of desire determine the dominant currency (or, in some cases, currencies) of sexual capital within a given field (Green 2008c; Weinberg and William 2009; cf. Martin and George 2006).[3] As that species of capital specific to the sexual field, *sexual capital* situates actors differentially in the status order, conferring advantage on those who possess it, including rights of sexual choice, social significance, and group membership, and, conversely, invisibility, marginality, and, in some cases, stigma on those who do not. Below, I focus individually on these core concepts and show their interrelationships.

## Sexual Fields

Sexual fields may be distinguished from one another on the basis of at least two elements. First, patterned variability in the patronage base of a given site, be it based in social or geographic factors, generally warrants an analytic distinction that designates each as its own field. For instance, a martini bar populated mostly by thirty somethings and a martini bar populated mostly by fifty somethings are best considered two distinct sexual fields, as are a punk nightclub in New York City and a punk nightclub in London. This is because demographic factors in the first example and geographic location in the second will produce mutually exclusive networks of actors—or *circuits* of participants—each with their own potential generational and local character. These circuits represent configurations of actors who rub elbows on a regular basis in shared sites of sexual sociality but who do not necessarily know one another by name. Despite their informality, such circuits are the lifeblood of any sexual field because they populate the field with a patterned assemblage of bodies (or, in cyber space, a patterned assemblage of profiles) that define the dominant structure of desire and represent the reference point against which actors engage in intersubjective comparison processes in an effort to discern their positions in the field (for more on sexual circuits, see

Adam and Green, chapter 5 in this volume). By hinging the boundaries of a sexual field on its *actual* participants, the analyst focuses on the interactional and representational elements of any given social assemblage without risking the reification of the field concept across social and geographic spaces. Nevertheless, in some instances, it may be analytically useful to consider highly similar sexual subcultures with mutually exclusive patronage bases as a single sexual field—for example, the fraternity culture in large state schools.

Conversely, similar patronage profiles do not necessarily make two or more sites the same sexual field because any given field depends on the existence of a distinct structure of desire and, in turn, distinct currencies of sexual capital. For example, while both the video music bar and the sports bar in downtown Atlanta may cater to a largely middle-class, heterosexual, twenty- to thirty-something profile, these sites represent two distinct sexual fields to the extent that each is organized by its own particular sexual status order, including both horizontal differentiation and vertical stratification.

*Horizontal differentiation and vertical stratification within a sexual field*

Like other forms of collective life, sexual sociality invites individual actors to make typological attributions of sexual capital to others, seeing in the sexual status order a composite of sexual "types" or distinct groups of sexual actors stratified within and between tiers of desirability. This differentiation can take two forms: horizontal differentiation and vertical stratification (Martin and George 2006). Horizontal differentiation distinguishes actors in nonhierarchical aggregations organized by a range of player characteristics, from socioeconomic background to sex to erotic theme, and can take form both within and across sexual fields. For example, the most basic horizontal differentiation within a sexual field can be seen in the case of heterosexual fields wherein players are male and female or in those lesbian sexual fields wherein players are identified as either butch or fem (Kennedy and Davis 1993). Other instances of horizontal organization arise when groups of actors are present concurrently within a given sexual field, one group having no more or less sexual capital than the other relative to a single structure of desire, or where there exist multiple, coincident structures of desire that afford value to both groups (e.g., men and women in a heterosexual sexual field). In this latter case, when the actors of a given sexual field possess desires that are, by and large, bifurcated and mutually exclusive, one has an instance of a "two-sided" field (Green 2008c) constituted by at least two distinct structures of desire—for example, men's and women's desires in the heterosexual field, butches' and fems' desires in a butch/fem lesbian field.

By contrast, vertical stratification arises when members of each group within a given field are sorted into hierarchical status positions or tiers of desirability (Green 2008c). These hierarchical positions typically reflect a distribution of sexual capital determined by the aggregated judgments of the *desiring* class (e.g., women's sexual capital in the heterosexual field will be determined by the aggregated judgments of *men* in the field), though this may not always be the case, as I outline below. In this latter instance, actors may achieve sexual status vis-à-vis association with and reception by members of their own class.[4]

In urban gay centers, Hennen (2008; chapter 3 in this volume) documents a form of horizontal differentiation represented by "fairies," "bears," and "leathermen." To the extent that each of these sociocultural types occupies a distinct sexual field, there is horizontal segregation across sexual fields. By contrast, if a group of fairies were to attend a leatherman event, vertical stratification is a likely consequence. That is, fairies in a leather sexual field will represent a distinct class of sexual actors with a systematic location in the sexual status order. Similarly, a man who does not conform to the leatherman structure of desire owing to physical appearance (perhaps he is too skinny), affect (perhaps he is effeminate), or style (perhaps he is too well coiffed or too fashionably dressed) will find himself inserted into a system of vertical stratification that renders him at considerable field disadvantage.

While sexual fields are often characterized by vertical stratification, this may vary by degree, particularly with respect to real-time, microlevel exchange. A number of factors account for this variation, including, perhaps most importantly, spatial and temporal distributions of sexual capital within a given field and, second, the content of the structure of desire relative to the patron base. In the first instance, for example, Tewksbury (2002) notes that competition in the bathhouse varies systematically over the course of a twenty-four-hour period, whereby prime-time hours are correlated with the widest distribution of sexual capital and, therefore, the most clearly defined, hierarchically stratified status order. By contrast, early mornings are populated by a decidedly different class of actors, most of whom have relatively less sexual capital when compared to their prime-time peers. Often enough, these participants frequent the bathhouse at off-peak hours precisely because they are more favorably situated in the distribution of sexual capital (Tewksbury 2002). In these hours, players in the top tiers of desirability have come and left (as it were). This implies not the absence of vertical stratification, but rather a kind of flattening out of the distribution of sexual capital toward the bottom. One important implication of this observation is that actors may become sensitized to temporal or seasonal variations in the distribution of sexual capital such that they coordinate their time in the field with the conditions that best meet their needs. Hence, actors who perceive themselves to be in a position of advantage in the sexual status order may target their participation in the field to prime-time hours, when they expect to encounter other high-status actors whom they would like to meet. Conversely, as in the case above, actors who perceive themselves to have a sexual capital deficit may target their participation for times of least disadvantage.

As well, the spatial configuration of a given sexual site may be correlated with the architecture of the sexual status order. The VIP room in a nightclub, for instance, may hold actors with a great deal of sexual capital and/or high social status, while the dark room in the bathhouse may hold actors with relatively little sexual capital.

A second reason for systematic variations in vertical stratification may stem from the structure of desire within a given sexual field. Some structures of desire articulate attractiveness in quite narrow and specific terms, while others have a much more pluralistic or democratic character. As an example, the swanky nightlife scene of Yorkville, Toronto, may be populated by heterosexual women and men with very particular sensibilities around partnership choice and for whom only a narrowly defined set of characteristics, including class status, produce collective interest. In these conditions, vertical stratification may crystallize in well-defined tiers of desirability and a palpable sexual status order. Here, actors are disposed to think of sexual sociality in quite subtle, hierarchical terms, related to class, age, race, and ethnicity.

Perhaps the most succinct description of these kinds of sexual fields is articulated by an actor on a Web site for gay male athletes who poses a mathematical equation for defining who can date whom: "You put yourself on a 1 to 10 scale. You can date guys one more or one less. So if you rate yourself as a 7, you go out with 6, 7 or 8." Or as another individual wrote of gradations in the sexual status order on the same Web site: "The one bedroom wants to move into a 2 bedroom, not a studio. The studio wants the one bedroom. The 2 bedroom wants a 3 bedroom, not a 2 bedroom." In this particular sexual field, the size and vascularity of the bodies of participants and the extent of their athleticism are all under scrutiny in a process of fine-grained discernment whereby actors must assess both their own relative sexual capital and that of the prospective partners for whom they may have interest.

By contrast, the parameters of desirability in other sexual fields may be more forgiving and less fine-grained, including both a wider range of eroticized types and, perhaps, multiple, coexisting structures of desire. For example, Hennen (chapter 3 in this volume) proposes that, at its inception, the bear sexual field featured an unusual degree of democratization that accommodated equally a wide range of bodies, from thin to obese. No body type was invested systematically with more sexual capital than any other. The big-city dance club with straight and gay patrons, a cabaret show at a vacation destination (Rupp and Taylor 2004), or busy coffeeshops may also cater to diverse publics such that no single logic of desirability prevails. Alternatively, the "tearooms" (Brekhus 2003; Humphreys 1970/1975)—men's public restrooms at the shopping mall, rest area, train depot, or university student center—are typically democratic spaces wherein desirability is extended to most men using the facility (Brekhus 2003; Green, Follert, Osterlund, and Paquin 2010). Hence, vertical stratification can take varying forms, materializing at one end of the continuum as a single, dominant, highly defined status order with definitive classes of actors and fine-grained, subtle assessments of erotic value and at the other end as a diffuse, relatively amorphous configuration with minor variations in sexual status between participants but definitive field effects on desire and practice nevertheless. Put in different terms, following Hennen (chapter 3 in this volume), the degree to which a sexual field can be captured by the metaphor of a "battlefield" or a "field of struggle" is subject to a rather significant degree of variability and is best posed as an empirical question to be researched rather than an assumption at the outset of field analysis.

Finally, one particularly interesting feature of vertical stratification is the degree to which actors cognize field players (and, often, themselves) in typological form, in terms of groups or classes of actors.[5] This propensity for typologization underscores the degree to which actors see the sexual field as a social order with its own particular cleavages. Consider, for example, the following random assortment of sexual types attendant to various sexual milieus, types that gain their legibility often less because actors self-identify with them than because they are so labeled: cougars, guidos and guidettes, chicken hawks, surfer boys, skate rats, Western women, bears, wolves, fairies, leathermen, clones, circuit boys, sluts, twinks, muscle Marys, butches, fems, geeks, jocks, lipstick lesbians, bridge-and-tunnel, girl-next-door, doms, subs, machos, rice queens, JAPS, switch hitters, blond bimbos, Jersey girls, sugar daddies, thugs, trannies, Mandingo, trade, hos, and players, to name only a few. While some individual actors may move between classifications, the classifications themselves provide a mapping of a social order within a given sexual field. As I suggest above, in some contexts these types are related in horizontal systems of differentiation, while in other contexts they are located within vertical, hierarchical forms of stratification. This observation becomes particularly important when considering the ways in which actors self-evaluate in a sexual field and, in turn, how such evaluations articulate with the rules of the game, including who approaches whom and how one responds to a given advance (e.g., "I'm not wealthy enough to attract the attention of this group of women"; "I'm not masculine enough or dark-skinned enough to be considered a 'thug'"; "I'm too old to try to date in that crowd"; "I'm too heavy to be desirable to the popular guys in high school"; "I'm too attractive to be receptive to the advance of this penniless guy"). Put another way, horizontal differentiation and vertical stratification in the sexual field materialize when individual characteristics (e.g., breast size, skin shade, clothing style, class status, ethnocultural background) are paired with cultural schemas, thereby distinguishing classes of players within the erotic worlds in which they circulate. And, moreover, once actors have ascertained the sexual status order and their own location within the field, they may modify their appearance, demeanor, and the like to be associated with a strata of actors to whom they attribute greater sexual capital (Green 2008c, 2011).

In this volume, Farrer and Dale (chapter 6 in this volume) give an instructive illustration of the ways in which race, nationality, and gender conspire to produce distinct group positions in the sexual field. In their work, present-day Shanghai represents an "ethnosexual contact zone" wherein the increasing penetration of national markets in global contexts creates historic encounters between previously segregated groups. Such ethnosexual contact zones produce sexual fields that bring together individuals and groups from distinct sociodemographic and cultural backgrounds wherein differences in ethnicity, race, nationality, and class are the basis for patterned sociosexual relations. These relations, however, cannot be read from the outset as isomorphic with or a recapitulation of larger differences in power and status that may characterize a given set of ethnic relations more generally, even as capitals typically distinguish one ethnic group from another. Rather, as Farrer and Dale show, sociosexual relations between ethnic groups can vary by gender and by the particular logics of sexual desirability endogenous to each sexual field—logics that, in some instances, map onto, complicate, or reverse existing interethnic power differences, an issue I return to below.

## Sexual Fields, Capital Portfolios, and the Role of Economic, Cultural, and Sexual Capitals

In my fieldwork, I have focused on the sexual social structure of urban gay male enclaves wherein sexual desire is the principal engine of sexual selection in many sites. Sexual social structure, however, need not be organized only or even primarily by sexual desirability. For example, in fields anchored to dating Web sites or mixers that appeal to marriage-minded users, sexual desirability may be one of many other factors of variable importance that shape patterns in partnership choice (Laumann, Ellingston, Mahay, Palk, and Youm 2004). Here, the economic and cultural capital of players, for instance, can be as or more important than sexual capital for achieving field significance. Accordingly, sexual fields can be more or less isomorphic with systemwide patterns of social stratification depending on the degree to which the field's status structure revolves around *sexual* capital.

Compared to the relatively straightforward case of a gay bathhouse or perhaps a college frat party, the sexual field gains added complexity when classes of field participants systematically value different *kinds* of capital. For example, if, as common wisdom has it, heterosexual men systematically value sexual capital in their female partners more than heterosexual women value sexual capital in their male partners, and, conversely, if heterosexual women systematically value economic capital in their male partners more than heterosexual men value economic capital in their female partners, then one has an instance of a two-sided field (Green 2008c) characterized not just by a horizontal bifurcation of sexual actors, each class attracted to the other, but, more importantly, a bifurcation of the necessary *capital portfolios* for sexual status. With regard to the importance of any given capital for field significance, we can imagine preference structures that run along two axes: an axis of sexual capital and an axis of cultural and economic capital. Put in graphic form (see fig. 1), we might then imagine a continuum of fields wherein sexual capital is the primary source of significance at the bottom right of the figure (e.g., the gay bathhouse), in contrast to those fields wherein economic and cultural capital are the primary sources of field significance, at the top left of the figure (e.g., the "marriage mixer," such as Web sites like JDate.com, designed for those explicitly looking for a serious long-term relationship and a marital partner). Somewhere between these two poles exists a field wherein both sexual capital and economic/cultural capital have more or less the same worth (e.g., the case of speed dating).[6]

Using similar axes, one might attempt to chart historical changes in the proportion of capitals that heterosexual men and women seek out in dating fields wherein both sexes are looking for marital partners (see fig. 2). For instance, using the findings of Buss, Shackelford, Kirkpatrick, and Larsen (2001) regarding mate preferences over the fifty-seven-year period between 1939 and 1996, we find the following among US men and women. On average, women are still valued much more for their sexual capital than for their economic capital, but somewhat less so over time. Conversely, men are still valued much more for their economic capital than for their sexual capital, but somewhat less so over time. Hence, the capital portfolios of desirable marital partners between the sexes are be-

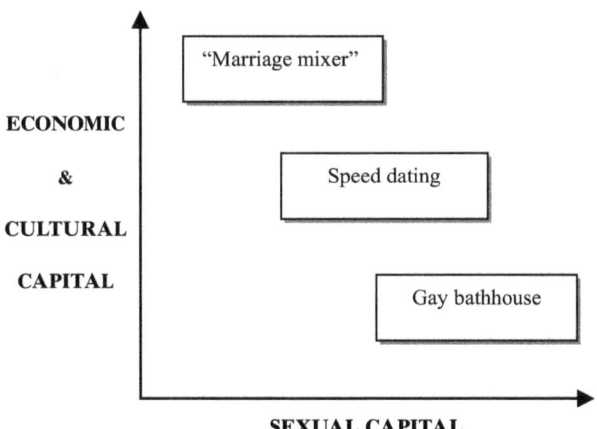

FIGURE 1. The relative importance of capitals across sexual fields.

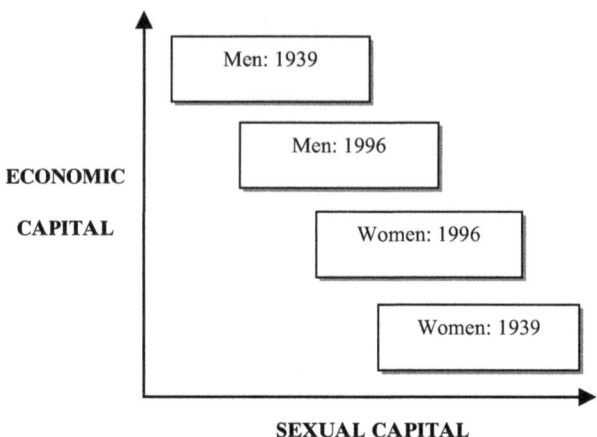

FIGURE 2. The relative historical importance of capitals by sex, 1939–96.

coming more alike over time, though significant differences in the characteristics that make men and women desirable to the opposite sex en-
dure. By a considerable margin, women continue to be valued more than
men on the basis of sexual and aesthetic qualities, while men continue to
be valued more than women on the basis of financial wherewithal and
professional position.

### Erotic Habitus and Structures of Desire: Minding One's Unit of Analysis

To the extent that individuals self-select into a given sexual field, they
come to the field with preexisting dispositions that predispose them to
favor a given kind of partner or type of sexual subculture. Elsewhere, I
have developed the concept *erotic habitus* (see Green 2008a) to capture
precisely these kinds of *individual-level*, subconscious dispositions that
shape and condition an actor's unique pathway through intimate life. In
this sense, it may be useful to focus on any given erotic habitus and its
relationship to the sexual field, not least because habitus are prone to
change over time in response to the field—a vital part of how fields "act
back" on participants. Nevertheless, once collective sexual life is under
way, desire and desirability are no longer a function of the habitus in a
direct, unmediated habitus-field interface. Rather, the habitus is twice
removed from establishing the logic of a sexual field because, first, sex-

ual fields are organized not by individual habitus but by their collectivization in the interactional and representational elements of the field
and, second, this collectivization of dispositions is not a simple additive
process but one akin to subcultural processes (Fischer 1976) associated
with the amplification and intensification of a given norm, a point I explore further below. Thus, the logic of a sexual field transcends the id-
iosyncrasy of any given erotic habitus, shifting the action from the intrapsychic level of the individual to field-level "hegemonic systems of
judgment" (Martin and George 2006), or what I refer to as a *structure of
desire* (Green 2008c; see also Weinberg and Williams, chapter 2 in this
volume).

Structures of desire typically communicate a sexual status order to
players, appearing in their simplest form in talk about who is desirable
and who is not but also in the fronts of patrons, observable patterns in
who is favored (and who is glossed over), the sign vehicles of the sexual
site that participants inhabit and, where present, the videos that play on
the screen, the décor, the name of the venue, its logo, representations
in the advertisements of the venue, and the appearance of bartenders
(Green 2008c, 2011). Hence, to use a very simple example, the gay leather
bar communicates a structure of desire through the fronts of patrons (often hypermasculine, leather clad, and in boots), the size, age, and race of
the bodies that garner positive attention (often beefy, thirty and above,
and white), the character of observable interactions among patrons, including interpersonal affect (gruff, masculine), the content of the videos playing on the video screens (leather-clad sex, S/M), the general atmospheric elements of the venue (usually dimly lit, dungeon-like, and
short on swank), the name of the venue (e.g., "Ramrod," "Spike"), associated emblems (e.g., a black leather boot, a clenched fist), and the fronts
of bartenders (usually hypermasculine, with burly bodies and dressed
in leather attire, boots, harnesses, and the like). These elements articulate an eroticized sensibility regarding the character of the idealized sex
partner and sexual practice. Thus, for instance, the décor of the leather
bar itself communicates an erotic idealization that corresponds to a
rough-and-tumble, aggressive, no-holds-barred sexuality and a partner
who can deliver (and take it). In a somewhat different valence, the structure of desire in a gay sports bar communicates to its patrons an erotic
idealization of male athleticism and a "straight-acting," "boy-next-door"
masculinity, both because the bar is dressed with sports paraphernalia
and television sets that broadcast seasonal sports and because *sports bar*

connotes heteronormative masculinity. On this latter note, we might say that sites articulate a structure of desire by dint of circulating as an object of discourse—that is, by dint of being associated with a particular *kind* of "place" (Green, Follert, Osterlund, and Paquin 2010).

Because attributions of sexual attractiveness often map onto and incorporate race, class, gender, age, nationality, and sexual orientation, structures of desire may reflect and, in turn, consolidate socio-ontological schemas. Such schemas act as shorthand for erotic value and can be consequential at the level of interaction and the patterning of field relations. In this sense, structures of desire are collective expressions of the objectification of the social order in the sexual dispositions of individual habitus returned to and transformed within collective life vis-à-vis the aggregation and intensification of schema of desirability among field participants. Put in different terms, collectively eroticized content is constituted in history first and, subsequently, transposed at the level of the individual vis-à-vis symbolic incorporation. Collective sexual life marks the return and transformation of this internalized history in the aggregated form of structures of desire.

This means that even as collective sexual life may incorporate socio-ontological schema, a sexual field is not a mere analogue of the social order or a mirror image of culturally or historically defined representations of attractiveness. This is so for the primary reason that, within a field, desire and desirability are oriented and shaped by processes that are internal to the field itself. Indeed, even if *individual* sexual desires could be deduced from race, class, or ethnic status, collective sexual life is based, not on individual desires, but on the aggregation of desires and attitudes. This fact means that desire and desirability arise, in part, as a function of *ecological* factors (Fischer 1976) that are independent of any given historical or cultural context. Here, the collective nature of sexual social life shapes desire itself in at least three ways: via the popularity tournament (Martin and George 2006; Waller 1937), socialization, and subcultural processes of amplification and intensification. I explore each one of these processes below.

*The popularity tournament*

As Waller (1937) observed of the "rating and dating complex" on college campuses, "here, as nowhere else, nothing succeeds like success" (730). Individuals deemed desirable to others gain added desirability by dint of their popularity. And by this logic one might add the inverse: those who garner little favorable attention in the field become even less desirable than otherwise. In either case, what is vital for a sexual field analysis is that interaction in the field itself—that is, the fact of sociality—has an effect on desirability above and beyond the desirability of any given characteristic or set of characteristics of a given individual alone. Put simply, those who are initially deemed desirable become more so, and, conversely, those deemed less desirable become even less so.

Moreover, with respect to Waller's conception of the popularity tournament, I would underscore the significance of *relative popularity*. That is, implicit in the popularity tournament is an ongoing process of discernment regarding one's own location in the sexual status order relative to others. Those deemed more desirable than ourselves in a given field become even more desirable to us because this discordance in desirability makes the higher-status partner less obtainable and also because the ability to obtain a higher-status partner puts our own desirability in a positive light.[7] Hence, "playing the (sexual) field" (Green 2011) occurs as actors take into account not just a measure of another's popularity (or lack thereof) but a corresponding assessment of one's own sexual capital relative to others'. The more popular a given player, the more desirable she or he is likely to become as individual partner preferences enter the force field of the sexual field. And status discordance itself may influence desirability as when an actor finds that his desired partner has more sexual capital than he. In turn, a higher-status partner becomes preferable to his sexual capital equal. In this way, desirability is shaped by the field and can be considered, in part, a field effect.[8]

## *Sexual socialization*

A second way desire is constituted as a field effect is through socialization processes, including imitation, assimilation, and, on a deeper, unconscious level, internalization. While it is certainly true that sexual actors self-select into particular sexual fields on the basis of preexisting desires, it is also the case that fields act to socialize desire and consolidate or expand a given erotic theme (Rupp 2012). As Martin (chapter 7 in this volume) writes: "*All* taste is cultivated taste; although some aspects of our sensory system develop in a nearly hardwired form, they are only the building blocks for a more complete sensory engagement in the world" (p. 174).

Hennen (2008; chapter 3 in this volume) offers a wonderful example of this process through his examination of the culture of leathermen
and, in particular, the practices of sadomasochism. He observes the ways
in which actors quite literally learn how to be doms and subs through
practice, imitation, trial, and error. Over time, novitiates gain increasing appreciation for the pleasure in pain, learning to eroticize particular acts of dominance and submission, and the erotic experience of giving control to or taking control of another. This is not to suggest that
such men entered the field as *tabulae rasae* with no prior affinity for this
genre of sexual practice. On the contrary, it is likely that individuals who
enter into and consistently engage in the leather scene come to the field
with a preexisting appreciation for it. Rather, it is to suggest that many
of the men who first encounter the leather, sadomasochistic sexual field
have yet to fully adopt its structure of desire, either in practice or in desire. Over time, however, exposure to the field produces a socialization
effect whereby individuals become familiar with, assimilate to, and eroticize more deeply its logic, until the desire itself appears natural, auto-
matic, and second nature. This socialization takes place on two levels:
the first is the conscious act of learning and becoming comfortable with
the leather/sadomasochistic repertoire as a kind of sexual script, and the
second is the actor's unconscious internalization of the field's structure
of desire in the erotic habitus such that it becomes a sexual disposition
independent of the field itself (Green 2008a). What may have been initially a passing interest in the world of leather S/M becomes a predominant source of sexual pleasure.

In my own research of the gay sexual district of Toronto, I came across
an interesting case that makes a similar point but from a rather different
angle. Mark, a twenty-six-year-old, stocky, balding white man moved to
Toronto and quickly came to the realization that his physique and clothing signaled to others that he was a bear in the gay sexual field. Because
he holds more sexual capital in the bear field than in other fields, Mark
finds that bear bars, parties, and events are the most welcoming of him.
There, he has developed a number of friendships with other bears, and
his social world, for the most part, is now confined to the bear subculture. But, as he astutely notes, it is not only his friendship circles that
have been shaped by the bear sexual field. In fact, he was not particularly attracted to hirsute, stocky men prior to his participation in the
bear subculture; over time, however, the field has cultivated in him a
taste for it, a process that he believes may not stop there:

I've been thinking that my status as a bear cub will probably shape my sexual future. Being born a bear cub will probably make me more popular in bear scenes, hence attracting me to them and eventually attracting me to bears. And since the bear community tends to lean to leather and kink, my guess is, being in that environment, I will eventually be dragged to that. And all because of something I didn't really choose. — Mark

In sum, sexual fields are part of the social process whereby taste is socialized in the deepest sense of that term, exposing and sensitizing the self to particular kinds of bodies, sexual themes, practices, and capital portfolios, and elaborating on and consolidating desires that preexisted the field, a process I touch on below.

## Aggregation, amplification, and intensification

Finally, a third way in which sexual fields shape desire is through a process of aggregation, amplification, and intensification (Fischer 1976) whereby otherwise diffusely distributed sexual interests and attitudes within a given population are brought together and, in a process of amplification and intensification, consolidated into structures of desire. As such, structures of desire are reducible to neither the desires of individuals alone nor a simple additive process whereby one might attend to the overlap of desires and attitudes across players. Levine's (1998) ethnography of the clone sexual subculture of the 1970s and 1980s in New York City demonstrates this process. Following the Stonewall riots in 1969, Greenwich Village became an unapologetic center for gay male sociality, attracting gay men throughout the city and the country to visit and in some cases take up residence. These men were largely white and middle-class and were socialized in childhood and adolescence to conceive of masculinity in terms of a gender script that emphasized aggression, muscularity, stoicism, and impersonal sex. As Levine astutely pointed out, despite their sexual attraction to men, gay men acquired the same masculine scripts as heterosexual men. Accordingly, they wrestled with this script in the construction of their own gender and sexual identities. Whereas older generations of gay men may have conformed to the gender-deviant "homosexual role" (McIntosh 1968) in a process of minstrelization (Levine 1998), the generation of gay men who came of age after Stonewall were markedly less apologetic about their sexual orientation and in this sense less beholden to heteronormative constructions of homosexuals as gender deviant. Once brought together in social space, this generation of gay men would enact their individually held masculine scripts, each interacting with and referencing others' enactments of masculinity. Over time, these enactments solidified in the form of a distinct sexual subculture that produced a cookie-cutter gay man (i.e., the clone) who both eroticized others and modeled himself in the image of post–World War II norms of masculinity, including hypermasculine clothing styles, affect, and sexual practices. Self-presentation, for instance, was blue-collar in appearance (granted, with a homoerotic twist), including clothing consisting largely of flannel shirts, tight denim jeans that highlighted the penis and testicles, and work boots or leather attire and motorcycle riding boots associated with the Hell's Angels. Bodies were tanned and weight trained in order to obtain large pectorals and biceps and lean, defined abdominal muscles. Moustaches and five o'clock shadows were *de rigueur*. And sexual practice, too, was markedly masculinized, deemphasizing emotional connection in favor of a rough, penetration-centered, impersonal exchange. In sum, as these particular gay men were brought together in social space, their individual, unconscious schemata around masculinity were consolidated and amplified, producing a sexual subculture that extracted from and magnified individual gendered sensibilities and dispositions in new kinds of intensified, institutionalized roles and practices, shaping everything from how one appeared, to whom one desired, to how one had sex. Put differently, a clone sexual field took shape that institutionalized a particular form of post–World War II masculinity in ways that built on and exceeded the individual desires of its participants.

In total, sexual fields both reflect and produce desire and desirability. Participants in sexual social life are neither fully preconstituted sexual actors nor lone atoms but rather agents whose desires and practices are shaped both prior to and in the process of field sociality (see also Weinberg and Williams, chapter 2 in this volume). This may occur through intersubjective assessments of one's own relative desirability within a given field whereby those perceived to be popular or more desirable than we are *become* more attractive over time and, conversely, those perceived to be less popular or *less* desirable become less attractive over time. It may also occur as individuals without a fully formed interest in a given sexual scene develop a taste for it following exposure to the dominant bodies, practices, and judgments of the field. And, when paired via sustained interaction, individual erotic dispositions can become amplified and inten-

sified with the effect of producing new structures of desire and new institutionalized norms of attractiveness within a given field.

It is important to note that, while the preceding discussion has focused
on the ways in which sexual desire is shaped by the sexual field, the same
principles are at work with respect to nonsexual elements of partner desirability. For instance, entrance into a particular heterosexual dating
subculture that prizes financial wherewithal among men may foster increased concern among women over their prospective partner's financial
portfolio. What may have previously been of only moderate interest now
becomes a major factor in partnering and by the same three processes
noted above—that is, the popularity tournament (wealthier men are
more popular and thereby become more desirable); socialization (wealth
becomes a crucial marker of status to which one becomes accustomed);
and, finally, amplification/intensification (having one house is no longer
enough since top-tier men all have at least two homes—one to live in and
one to summer in).

In this way, sexual fields are related but not reducible to the broader
terrain of social stratification and cultural representation, and neither
are they simply an additive product of the preexisting sexual desires and
attitudes of a given set of individual actors within the field.[9] Rather, sexual fields demonstrate a degree of autonomy from both the broader social structure and individual dispositions insofar as they (re)socialize
constructions of desirability and sexual repertoires through the collectivization of individual desires and attitudes and subsequent processes of
socialization, amplification, intensification, and transformation.

## Objectivity, Subjectivity, and Structures of Desire

To the extent that structures of desire underpin the logic of social stratification, they produce an objective outcome in the form of a sexual status
order. Subsequently, in order to play the sexual field, actors must become
cognizant of the field's structure of desire, situating themselves and others
in relation to it (Green 2008b, 2008c, 2011). By definition, then, a field's
structure of desire possesses both an objective and a subjective element.
On the one hand, an actor is subject to the patterning of sexual preference and selection within the field, the latter impinging on her experience
regardless of her awareness of it. This is the objective component of a sexual field. On the other hand, the determination of the desirability of oth-

ers entails a subjective (but surely not random) process based on observation and inference without parallel in other kinds of fields wherein status is formally codified and conferred through institutionalized, public status markers. This is perhaps what most sets the sexual field apart from fields more generally and an issue for which the sexual field analyst must pay special attention. It is to the subjective process of discerning a sexual status order, and one's location within it, that I turn below.

As I have noted elsewhere (Green 2011), there are at least six key moments in the process by which an actor apprehends a structure of desire and corresponding sexual status order, of which the first four are most critical for the present purpose: (*a*) a recognition of the sexual field (i.e., the sexual actor must conceive of the site as a social space wherein individuals compete for status and sexual selection); (*b*) a formulation of the *generalized other* (Mead 1934) within the field, including knowledge concerning its particular structure of desire or, in different terms, a given field's collective valuations of sexual attractiveness; (*c*) a formulation of one's own position within the sexual status order vis-à-vis intersubjective feedback and the development of a looking-glass self (Cooley 1902); and (*d*) an assessment of others' positions within the sexual status order, including dispositional attributions based on inferences made from personal observation. Note that each of these four moments arises as part of a subjective process whereby actors formulate *a theory* of the field's structure of desire that is based on their perceptions of sexual value, including cumulative observations made over time and across space. But, to the extent that such theory building will vary between individuals and will capture, imperfectly, the patterning of sexual selection at any given time and space coordinate, the composition of a structure of desire is little more than an educated guess in the minds of each participant.[10]

One interesting dimension of the process of cognizing a structure of desire is that these structures are not only aggregations of desire but also aggregations of ideals *about* desirability. In this sense, structures of desire can operate as "governing fictions" that organize how one attributes sexual capital to others and, subsequently, how one negotiates the field. For this reason, it is possible that a status order may take shape in which a class of actors will possess a degree of sexual capital incommensurate with the attractiveness that many individual players in the field attribute to them. Thus, we have a case of "pluralistic ignorance" (Waller 1937, 733) insofar as each actor believes that most other actors want X when, in fact, most actors would prefer Y. Or, alternatively, actors may find their desires resocialized by a structure of desire such that a group of actors who were previously unappealing become appealing (see above), and vice versa. Indeed, it is likely that most sexual fields possess structures of desire and, in turn, sexual status orders that reflect *both* the actual, first-order desires of actors, on the one hand, and constructions of what actors believe is desirable en masse, on the other—that is, a second-order desire.

One example of this phenomenon can be seen in lesbian life in North America in the 1940s and 1950s, and here I draw primarily from Kennedy and Davis (1993), who conducted ethnographic work on a lesbian community in Buffalo, New York,[11] and the delightful film about Canadian lesbians from this time period, *Forbidden Love*. Then, lesbian sociality was organized rather strictly by a two-sided sexual field composed of butches and fems. Queer women were classified as either butch or fem, and gender ambiguity was not generally tolerated. Butches were to desire and couple with fems, and fems were to desire and couple with butches. Assimilation to the lesbian community all but required that one conform to one classification or another, and the sexual field was organized accordingly.

While we do not have definitive sources to determine the actual desires of all butch and fem lesbians, what is clear is that not all women felt fully comfortable with this kind of bifurcated, butch-fem structure. In fact, while some women were at ease with appropriating the identity and role of one sexual type over the other, some women felt that the binary categories were an artificial imposition to which they had to conform lest they face alienation in the sexual field. In some cases, women would actually shift from one category to the other, but rarely in the context of a butch-fem relationship, as the transition would call into question the identity and role of the partner. One question that inevitably emerges from this time period is, while, as a rule, butches partnered only with fems, and vice versa, were there instances whereby some butches found other butches more attractive than fems and some fems found other fems more attractive than butches? If structures of desire can work both as an aggregation of what actors desire and as a representation of what is deemed collectively desirable, then, in the North American lesbian sexual fields of the 1940s and 1950s, the two-sided structure of desire may have corralled some butches into partnerships with some fems, and vice versa, even when these arrangements did not reflect their actual, first-order desires, or their strongest desires, or at least their only desires. Undoubtedly, a butch-fem structure of desire reflected the true desires of many women, but it may have also operated as a governing fiction whereby butches came to believe that fems were more desirable than butches and fems believed that butches were more desirable than fems and, thus, the patterning of sexual partnerships followed suit. Here, either pluralistic ignorance prevailed as butches and fems followed the normative, idealized pattern of opposite-gender selection, or the structure of desire acted back on their desires such that fems *became* more attractive to butches and butches to fems following field socialization.

Another instance of this phenomenon can be seen in Armstrong's (2010b) study of "the slut" in college sorority life. Sluts, by virtue of their promiscuous reputations, lose favor within the Greek sexual field and incur a sexual capital deficit when compared to their nonslut sisters. What is particularly interesting in this research is the fact that sisters acquire the stigmatized label *slut* less from the quality and quantity of their sexual encounters with men than from the assessments of other sorority sisters. Hence, when a sister becomes marked by other sisters as a slut, she is devalued by the fraternity brothers. In turn, the question arises, on the basis of this label, to what extent do fraternity brothers pass up opportunities to date or have a sexual encounter with a slut even when, on any given occasion, the latter may be more sexually attractive than her "good-girl" sisters? It is likely that some fraternity brothers avoid intimate relations with the sluts less as a consequence of their own desires than because of the lack of desirability of these women to others. That is, the prevailing structure of desire within Greek campus life may operate as a governing fiction to the extent that fraternity brothers believe that the sluts are less desirable than the good girls as hookup partners and most certainly as dates. Alternatively, the structure of desire may operate to transform the brothers' desires altogether—that is, whereas the slut was once a source of sexual interest, now the field has dampened this interest or replaced it with desire for the good girl.

The potential shame or loss of status that may result from sexual association with the slut is related to a broader set of implications with respect to structures of desire and sexual fields. In this particular instance, heterosexual men's attraction to women would seem related, in part, to the fantasy of the latter's potential access. Women who are either "omni-available" or, by contrast, *un*available may incite both male heterosexual desire and, at the same time, scorn.[12] This brings to the forefront the more general issue of the social organization of the sexual field with respect to ambivalence and contradiction in desire and desirability, particularly those fields wherein shorter-term sexual relations are normative. To the extent that sexual desire and desirability are constituted as unconscious dispositions, and insofar as such dispositions are aggregated as an organizing principle of partner preference in collective sexual life, so they become relevant for field analysis. For instance, in my earlier work on the sexual capital of black gay men in a largely white-dominated, middle-class sexual field of Manhattan, I observed that some black men achieved high sexual status when they possessed a front that connoted dominance and aggression—for example, the "Mandingo man" and the "thug" (Green 2008c). Nevertheless, while these men acquired considerable sexual capital in the field, they at the same time perceived themselves to be devalued by white men as prospective long-term partners. My reading of this paradoxical status hinged on the extent to which structures of desire collectivize unconscious, psychodynamic preoccupations with power relations in the context of sexual fantasy. In the most general sense, sexual desiring may draw on a range of cultural and historical representations of a given group, transposing these representations onto preconstituted psychodynamic dispositions related to dominance, submission, incorporation, evisceration, and humiliation (Benjamin 1988; Stoller 1985). This transposition renders not just certain kinds of sexual acts sexy but certain kinds of sexual objects—for example, the "whore," the "thug"—highly erotic even while highly stigmatized or otherwise marginalized (McClintock 1995; Weiss 2011).

What these examples demonstrate is that structures of desire must be treated with analytic care insofar as they may differentially (*a*) reflect the desires of field participants, (*b*) provide a collective valuation of desirability that may or may not reflect actors' real desires (but will be consequential in any case for field practice), (*c*) resocialize the very substance of what an actor finds to be desirable, and (*d*) reflect a collectivization of psychodynamic dispositions related to human eroticism, including those associated with shame, ambivalence, and unequal power relations. Insofar as these possibilities may be present to varying degrees across sexual fields, it becomes an empirical question whether and to what extent some sexual fields are more likely than others to tilt the balance of field selection by one mechanism or the other. As well, these examples demonstrate that sexual capital should be understood not as simply the sexual value accruing to an actor on the basis of her individual characteristics (what Hakim [2011] refers to as a personal and portable *asset*) but rather as an outgrowth of the field's structure of desire and its hegemonic system of judgment. In this latter case, sexual capital is a collective assignment of sexual value, an issue I discuss further below.

## Sexual Capital

While varying in importance across sexual fields (see above), *sexual capital* is generally associated with an individual's location in sexual social structure, if only because others' evaluations of his or her status are influenced by what they think others think of him or her. Sexual capital indexes the degree of power an individual or a group holds within a sexual field on the basis of collective assessments of attractiveness and sex appeal. Thus, the common expression, "he/she is out of my league," is the colloquial way of suggesting a sexual capital discordance between the desiring actor and the desired actor wherein the desirer is located too low in the field's tiers of desirability to obtain the interest of the desired.

For the sexual fields framework, the analytic value of sexual capital rests on the concept's ability to capture two important elements of status: first, the degree of desirability one has within a given sexual field and the corresponding capacity to reap the field's rewards and, second, the extent to which this desirability is interconvertible with (but irreducible to) other forms of capital. With respect to this second element, sexual capital can be parlayed into financial benefits (economic capital), social contacts, including access to networks of influence (social capital), and even, in some cases, cultural distinction (symbolic capital), as when a porn star parlays her sexual capital into name recognition. This element of convertibility makes sexual desirability not just an index of power within a field but a structural bridge that can connect one field with another.

To the extent that sexual fields are distinguished by structures of desire, it follows that what constitutes sexual capital in one field may not constitute it in another field. Accordingly, sexual capital, like other capitals, is field dependent and must be considered, in part, *a property of a field* rather than a property of an individual. For instance, while male (and, for that matter, female) bodybuilders may have a great deal of sexual capital on Venice's muscle beach, they are not likely to enjoy the same status among members of the Classical Music Lovers' Exchange.[13]

Yet, once a structure of desire takes form, the reigning "hegemonic systems of judgment" locate sexual capital in the characteristics of people. In this sense, sexual capital is both a property of the field and a property of the individual and cannot be reduced to either.

Sexual capital typically accrues to individuals and groups along at least three intersecting axes: the appearance of the face and body, affect, and sociocultural style (Green 2008b, 2008c). As I note above, characteristics that confer sexual capital in a sexual field are neither universal nor independent of field context and therefore cannot be presumed *a priori*.[14] Nevertheless, it is useful to outline categories of attributes that typically confer sexual capital.

Physical attributes of the face and body that contribute to sexual capital can include height, weight, skin shade, the length, color, texture, and style of the hair, the shape of the face, the fullness of the lips, the width of the shoulders, the length of the neck, the fullness of the bust, the ratio of hip to waist, the length and size of the legs, and the size and shape of the buttocks, among many others. But bodies themselves are carried and animated in a variety of ways that communicate affect and can be as important as physical attributes in determining sexual capital. In fact, very similar bodies can accrue radically different degrees of sexual capital within a sexual field on the basis of the body's bearing, whether it stands erect or slouches, whether the gate is strong and swaggering or deferential and demur, whether the gaze is solid, steady, and in command of its wants or shy, unsteady, inexperienced, or overly eager. As well, affect is surmised in gestural repertoires that communicate masculinity and femininity, including the positioning of the legs when one sits, the character of gesticulation, the positioning of the head when one speaks, how much is spoken, and variations in enunciation of language. As a gestalt, these affective characteristics communicate to others who we are as gendered, racialized, and classed individuals, components many of which are central to erotic attribution.

Finally, sociocultural styles can provide an important attribute of sexual capital. Like affect, dress and accessories communicate race, class, gender, age, lifestyle, and sensibility. So, too, the manner in which clothing and accessories are worn can communicate a great deal, such as a baseball hat worn forward, backward, or sideways. Moreover, clothing and accessories have different connotations from one body to another: a fur coat on a man has a very different connotation than does a fur coat on a woman; a large gold necklace communicates a different message when it is worn by a white woman than when it is worn by a black man.

### Currencies of sexual capital

While any given characteristic can possess erotic value, characteristics that confer sexual capital are often of the typological character—that is, they exist not in isolation but rather in *combinations* that specify an erotic type or thematic (cf. Waller [1937] on high-status fraternity men). This occurs because the audience of a given site is typically composed of individuals who share socioerotic schematics. In a sexual field, the combination of physical, affective, and stylistic attributes that confer erotic value constitutes a *currency of sexual capital*. Referring back to Levine's (1998) ethnography of the New York City gay clone subculture of the 1970s, one finds a clear example of a currency of sexual capital whereby a cluster of valorized characteristics characterized the field's "leading men"—including a hard, muscled physique, youth, hypermasculinity, facial hair, and a working-class style. This erotic aesthetic was so highly coordinated that it gave rise to the subcultural classification *the clone*. Here, the clone structure of desire was characterized, not by one particular physical or affective trait, but by an erotic thematic. Hence, white, twenty- to thirty-something men who were hypermasculine in appearance, with hard, tanned muscular bodies, and who could be read as working-class had great advantage in the field. All other men were merely inferior facsimiles in descending order.

### Distribution of sexual capital

Because sexual fields produce an arena of relations wherein sexual capital is of relative value, the sexual status order is subject to change as actors with varying degrees of sexual capital cycle in and out of a given site. As outlined above, sites that provide real-time sexual sociality, such as a bar or a house party, possess temporally fluid status orders wherein the distribution of sexual capital can recalibrate by the hour (see, e.g., Tewksbury 2002). The concept itself is probably most useful in these types of contexts as it may help make intelligible the logic of social interaction among on-site actors, including who approaches whom and when and how they approach. As I have written elsewhere (Green 2011), strategies of approach and deference in the field are organized around the distribution of sexual capital as actors take account of their own sexual capital vis-à-vis other actors. When an actor deems herself to occupy a position of low desirability, she may be less likely to pursue a desired partner. Alternatively, an actor who feels he has equal or greater sexual capital than most players in the field may feel freer to make an advance and become less receptive to the advances of others.

There is a more serious implication of low sexual status that may be relatively unexplored in the literature on a host of topics, from mental health, adolescent pregnancy, and the social determinants of sexually transmitted infections to rape on college campus. One's location in the distribution of sexual capital, over time, can produce enduring psychological states related to self-esteem and perceptions of assimilation (Green 2008b). For instance, an actor who repeatedly feels that she possesses little sexual capital in a given sexual field may develop negative reflected self-esteem (Thoits 1999) and, in turn, use sexual availability as a way of attracting others (Akers et al. 2009; Eisenberg, Neumark-Sztainer, and Lust 2005). Alternatively, actors with low sexual capital may lose agency in the course of a sexual encounter with a person of perceived higher status, becoming less able to talk about his own sexual satisfaction and more willing to please his partner, even when this can put him at risk for sexually transmitted infections, including HIV (Green 2008b, 2008c, 2011; Murray and Adam 2001; Poon and Ho 2008; Wilton 2009). Similarly, there is research to suggest that sexual status is related to one's ability to negotiate safer sex and, in the case of college women, to deter sexual assault (Armstrong, Hamilton, and Sweeney 2006).

To summarize, the sexual fields framework is composed of a set of sensitizing concepts that illuminate the structures and processes associated with collective sexual life and sexual stratification. But sexual fields are themselves social spaces that can be conceived at multiple levels of analysis, each with its own analytic jurisdiction, yet all interconnected. Below, I turn to a specification of these levels of analysis and offer some preliminary speculation as to their interconnections.

## Levels of Analysis

In the study of sexual fields, a series of empirical and theoretical lines of inquiry are of immediate import: (*a*) What is the relationship of sexual desires to the sexual field? (*b*) What kinds of capital confer value in

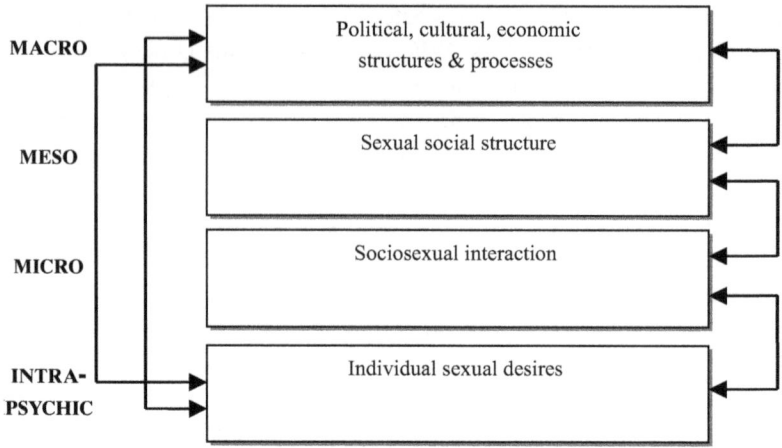

FIGURE 3. Levels of analysis in collective sexual life.

a sexual field, why and how are these distributed across actors, and with what effects? (*c*) What is the structure of a sexual field with respect to its circuits (for more on circuits, see Adam and Green, chapter 5 in this volume) and horizontal and vertical stratification? (*d*) How do sexual fields relate to one another, to other kinds of fields, and to larger structures and processes, such as immigration, gentrification, urban renewal, and the rise and fall of sexually transmitted infections? Thinking about these questions more abstractly, we might model them at four interconnected levels of analysis (see fig. 3).

At the intrapsychic level, individuals develop sexual desires that typically focus on certain kinds of people, contexts, and interactions. As I note above and elsewhere (Green 2008a), it is nearly impossible to model sexual desire with much predictive validity because there is so much variability between people and because processes other than those directly observable, including primary process, are likely to shape the things we find erotic. Nevertheless, to be sure, the erotic imagination is socialized, changing over time and from one context to another. While the sexual fields framework is primarily a tool for analyzing collective rather than individual sexual life, it is nevertheless critical to think about the intrapsychic level of individual sexual desires, both because individuals entering the field come with some of these desires preconstituted and because the field itself can act back on these intrapsychic desires and transform them. Hence, there is an important interface between individual desire and collective sexual life.[15]

Moving upward one level of analysis, microlevel, interactions in a nightclub, on a street corner, or in the virtual field of an Internet chat room represent social structure in the making: Who is being paid attention by whom? Who initiates conversation and how? Who is rebuffed by whom and how? What are the temporal patterns of sexual sociality over a given evening, a given week night, a given season? So, too, the analyst will want to attend to the range of sociospatial configurations that can emerge in interaction, as when, for instance, similarly positioned actors in the sexual social structure cohere in homophilic segments, with more attractive actors located in cliques at the center of interaction and less attractive actors floating at the sidelines. In turn, the analyst will want to be mindful of how sexual actors manage the self and jockey for position in light of differential sexual status.

At a greater degree of abstraction, the analyst can attend to the aggregation of sexual attitudes and appreciations in the form of a structure of desire, a currency of sexual capital, and the attendant sexual field, as noted at length above.

At a still greater degree of abstraction, any given neighborhood can constitute a *sexual district* with multiple sexual fields of varying character. The status order of a given sexual field within a given sexual district may not coincide with the status order of another sexual field, and, in fact, one field may exist precisely because another does not accommodate the desires of local players (see Hennen, chapter 3 in this volume). The gross relation of these sexual fields to one another is part and parcel of the analysis of the sexual social structure of a given sexual district.

And, finally, at the broadest level of analysis, sexual fields are shaped by and imbricated within social, political, and economic processes and structures, including local configurations of commercial and public space, the culture of neighborhoods and the vicissitudes of local economies, local and federal policies related to sexual regulation and sexual citizenship, patterns of immigration, gentrification, and urban renewal, changing demographic configurations, and the rise and fall of sexually transmitted infections, to name only a few.

In sum, the phenomenon of sexual stratification is subject to the full scale of sociological analysis and will require attention at each of these levels—from the intrapsychic up through the macroscopic—if it is to be fully understood. The sexual fields framework provides one systematic approach to thinking sociologically about sexual stratification and the social contexts within which desire and desirability are consequential. But sensitizing scholars to the structures and processes of sexual stratification will surely open up many more new lines of inquiry than it resolves. How future scholars of the sexual field will apply and develop the framework remains to be seen, but, to be sure, much work remains ahead.

## Notes

1. In some instances, it may be analytically useful to analyze the private bedroom of the monogamous couple as a field, whereby each jockeys for status relative to the other and, in turn, establishes a kind of status order that shapes sexual identity and practice.

2. Sites, as the spatial nodes of a sexual field, may be conceived at multiple levels of analysis. At the broadest level of analysis, one may wish to refer to the gross composition of physical locations of sexual sociality within a given bounded territory—i.e., a *sexual district.* Alternatively, at a more microlevel of analysis, one may wish to consider a particular site of sexual social life, such as a bar, a park, or a barn dance. As I elaborate in my discussion of structures of desire, such sites are important objects of analysis because they often communicate the character of a given sexual status order, including the atmospheric elements of décor and the meanings attributed to the space itself—i.e., the "place" of space (Green, Follert, Osterlund, and Paquin 2010).

3. The term *sexual capital* is analytically interchangeable with *erotic capital,* though, for an exception, Hakim's (2010, 2011) *erotic capital* represents a much broader version of the concept and a topic of critique. See Green (2013).

4. For instance, Armstrong (2010a) notes that the sexual capital of sorority sisters is, in part, shaped by the sorority members themselves. For more on this, see my discussion in this chapter of sexual capital.

5. This process is consistent with research in cognitive psychology and the principle of cognitive economy. For more, see Rosch (1978).

6. One implication of this typology is that, when a sexual field is bifurcated between groups that possess highly distinct preferences in terms of capital portfolios, it may be tempting to think of a two-sided field as two entirely separate fields that happen to arise in the same site at the same time. But this formulation may present more problems than it resolves because, as Waller (1937) notes, desirability itself can arise, in part, as a function of one's popularity. For example, among heterosexuals, a woman's attraction to a man can come, in part, as a function of his popularity among other women in the field. What is more, here, pop-

ularity can index, not only attractiveness to the opposite sex, but also, as Armstrong (2010a) notes in a parallel formulation, a given individual's social status among his or her same-sex peers. Hence, in this regard, desirability can arise within the interactional setting of a sexual domain best conceived as a single sexual field.

7. Of course, this may not necessarily be the case at the level of *individual* preferences. As Martin and George (2006) note, for some individuals, desirability is a "disutility" insofar as a potential partner's added attractiveness, relative to one's own, can make him harder to attract and harder to keep.

8. Determining desirability at the level of the individual, however, may not abide by the same processes as those implied by the popularity tournament or by a market analysis. On the potential utility of obtaining a partner who is deemed *less* attractive than oneself, see Martin and George (2006).

9. A second reason that sexual fields are not simply extensions of other systems of stratification takes us to the complexity of human desire and desirability. For the same reason that Wrong (1999) rejected the "oversocialized man" and the gloss of psychological processes in Parsonian structural functionalism, sexual desire cannot be collapsed into social learning or capitalist relations of production (Chodorow 1994). In fact, as I and others have argued elsewhere (Epstein 1991; Green 2008b), social learning models such as scripting theory are limited in their ability to explain the content of a person's sexual desires. This is not at all to suggest that there are no learning components to sexual desire, no less sexual practice. Quite the contrary, the sexual fields framework is premised on such a possibility, as when the field acts back on individual erotic habitus, resocializing sexual desire and practices. However, the empirical record demonstrates that humans are predisposed to acquire at least some of their sexual desires in the absence of express inputs from scripts or class background or other learned cultural materials. The case of same-sex attraction is itself an instructive example of a genre of sexual desires for which many lesbians and gay men had no prior knowledge at the time they found members of the same sex desirable.

What is more, as a century of psychodynamic literature and research attests, sexual desires are replete with tenacious psychic preoccupations, including preoccupations with power, humiliation, dominance, submission, annihilation, and identification (Benjamin 1988; Chodorow 1994; Dor 2001; Freud 1961; Green 2008b; Stoller 1985; Simon and Whittier 2001). In this sense, sexual desires draw so deeply from an individual's psychic biography, including his or her family relations, and from intrapsychic processes that defy logical organization or prediction that any systematic account of sexual desiring is doomed to failure. Without a doubt, a theory that posits a one-to-one relationship between culture or social structure and sexual fantasy, no less sexual stratification, is dubious from the start.

10. To be sure, not all formulations of the sexual status structure are equally

perceptive. In my study of an urban gay and bisexual sexual field, for example, I accumulated a systematic catalog of all street-level representations on three blocks of the main street of the Gay Village over the course of four years. I found that nearly nine of ten images of men were of white, fit, athletic men ranging from twenty- to thirty-something years old, usually advertising a bar event or the local sex shop. While most interviewees recounted a similar distribution of representations when asked (upward of four/five), a few respondents had different perceptions. One respondent, for example, reported that the majority of images on the main street of the Gay Village featured men of color—black men in particular. This observation is factually untrue.

That said, however, the accuracy with which a given actor formulates a theory of a sexual status order may be less important than the fact that he or she formulates one and, subsequently, positions himself or herself within it. In this sense, to follow Thomas and Thomas (1928): "If men define situations as real, they are real in their consequences" (572). This is so because, once actors formulate a theory of the logic of desirability in the field, they are likely to develop lines of action commensurate with their theory, evaluating both their own sexual capital and that of others from within its scope.

11. I am indebted to John Levi Martin for pointing me to this example.

12. I am grateful to Elizabeth Armstrong for this insight.

13. The Classical Music Lovers' Exchange is a nationwide organization founded in 1980 to provide the community of classical music lovers access to one another.

14. All characteristics conferring sexual capital are saturated with culturally constructed meaning, though some of these characteristics—such as age—may be somewhat less subject to cultural variations because they are more subject to hardwiring. Indeed, should we concede the contentious point made by evolutionary psychologists that some physical characteristics are innately desirable— e.g., a particular female waist to hip ratio—the meaning of such characteristics, nevertheless, will be mediated by culture, history, and one's own embodiment such that their sexual value is always, to some degree, field dependent.

15. For more on this interface, see Green's (2008a) work on the erotic habitus.

# CHAPTER TWO

# Sexual Field, Erotic Habitus, and Embodiment at a Transgender Bar

Martin S. Weinberg, Indiana University
Colin J. Williams, Indiana University/
Purdue University Indianapolis

## Mabel's Bar

W e first came across Green's (2008c) ideas on collective sexual life while working on a study of a bar in San Francisco that catered to trans women (persons assigned male status at birth who do not wish to live as men) and their male admirers. The bar (which we refer to as "Mabel's") located in the Tenderloin—an area that contains many cheap hotels and rooming houses as well as small neighborhood bars, cafés, and restaurants. The inhabitants of the area include a number of working-class Asian immigrants and a poor African American population, and it also serves as the epicenter for the city's homeless. We were accepted at Mabel's because our other studies in San Francisco had made us known to persons in the city's "sexual underground" (Weinberg, Williams, and Pryor 1994, chap. 2).

Because the bar was located just down the street from where we stayed in San Francisco, we frequented Mabel's often over a period of many years. As a sexual interest in trans women had rarely been studied,[1] we started some preliminary ethnography, observing the interactions between the men and the trans women (as well as the interactions among the trans women).[2] In addition to overhearing their verbal interactions, we had many casual conversations with both the men and the trans women and observed a variety of nonverbal interactions (e.g., flirting through body language, touching). These ethnographic experiences provided data as well as the basis for an interview that would provide additional material. The investigation became, in Green's (2008c, 2011) terms, an examination of the dominant structure of desire at Mabel's and the erotic habitus that developed as a consequence of interaction in this sexual field. This examination fit well with another interest we had begun to pursue, the phenomenon of "embodiment" and the incorporation of social structure through bodily practices (see Weinberg and Williams 2005). Accordingly, we describe how interaction at Mabel's between the trans women and the men leads to intersubjective rapport through different types of embodiment. These processes of embodiment reflect and incorporate the field's structure of desire and, in turn, have the capacity to act back on the erotic habitus itself. In this way, we view embodiment as the means through which the field's structure of desire becomes objectified in, and extends, the men's erotic habitus.

## Observations in the Bar

Mabel's was a fun bar. Soulful music played from the jukebox, and sometimes a few people danced on the small dance floor at the back of the bar. There was an air of congeniality, sounds of laughter, and smells of perfume. There was the touch of the trans women who walked past or who gently touched a man sitting next to them. Sometimes they would hug or kiss on the cheek men whom they knew or would fondle their genitals. There was also a sense excitement expressed in the verbal negotiations that could lead to sex between the men and the trans women. Many of these interactions were commercial—centered on the exchange of sex for money. However, not all the trans women at Mabel's were sex workers; noncommercial hookups also occurred between the trans women (even those who did sex work) and the men attending the bar.

As Green has proposed, sexual fields possess three invariant structural features. One is a *structure of desire*. In the case of Mabel's, the erotic habitus of its male patrons reflected an erotic disposition toward a gendered sex appeal—mainly one of femininity. This disposition preceded patronage at Mabel's and therefore can be seen as part of the men's preexisting habitus. At Mabel's, however, this disposition was extended to include women who have a penis. The bodywork of the trans women—namely, their dress, posture, style of speech, and comportment—incorporated these features as they pursued a dramatic style of womanhood while at the same time disguising outward signs of maleness.

This particular structure of desire, institutionalized in Mabel's, produced the field's currency of erotic capital possessed by the trans women. Its convertibility was through financial transactions: the trans women parlayed their gender presentation and sexual availability into cash. Thus, the "bifurcation of . . . *capital portfolios*" that Green (chapter 1 in this volume, p. 34) says occurs in typical heterosexual situations is parodied at Mabel's even though the interaction is between two genetic males.

How successful this interaction is relates to Green's (2008c) second invariant feature of a sexual field—*tiers of desirability*. Thus, within a field, individuals assign (to themselves and others) a ranking based on the capital they possess. At Mabel's, those trans women who produced the most successful femininity occupied the highest tier of desirability in the competition for the men.[3] This could lead to concerns among them as to how well they achieved femininity. For example, in referring disparagingly to potential clients, one trans woman said: "The worst are men who change their minds [and choose some other trans woman] because I'm not as feminine."

The trans women who possessed the greatest erotic capital at Mabel's were those who were younger and those who were Asian, who generally exhibited the most successful feminization and thus had an advantage in hustling. At times, the competition between the trans women led to conflict and the trading of insults especially referring to suggested rank on the tier of desirability. Accordingly, we heard negative comments on hair, makeup, dress, and comportment, remarks such as, "You don't pass," "You'll never make a wife," and "You don't make it in women's clothes." On the whole, however, the camaraderie among the trans women was striking (cf. Sausa, Keatley, and Operario 2007). Also, concerns could occur not only about being placed "too low" on the tier of desirability but also about being placed "too high"—namely, when men with a sexual interest thought they were "real women" (we use the terminology used in the bar rather than currently accepted academic nomenclature, such as *cismen* and *ciswomen*). This concern was reflected when there was uncertainty about whether a potential client/partner knew that the individual in which they were interested had a penis. Some of the trans women were apprehensive that, if the men found out at a later point, it could lead to an assault. Thus, they were heard informing potential clients/hook-ups, "You know I'm a boy?" Or the classic retort to being asked whether they were "a man" was often, "No, but I have a cock."

Moreover, the ranking structure at Mabel's could be an unstable one. This is related to Green's third and final invariant feature of a sexual field—*the distribution of erotic capital.* There was an obvious change in the distribution of erotic capital according to the day of the week, the time of day, and even the month and week of the month. More trans women, and a greater variety, were there in the evening and on week-end evenings. There were also more men during the period of the month when unemployment, social security, and disability checks were received, with the availability of this money further facilitating potential hook-ups. Finally, the summer months provided an additional source of men—tourists who found their way to the bar. Thus, the sexual field at Mabel's expanded and contracted as the numbers and proportions of different types of customers varied, with a resulting recalibration of the tiers of desirability. If there were few men or too much competition because of a high trans to nontrans ratio, those with less erotic capital had their capital's value reduced even further. Consequently, some of these trans women would leave the bar to seek customers on a nearby street. Also, when the trans women found sex partners in the bar, they would leave and go elsewhere—often to a nearby parking lot, where they had sex in a car. Thus, there was often a flow of bodies to and from the bar that added to the aura that indeed something exciting was going on there.

### Interviewing the Men

In addition to the observations, we conducted interviews with forty-three of the men who were in attendance at the bar. We obtained back-ground information, and we sought information about the nature of the erotic habitus they shared, how it was embodied, and how it was realized in the sexual field provided by Mabel's.

We interviewed the men while they were standing or sitting at the bar or at one of the tables and recorded their responses in written form. Over a series of evenings, each of the men who were in attendance was approached. We informed the men that we were researchers associated with the Kinsey Institute trying to learn more about the "tranny bar" scene. Many of them had seen us hanging out at the bar, and many knew that we were Indiana University sex researchers as we were open about this. Only one patron did not wish to talk to us, and all the interview conversations proceeded in a friendly manner. The interviews lasted from twenty to thirty minutes. We also conversed informally with the same men at other times in the bar. The results of the interviews and conversations dovetailed nicely with the ethnographic observations; they provided information about how the men constructed the meaning of their association with trans women and any sexual interaction that had occurred.

The forty-three men we interviewed ranged in age from twenty-one to fifty, with a median age of thirty-four. In terms of race/ethnicity, there were equal numbers of white and nonwhite participants. Educationally, just over two-fifths reported being college graduates. We considered over half of them to be sexually interested in the trans women (determined by whether they said they had engaged in sexual activity with a trans woman [about a third of those interviewed] or had an interest in engaging in sexual activity with a trans woman but had not yet done so [another third]). Of these men who had sex or wanted to have sex with a trans woman, half defined as "heterosexual" and the other half as "bisexual" or "probably bisexual."[4] The remainder of the men we interviewed indicated that they attended the bar because they found it curious and exotic but that they did not wish to have sex with any of the trans women.

Of the men who reported having engaged in sex with a trans woman, both the number of times and the frequency of sex with them were low (i.e., one to two times and generally not more than once in a month, although one man said that he did this a couple times a week). The most common sexual activity, reported by about two-thirds of this group, was receiving fellatio from the trans woman. A third said that they had been given a hand job, one said that he had performed a hand job, and over a third told us that they had been the inserter in anal intercourse with a trans woman. Although all these men saw sex with a trans woman as casual and not part of a relationship, some were able to obtain the sex without charge (e.g., when the trans woman was not a sex worker or when the trans sex worker was inebriated and/or seemed to fancy them), while others had paid. Over half the men who reported sex with a trans woman said that they had paid, and the median payment was $50. When they were asked what their preference would be if given a choice of sex partners, all but one said that a "real woman" was their first preference, and the single remaining person said a man.

When we add to those who said that they had had sex with a trans woman, those who indicated an interest in doing so—over three-quarters of the combined group—said that their first preference was "real women," one said men, and the remaining four reported an equal preference either for a trans woman *or* a real woman or for a trans woman *or* a man. No one chose trans women as their sole first preference. For those who said that they had a second preference, however, *all* of these men said that it was trans women.

We could clearly distinguish two types of erotic habitus among these men. One was exhibited by the *straight men* (those who defined themselves as heterosexual). The second was displayed by the *bisexual men* (those who defined as bisexual or probably bisexual). These labels, however, are superficial in describing their sexual interest, and we will specifically examine how their erotic habitus is embodied so they are able to perform (or contemplate performing) sexually in this particular field (see also Green 2008a).

## Sexual Embodiment

Within the context of the sexual field, *sexual embodiment* (Jackson and Scott 2007) can be conceptualized as the individual incorporation of the field's structure of desire. The first dimension of sexual embodiment in this framework is *objectified embodiment*. This designates when one's body is the object of another's desire. The fieldwork made clear that this experience was more likely to be the case for the trans women and less likely to be the case for the men, who were usually uncertain about being the object of the trans women's desire. Many of the men mentioned that they knew that they were a "trick" and that any attraction toward them was probably feigned or counterfeit. On the other hand, the trans women were usually assumed by the men to be genetic males with a sexual preference for other men as sex partners, so the men could be made to feel that their body was desired. We saw this happen in the bar (e.g., through fondling, compliments, and rapt attention). What were taken as signs of the trans women's personal sexual interest or lack thereof fed into the reflexive embodiment of the men. Thus, the process was a kind of intersubjective dance whereby one's perceived desirability and the desire of the other became inextricably intertwined.

When asked what drew them to the bar, the straight men first noted the ease and fun of associating with the trans women. Stan (all names of participants are pseudonyms), a thirty-three-year-old white man with a high school education, summed this up thusly: "It's more comfortable here than straight bars; the girls [trans women] are nicer." He visited the bar almost weekly. Dwight, a college-educated white man in his forties, said: "They [the trans women] are only interested in you as a man, not marriage material. They make you feel wanted, and that's cool." As the last comment illustrates, another aspect of interaction that the men found positive was how flattering the trans women's attentions could be, even though they knew they were ordinarily the targets for commercial sex. Dwight continued his comments by saying: "They make you think you have a big cock even when you don't." Carl, another college-educated white man in his forties, said: "[The attention from the trans women] doesn't bother me; I find it flattering."

Sexually forward behavior, of course, is often part of what also attracts men to female sex workers. Our observations, however, were that, in general, the trans women related to the men in a warmer and friendlier way and tended to be less personally abrasive than female sex workers who worked the same area of the city. This perceived difference in the nature of the sociability of trans women versus real women was a major factor in attracting straight men to this bar. Dwight, again, put it directly: "They verbalize the sex acts; real women don't." Andrew, thirty-one, a white man who had a law degree, emphasized this sexual explicitness: "They get into very suggestive and explicit talk, like, 'How big is your dick?'" He added: "They're unusual, provocative, and overtly sexual." We also received direct comments from the men comparing them to female sex workers. Alvin was a twenty-five-year-old black man who was one year short of college graduation. He reported that what he liked about the trans women was that "there was no time limit [for the sex], the opposite of what happens with a female prostitute."

The bisexual men also mentioned, like the straight men, the ease of sexual interaction with the trans women. Two of the bisexual men, John and Alan, had this to say. John, a thirty-one-year-old white man who had a high school degree, said that he liked "their honesty, their looseness": "They're not having any hang-ups about sex." And Alan noted: "Most real women haven't been taught how to give great head."

A second dimension of sexual embodiment is *sensory embodiment*. It refers to the capacity to be sensually aware of another's body, to engage in the interpretive work whereby another's embodiment is seen as erotic.

This is accomplished through the sexual field, which creates a logic of practice whereby the men can sexually respond to the elaborate gender presentation exhibited in the trans women's appearance and behavior. Most trans women feminize their bodies in various ways: some have developed breasts as a result of hormone treatments or implants; most wear extremely sexualized feminine apparel (e.g. a tight dress, spike heels, heavy makeup, a wig); and most use their bodies in a seductive way, caressing the man, leaning into him, groping and stroking his penis. It is not difficult for the men to mobilize fantasy scripts involving gendered embodiment so that they become sexually aroused in response to the trans women's flirtatiousness. This illustrates, as Green (chapter 1 in this volume) notes, that field's function to structure and intensify desire by bringing erotic interests together. Thus, the appreciation of women with a penis is increased by the collective nature of the sexual field.

The major attraction provided by the trans women to the straight men was the experience of sensory embodiment. Stan, who, we quoted before, said: "They have great bodies, like women on display, but more so than any real woman would reveal." Curtis, a thirty-eight-year-old black man with some college education, had this to say: "I fantasize about men looking better than women."

More than their bodies, what seemed most sexually attractive to the straight men was the trans women's "presentation of gender," the most valuable currency of erotic capital at Mabel's. Jim, a thirty-three-year-old white man with a college degree, sounded like a sociologist when he noted that his attraction centered around "how they manage to create gender." Again, the Asian trans women were singled out. Fred, a twenty-six-year-old white man with a college degree, said: "The Asian ladies appeal to me. . . . They're nontraditional and walk a fine line between what is acceptable and what is not." What seemed to be a common experience was voiced by Robert, a thirty-seven-year-old white man with a master's degree, who said: "The more feminine they are, the more interested I am, and the more drunk I get, the more feminine they become."

In effect, the straight men's desires and the trans women's appearance merge to produce a fantasy woman. As noted, this fantasy was carried further in that the trans women decidedly did not act like the image many of the straight men had of most women. Thus, while the straight men might prefer what they refer to as a "real woman" (i.e., a genetic female), they noted that they wished real women looked and acted like the trans women did. As one said: "Wow, the mind of a man and the body of a woman; it doesn't get better than that!" This illustrates again the appeal of the illusion—in their embodiment, the trans women fit into the eroticized schema the straight men had of an attractive woman. The usual reserve expected from a woman, however, was not forthcoming. Rather, excitement was aroused when such an icon exhibited the blatant, sexually direct demeanor of a man.

For the bisexual men, sensory embodiment was also effected through the trans women's gender presentation. Thus, Clark, a forty-one-year-old white man who had a high school education, said: "The more I look at them, the more they turn me on—the way they're dressed—very sexy." This sentiment was echoed by Lee, a thirty-four-year-old Asian man who had two years of college, who reported: "The longer you sit here [in Mabel's], the more you view them as women." Jorge, a forty-seven-year-old Hispanic man with a Ph.D., adds another dimension to the attraction of effeminacy: "The more feminine the better; the more trampy the better. . . . I like trampy women too." Ray, however, a forty-seven-year-old white man with some college, had a different point of view. In his words: "The girls who are tacky and gaudy—it's a turnoff."

The reaction to the unique sexual embodiment of the trans women, however, was what created the major difference between the bisexual and the straight men. Unlike the straight men, the key attraction for the bisexuals was that trans women had both "tits and a cock," which was the core of their sexual excitement. Among the straight men, the trans woman's penis was not mentioned as an attraction and was apparently ignored. In contrast, because their attraction did include the penis, the bisexual men often sought to incorporate it into their sexual activity with a trans woman. Thus, some of the bisexuals, as well as receiving fellatio and performing anal intercourse, also reported performing fellatio on a trans woman. Many referred, like Eddie, to the unique sexual embodiment of the trans women: "I freak with them. It's been a fantasy since I was sixteen—a beautiful woman with a dick!" Byron, a twenty-eight-year-old single white man with a tenth-grade education, noted: "Breasts and a cock is so intriguing, so feminine, but still with male genitalia." A final example from Lee: "I'm only turned on to a beautiful woman with a cock. If they can pull a cock out in my face, I'm in ecstasy."

The final dimension of sexual embodiment is *sensate embodiment*. This refers to the self-awareness of one's own body—the "reflexive engagement with . . . [one's] own embodied state" (Jackson and Scott 2007, 100). Given the hegemonic erotic habitus of the dominant culture, both straight and bisexual men were aware that sex between men was denigrated. This affected how they interpreted the penis lurking under the female appearance of the trans woman. If the man self-defined as bisexual, dissonance or concern over his sexual orientation/identity was less likely than if he self-defined as heterosexual. The sensate embodiment could be perplexing for the man who defined as straight—being erotically turned on by an attractive woman but one who in reality has a penis. Thus, the most common sex act the straight men experienced was receiving fellatio. (As already noted, none of the straight men reported ever having performed fellatio on a trans woman.)

Of the straight men who reported not having engaged in sex with a trans woman (but who were interested in doing so), there was an emphasis placed on the beauty and femininity of the trans women, especially their appearance as real women. These men were also most interested in receiving fellatio. Some, however, did state directly that the trans women's penis was a barrier to any sexual interaction. For example, Robert loved the illusion, but, when it came down to whether to engage in sex with a trans woman, he said: "I don't like to think about it." Fred said: "Because they have a penis, this has prevented me from approaching them." And Curtis said: "I try to find an excuse to pursue it [sex], but my conscience [because of the trans woman's penis] doesn't allow me." Art, a thirty-two-year-old black man with a college degree, is interested in having sex with a trans woman but summed it up as follows: "Yes [I'd like to have sex], but she'd have to have breasts, and I would try not to think of her having a penis."

Because of the dissonance provided by the penis, a smaller proportion of the straight men reported having engaged in sex with a trans woman as compared to the bisexual men (only about a quarter of the straight men who had this interest compared to approximately two-thirds of the bisexual men). The bisexuals also showed a greater sexual openness than did the straights. For example, in terms of a choice of a sex partner, the bisexual men were not as likely as the straight men to say that their first preference was a "real woman"; they were likely to be broader in their preference (e.g., "a man *or* a trans woman" or "a woman *or* a trans woman"—with no difference in preference within each of the pairs). In addition, of those who reported having had sex with a trans woman, fewer bisexual men than straight men said that they paid for the sex, and the bisexual men also ended up paying less when payment was necessary. This may be related to the greater comfort in socializing with the trans women and the possibility of sexual reciprocation coming from the bisexuals. As with the straight men, all the bisexuals who had engaged in sex with a trans woman said that they enjoyed it.

For the sexually interested bisexuals, the sensate embodiment was often reflexively related to crystallizing or validating their sexual orientation/identity. Thus, some said that sexually relating to a trans woman confirmed a bisexual sexual orientation/identity. Arthur, a twenty-nine-year-old black man with a high school diploma, had this to say: "My interest in the girls here makes me bisexual." Leroy, a twenty-two-year-old black man with one year of college, was able to specify what type of bisexual he was: "I'm bisexual but more of a straight one, so a guy who looks like a woman turns me on." On the other hand, in a few cases, an interest in trans women was used as a basis for denying a "homosexual" interest per se, thus invalidating a self-identity as "gay." As Jake, a twenty-six-year-old white college graduate, said: "I'm only turned on by the Asians. And it's a way to deny my homosexuality." Arthur said that he was "bisexual" rather than "gay" because he was able to think of the trans women as women. This was possible even though the trans women had a penis; their feminine appearance and behavior made it seem different from having sex with a man. Finally, there were those sexually interested in trans women who saw sexual orientation/identity as irrelevant in explaining their interest. Thus, Roco, a twenty-one-year-old black man with two years of college, said: "Tits and cock isn't an issue—it's the person."

## Discussion

This chapter provides a glimpse into a particular sexual field that facilitates the collective sexual life of trans women and the men who have a sexual interest in them. The two parties occupy complimentary positions as patrons of a bar we refer to as Mabel's. We have described the structure of desire at Mabel's, the tiers of desirability, and the currencies of capital highlighted in this field. We have described how men patronizing Mabel's internalize the field's structure of desire through three different forms of embodiment whereby the erotic habitus is resocialized and often expanded to permit a broader range of objects of desire than might otherwise be the case.

Our overall impression of the men at Mabel's was that they were seeking titillation and/or casual sex at a reasonable cost and had located a so-cial environment that had this to offer. It provided a sexual field with a sexual opportunity structure in which the seductive skills of the trans women were displayed for commercial and recreational ends, one where a man's erotic habitus was extended to include trans women through the illusion of an attractive and easily available genetic female. Most of the men knew that a play was being performed and what the available roles and the prevailing scripts were. This added to the fun and adventure of this sexual field, and it took the hard edge off any underlying commer-cial transactions.

As we have described, the three forms of embodiment help explain the process by which men who were sexually interested in trans women deconstructed the relationship between gender and sexual arousal, then put it back together again, valorizing the extremely feminine presenta-tions. This was enabled by a field in which tiers of desirability were or-ganized by traditional scripts (namely, currencies of attractiveness and femininity). The desirability of trans women, then, involved a "field effect" that altered the character of sexual arousal and pleasure among the men.

Despite desiring trans women, potentially many of the men could have concerns about their sexual orientation/identity. The atmosphere of Mabel's, facilitated by the collective gendered presentations of the trans women that produced a hyperfeminine, seductive context, how-ever, aided the straight guy's ability to overlook the trans women's pe-nis. By accomplishing this, not one of the heterosexually identified men voiced concern over whether they were "really straight."

Also, for the bisexual men, we found that sexual relations with a trans woman worked to validate a bisexual self-identity—given their attrac-tion to the penis as well as to the female body features, especially the breasts, of the trans woman. Thus, both the straight and the bisexual men seemed to have little in the way of concern over their sexual ori-entation/identity. In fact, one role that Mabel's played was to isolate the men from the conventional world so that questions of self-identity could be situated at Mabel's or, as is probably more common, could lose their salience (Stryker 2008). For as one man summed up about his weekly visits to Mabel's: "It's just like that bar in the Star Wars movie—like go-ing to another world." (For a similar comment, that such bars are like "fantasy island," see Caceres and Cortinas 1996.)

Overall, then, this study shows the complexity of sex, gender, and sexuality as they interact in a particular form of collective sexual life. It illustrates the relationship of objective and subjective elements of the sexual field (cf. these aspects in gay baths in Weinberg and Williams [1975a]) and the ways in which these cocreate desire and desirability. That is, Mabel's provided an erotic oasis with an objective status order that reflected a particular desire and, at the same time, constructed it, thereby reproducing the field itself.

## Notes

1. For a review of some of the studies that have been done, see Bockting, Miner, and Rosser (2007).

2. The sexual sites (Green 2011) in which these interactions occur can vary, e.g., from parties in New York City (Mauk 2008) to street locales for the homeless in Los Angeles (Reback and Larkins 2006).

3. On the other hand, the desirability of the men was based on the appearance of financial capital (e.g., being generous in buying drinks for the trans women) and acting like a "gentleman," which validated the trans woman's status as a "lady." When a man exhibited what could be considered crude verbal or physical behavior (e.g., grabbing), we heard him being told that "a gentleman doesn't treat a lady like that."

4. A study of clients of trans women in the Netherlands Vennix et al. 2000) also found half identifying as "straight" and half as "bisexual." The same was found for Latino and black men in another San Francisco study (Coan, Schrager, and Packer, 2005).

# CHAPTER THREE

# Sexual Field Theory

## *Some Theoretical Questions and Empirical Complications*

Peter Hennen, The Ohio State University at Newark

In their attempts to theorize the sexual, sociologists seem to invite ca-
lamity. Consider for a moment the consequences of success. Would
anyone want to live in a world where all the mysteries of carnal delight
have been solved? With inscrutable Eros held captive and dragged into
the glaring light of day? Perhaps the appeal of a comprehensive theory
of human sexuality with unlimited scope conditions, traversing all levels of analysis, is entirely academic. The best example of this type of sexual theorizing gone wild is found in market approaches that unproblematically reduce human sexuality to cost/benefit analyses while failing
to question the pertinence of market metaphors or to acknowledge the
complexities of "trans-individual consistencies in sexual desiring" (Martin and George 2006, 121). At first blush, it seems that the passion of
sexual market theorists cannot be restrained. In their mad lust for clar-
ity, they proudly thrust the formidable key of science into the quivering
lock of human sexuality. A few expert moves (a conceptual manipulation
here, a wildly impulsive operationalization there), and oh—the lock is
undone! The heavy breath of anticipation reaches its climax as the black
box of desire is opened to reveal—*mathematical formulas.*

Sexual field theory approaches its subject with far less bravado but
also with significantly less risk of the kind of disappointment that seems
pervasive in market-based approaches. As Green has observed: "A sex-

ual field is organized by desires and, in turn, resources that defy abstract formulation" (2008c, 29). Field theory's potential for a very different kind of success is linked to its fundamentally pluralist approach. It rejects any notion of a singular, definitive sexual field and instead acknowledges multiple and distinct sites of shared and mutually recognized desires, each tied to specific forms of sexual capital. It also refuses any attempt to reveal the precise contents of the black box of sexual desire, focusing instead on a more rigorous investigation of collective structures of desire (and desirability) and how these shape individual desire and expression (Green 2008c, 31).

In this chapter, I draw on ethnographic data from two communities of gay/queer-identified men (gay leathermen and bears)[1] to present a partial reading of the initial phase of a sexual field—that is, of sexual field *formation*—and how this reading squares with the several analogical models previously advanced. The question, "Where do fields come from?" is intimately bound up with the question, "What is a field?" and in what follows I shuttle back and forth between the two. Martin (2003, 28–30) has identified "three senses of field": as an *area* wherein people or institutions are strategically positioned with respect to each other, as an *organization of forces* (readily analogous but not reducible to a magnetic field of force), and, finally, in the Bourdieusian sense, as a field of struggle, contestation, and competition within a hierarchically ordered system.

In addition to examining the goodness of fit between my data and existing conceptual field models, I devote special attention to three specific theoretical/conceptual points. First, I want to examine the temporal relationship between sexual field formation and field-specific forms of sexual capital. In this first section, I introduce the idea that fields do not merely accommodate the expression of preexisting desires; they are also productive of *new* desires. While it is no secret that sociality is exciting, the point I highlight here is that under certain circumstances a powerful erotic component of the social is realized that facilitates new patterns of desiring. In this section, I also articulate the temporal/historical relationship between sexual fields and their associated forms of capital. Here, the suggestion is that fields emerge from other fields and that one cannot account for many of the particular characteristics of a given sexual field without careful attention to its antecedent fields and the changing dispositions of field participants over time. In the second section, I challenge and complicate the assumption that fields (and sexual fields in particular) are necessarily structured hierarchically. Toward this end, I make the case for a partial rejection of the Bourdieusian concept of field, arguing that in some instances a field of force metaphor better serves the analysis. I follow this theoretical argument with empirical support from both the leather and the bear cases. In the third and final section, I turn my attention to an observation that may have important implications for qualitative researchers working with sexual field theory. Here, I illustrate by way of a personal anecdote the importance of attending to the often very subtle signaling that takes place both within and between fields. I feel that this is a neglected methodological point for two reasons. First, because much of this signaling is an effect of the "erotic habitus" (Green 2008a), it operates below the level of conscious thought. Thus, researchers cannot expect field participants to produce conscious accounts of this signaling in interviews. Second, if the intricate details of these signals are not attended to, they can easily escape the notice of researchers, particularly those who are not active participants in the fields they are studying.

## Bodies in History: Sexual Field Formation and Sexual Capital

While Green comments on the constitutive elements of fields in terms of the aggregation of sexual desires and erotic preferences (2008c, chapter 1 in this volume), my concern is with the aggregation of actors. How is it, to apply Green's phrase to a different context, that the overlapping desires of individual actors "aggregate up" to a new field? Under what empirical conditions does this occur? In pursuit of these questions, I would like to look at two specific time points, using selected data from two of my case study communities. I will attempt to shed some light on the question of field formation with an emphasis on the specific historical conditions that inform each of these cases, the importance of antecedent events and prior fields, and, most importantly, how these affect the production of desire. I look first at a particular ensemble of individual actors, that is, men recently discharged from military service in World War II, and the social components of what would eventually come to be recognized as the field of gay leathermen. Second, in a move that would eventually result in the formation of the bear sexual field, I look at a peculiar development among another ensemble of social actors, this one involving leather, colored hankies, and adorable little teddy bears.

The story begins in the late 1940s, primarily but not exclusively in

California. When I initially published my research on the origins of gay leathermen's sexual culture (see Hennen 2008), I conceived of the raw materials of this field in terms very similar to D'Emilio's (1983). I assumed that this community was fueled primarily by the dislocated masculinities of men who had enjoyed their first same-sex experiences while serving in the military, that is, men who had discovered their same-sex desires during the war. I still believe this to be a significant component. For some enlisted personnel, the war years represented a unique period of sexual experimentation and discovery, some of which was no doubt prompted by the psychological pressures of combat. In the context of postwar stereotypes about the effeminacy and pathology of the homosexual, the new pleasures these men were experiencing must have elicited considerable anxiety, especially regarding their masculinity. In this context, the formation of a homosexual community heavily invested in the derogation of the feminine makes sense.

However, I have recently been moved to think more carefully about another group of veterans—a group of men whose experience becomes fully legible only with the adoption of a sexual fields approach. I am referring here to those men whose postwar dislocation had no necessary connection with the discovery of same-sex pleasures but was rather based on the psychological trauma of war, experienced in a highly charged homosocial, but not homosexual, context. I suggest that the horrors of war had so traumatized these men that they found it necessary to seek out the company of men with similar experiences, to organize a furtive alternative culture rather than return to the mainstream.

This is suggested by the numerous examples of "wounded masculinity" I encountered, both in my historical research and in the field. Here is a reminiscence from Thom Magister, a prominent player in the California leather scene during the 1950s, as he recalls his early encounters with such men:

> Hitchhiking back to Hollywood from downtown L.A., one afternoon I was picked up by an ex-Marine who had joined the many others who became the core of what we later called outlaw bikers. These men, *both gay and straight*, had been damaged by the war and felt that they could "never go home again." Tortured and tormented often beyond anyone's comprehension, *they drifted together in a mutual loss of innocence.* They had been mere boys when they left home to serve Uncle Sam in his great war against the Axis nations. Six

years later they came home broken men with nowhere to go and no reason to go there. (Magister 1991/2001, 93 [emphasis added])

A great deal of what is be important (in terms of sexual field theory) can be obscured in a twenty-first-century reading of this passage. It is surely a mistake to frame this description in terms of stabilized identity categories like *leatherman* or *gay leatherman* as neither of these identities had achieved widespread social legibility in the early 1950s. In fact, I would argue that the emphasized phrases directly refute such a reading. What seems much more important to Magister is the *field*, in this case, a shared social symbolic space, inhabited by men with similar experiences of violence and trauma as well as a shared sense of dislocated masculinity.

Later in his essay, Magister relates how his new friend, a powerfully built and masculine ex-marine named Charley, had been tortured and castrated while a prisoner of war in Japan. When Magister met him, Charley "hung out at a biker bar with his war buddies and their partners" (Magister 1991/2001, 93). He also notes that, despite Charley's mutilation, they enjoyed a relationship that was clearly more intimate than a conventional male friendship. In fact, Magister reveals that Charley became his long-term partner and provided him with the meticulous "old guard" BDSM (bondage/discipline/sadomasochism) training that enabled him to eventually become a prominent leather master.

This type of empirical detail strongly recommends a sexual fields approach and complicates the notion that same-sex desire in the postwar years was the result of soldiers' discovering their sexual natures through opportunities afforded them during their years of service. The alternative sexual fields reading I am proposing here shifts the focus to the particular social dynamics and practices of a particular group of actors at a specific place and time who aggregate up to a new sexual field through (in this case) a shared sense of psychological trauma, or perhaps more accurately the problematic intersection of this shared sense of trauma with their prior investments in a particular construction of masculinity.

One element of gay leather culture that corroborates the transformation-through-trauma view is its close association with bondage, discipline, and sadomasochism. Another is the remarkable way it has decentered insertive intercourse, to the point where, based on the words of one of my interview subjects, garden-variety anal intercourse comes to be seen as "just another fetish" (Hennen 2008, 175). This implies a radical reorganization of sexual capital, something I was able to document. What is prized most in BDSM play among gay leathermen is a sense of presence in the scene, an ability to engage in deep embodied connection with your partner (which is often nongenital), and technique, technique, technique—especially but not exclusively in the top, or the one running the scene. This type of play is, on the one hand, highly rationalized and, on the other, capable of delivering a sense of profound and powerful connection between the players. This passionate connection is all the more intriguing in light of the fact that it is so obviously a *novel* pleasure, produced by a particular set of actors with a shared history at a particular point in time.

Of course, this approach raises as many questions as it answers. Magister, after all, was not himself subject to the horror of war and did not share a bond of past trauma with these men. Yet he found himself strongly (and surprisingly) attracted to the field. As Green notes: "Sexual actors may learn to like an erotic world as they develop its habitus through a process of deliberate inculcation" (2008c, 31). One can scarcely imagine a more deliberate process than the one undertaken by Magister in his training to become a leather master. What insight might sexual field theory offer here? My sense is that Magister's desire actually strengthens rather than weakens the viability of the sexual fields approach, in that his willingness to submit to this deliberate process occurred only after a positive encounter with an established sexual field, one whose collective and social nature invested it with its own self-renewing energy. While he was not a player in the formation of this particular field, Magister found himself intensely interested in the finished product. Without extending the analogy too far, one might say that this corresponds roughly to the difference between the original conditions constituting the field of force around a magnet and the metal shards that are subsequently attracted to it.

My field work, conducted in 2001, corroborated the idea that in at least some cases identification as a combat veteran remains as important (if not more important) to members of leather clubs as identification based on sexual orientation. Among the approximately twenty members of the Sentinels (the pseudonymous name of the gay leather club I studied), three men corresponded to some degree with the wounded profile described by Magister. Most prominent among these was Billy, a Vietnam veteran whose belligerent and sometimes violent behavior was widely acknowledged. Billy, I found out, was considered dangerous by many of my fellow leather campers. One of the other members of the Sentinels told me that Billy had been thrown out of the play cabin by the dungeon master at the previous year's event because he was abusing the man he was playing with, thereby violating the "safe, sane, and consensual" rule that is a fundamental principle governing all responsible leather sex play. A second man strongly identified as a Viet Nam veteran, telling me shortly after we met that he had been damaged by Agent Orange. A third man, Wayne, also made a point of referring repeatedly to his status as a Vietnam vet. Although he was clearly in better psychological shape than Billy, it became apparent to me that there was a unique bond between these two men. While in the play cabin, I observed the following.

Billy was naked, leaning back in one of the cabin chairs. Wayne was crouched before him and seemed to be rather tentatively giving him some head—I say *tentatively* because Billy was babbling nonstop about some Vietnam experience.

I thought this was extraordinary, one of the most arresting images I witnessed during my time in the field. In its own humble way, it speaks to the presence of an ethic of healing within leather culture; there is a sensitivity toward psychological pain here and a willingness to attend to it through erotic contact. In terms of sexual field theory, what strikes me as most significant is the way the situation clearly contains both homosocial and homosexual elements, without obviously privileging one over the other. The boundary between these two ways of relating, so vigorously policed in most other aspects of men's lives (including many gay men's lives), is here effectively blurred with a kind of quiet indifference that I find compelling.

What all these examples suggest is that field theory marks a significant advance over prior approaches that emphasize the ability of the social environment to liberate already-existing preferences (D'Emilio 1983). Under certain conditions, fields clearly *constitute* desire as well while fostering the development of new pleasures and new forms of sexual capital. Furthermore, once the field of force metaphor is taken seriously, theorizing desire becomes less a matter of analyzing the desire itself and more a matter of attending to its effects. Indeed, it may be that an incurious attitude toward what a desire *is*, as opposed to what it *does* and how it does it, can bring the theorist into more meaningful proximity to sexual actors. Perhaps the inscrutability of sexual desire is itself

an essential element of an erotic field of force. That this power is man-
ifested in widely varying ways, with varying strength and range, is an
unsurprising but heretofore highly problematic element of sexual theorizing. Unlike earlier approaches, sexual field theory is exquisitely positioned to appreciate these complexities.

*    *    *

Now, about those tiny teddy bears . . . The instrumentality and emphasis
on the technical aspects of BDSM play, along with the elaborate system
of sexual signaling known as the "hanky code" (whereby patrons in a
leather bar could discern the sexual and fetish interests of potential partners by the color and placement of pocket handkerchiefs), provoked a
new, discontented disposition from within the world of gay leather sex in
the late 1980s. This eventually led to what is now recognized as the bear
community—a new sexual field with new forms of sexual capital. How
best to explain this development?

Andreas Glaeser (2010) has suggested that it might be helpful to think
of social actors not as originators but as *collectors*. In other words, there
is an important cumulative dimension to any individual's life experience
that "collects" temporally and shapes both individual and (to the extent
that individual experience is shared with other members of a generational cohort) collective behavior. Any innovations that social actors advance are always shaped by the sum total of their prior experiences, that
is, whatever joys, frustrations, misunderstandings, fears, values, beliefs,
and behaviors they have collected over the life course. Bourdieu reminds
us that, under normal circumstances, this collecting process occurs without conscious awareness: "The habitus—embodied history, internalized
as a second nature and so forgotten as history—is the active presence
of the whole past of which it is the product" (1990b, 56). Under what
circumstances is this "forgotten" history recovered? How is it then de-
ployed toward conscious change?

To answer these questions, I work backward from a comparison of
the contemporary sexual cultures of bears and leathermen. On the one
hand, there is clear continuity between the two fields, especially with respect to a shared concern with rejecting effeminacy and maintaining a
legitimate claim to masculinity. On the other hand, there are clear dispositional differences between leathermen and bears. Shared generational experience clearly played a role in defining the point of departure:

the ravages of AIDS and AIDS wasting syndrome resignified the larger, fleshier bear body as healthy, virile, and safe, a symbolic shift that intersected auspiciously with the slowing metabolisms and expanding waistlines of the Stonewall generation. But, if we can speak of a bear sexual field, it was also clearly forged in resistance to the perceived instrumental, coldly objectified sexual field of the leatherman, a field wherein the hard, muscled body remained the ideal and the fleshier body was increasingly stigmatized. On this view, individual actors within the field of gay leathermen collected negative attitudes toward the field, insofar as they increasingly came to feel alienated from it, culminating in an individual rejection or "turning away."[2]

This was achieved at least in part through an aggressive yet rather amusing challenge to one of the time-honored traditions of gay leather culture. As it evolved, the hanky code became an elaborate system of sexual signaling. Given the color and placement of pocket handkerchiefs, leathermen could discern in some detail the sexual interests of other men from across a crowded bar, sometimes completely obviating the need for conversation. According to the historian and founding figure Les Wright, sometime during the early 1980s men frequenting leather bars in San Francisco and other cities began placing a small teddy bear in their shirt or hip pocket, instead of the requisite hanky. This, says Wright, was a way of saying: "I'm a human being. I give and receive affection" (1990, 54). Not willing to be objectified and reduced to an interest in one specific sexual activity, these men sported teddy bears to emphasize their interest in a less instrumental sexuality (Wright 1997b, 21).

Although some might see this as an ostensibly trivial, perhaps even precious tactic for registering dissent, from a sexual field perspective it acquires formidable significance. First, by directly attacking a richly symbolic practice of the gay leather community, the move suggests a broader challenge to the agreed-on (doxic) tenets of the leather field. This, along with collected discontent, enabled a more formidable disruption—one that challenged the taken-for-granted "doing" of gender in leather bars (West and Zimmerman 1987). In short order, bear culture articulated a softer, more sociable masculinity as an alternative to the instrumentality of leather culture. Second, as a visible practice, this tactic allowed individual actors to see that they were not alone in their discontent. Adorable little teddy bears made it clear that, in their turning away from the perceived objectification and rationalization of leather sexual culture, these individual men were not alone. The turning away, initially an individual act of rejection advanced in specifically sexual terms, was thereby allowed to acquire an additional erotic appeal in light of the indisputable evidence that there were others so disposed. To return to the magnetic metaphor momentarily, it is as if an individual metal shard acquires, over time, a charge that renders it immune to the field of force that formerly determined its course. Propulsion outside the field is (again, very roughly) analogous to an individual act of resistance, a saying no, a turning away. Perhaps a more apt metaphor is this: It is as if, in a desperate act of rejection, one jumps off a cliff and on the way down discovers other similarly discontented jumpers in the air. Suddenly, a new set of relationships and meanings (a new field) seems possible. There is no longer any need to hit the ground.[3]

And so the game is on. Bears can now play a new sexual game, with new sexual capital. Extra weight, hair, and age are refigured as sexy. But, as one of my interview subjects reminded me, being a bear is "90% attitude, 10% looks" (Hennen 2008, 97). That attitude, in explicit contrast to that of the leatherman, is gregarious and emotionally open, favoring a "regular guy" masculinity over the dramatic hypermasculinity of the leatherman. As in the case of the leathermen before them, for bears the playing of the new sexual game *itself* generates desire as well as structure—that is, the implicit and explicit rules of the new game. Conventions like the "bear hug," "nuzzling," and "cuddling" emerge in bear sexual culture to replace the technical and fetishistic practices that earlier evolved through a similar process in the leather sexual field (Hennen 2008, 122–30). This phenomenon of creating desire through practice, evident in my description of the leather case as well, brings up what I think is an undertheorized point. Much of the literature I have encountered on sexual field theory (and field theory in general) seems to suggest a certain chronological relationship between field and capital. An unsympathetic account might reduce this assumption to something as simplistic as "first comes field, then come capital," or perhaps the reverse. This is surely not what is intended in most of the extant literature, but I do think that the temporality of field and capital remains a neglected topic in field theory. I hope that the two narratives of field formation offered above suggest the need to attend to this matter. At its most rudimentary level, and at the risk of reviving market metaphors, one way of conceptualizing capital is as an agreed-on way of valuing. By the same token, a rudimentary conception of a field might define it as a place (whether physical, virtual, or symbolic) wherein this agreed-on valuing occurs. Thus, I would suggest that there is an inescapable simultaneity between the recognition of novel forms of sexual capital and the recognition of an attendant sexual field. Furthermore, I see the relationship as not only simultaneous but also symbiotic. Here, I am drawing on Bourdieu's (Bourdieu and Wacquant 1992, 131) notion of limited agency and Giddens's (1986) notion of structuration.

While Bourdieu argues that embodied principles are "placed beyond the grasp of consciousness, and hence cannot be touched by voluntary, deliberate transformation, cannot even be made explicit" (1977, 94), he makes exceptions for times of crisis (understood by him as periods of widespread disruption in objective power relations), during which the contours of habitus become at least partially accessible and amenable to change. Following Bourdieu, I want to suggest that periods when novel forms of sexual capital accompany new field formation represent moments of heightened yet not fully developed consciousness for individual actors, specifically with respect to the erotic habitus (Green 2008a) and the limited (but real) possibilities for deliberate refashioning that periods of crisis temporarily illuminate.

Contributing to the erotic energy of the new field is the realization that the individual's initial refusal is significant—this is affirmed when it is corroborated by the discovery of similar dispositions in others. It demonstrates that the individual is not alone and that this realization is exciting, both in an erotic and in a more traditional sense. So perhaps a partial answer to the question, "How does an ensemble of actors aggregate up to a sexual field?" is that it is determined by the lack of fit between the specific social/symbolic features of a given field and the habitus that develops in resistance to it. This in turn prompts the individual to assume the enormous risk of saying no, of rejecting the rules of the game in the existing field. This individual act, which is never trivial but perceived by its initiator as little more than an act of desperate destruction, is validated as meaningful once other similarly disposed defectors from the original field are recognized. At this point, the force of resistance is transposed to attraction, enabling the formation of a new field. While this process partially explains certain types of field formation, it also helps explain ways in which the process is constrained. Multiple and rapid subdivisions of a given field are unlikely because all such divisions require a similar process of collecting discontent in the existing field over time and a subsequent turning away, which comes about only after an extended period of alienating social/sexual experience, and which produces a new field only if social and historical conditions favor it.[4] Here again, field theory demonstrates the eminently social character of desire in new and productive ways.

As described above, a feature common to the formation of both the leather and the bear fields is that they are born of disruption, resistance, and trauma. In both cases the collection of discontent enables resistance, and in both cases resisters, on finding others so disposed, are able to establish their own field, governed by a new set of internal valences. Of course, all this happens below the level of conscious deliberation, promoting the idea that the new field and its governing rules are only natural.

As I conclude this section, an additional note of clarification is in order. Much of the vocabulary that I have employed thus far suggests that my understanding of fields clearly favors the field of force metaphor over the "field of struggle" model. Two points obtain here. First, I do not mean to suggest any kind of neat analogy between social and physical entities. I am not suggesting that a kind of social physics should or can accompany field theory; along these lines, Martin (2003, 29) warns against "sloppy importations from other disciplines." My use of analogies with magnetic force, for example, are intended for heuristic purposes only and are not meant to be interpreted literally. Rather, the *force* in the field of forces model I am advancing here refers to the force of meaning—specifically, the intersubjectively shared sense-making schemes that govern a field. Second, my use of this vocabulary is more appropriately understood as a challenge to the assumption that fields (and perhaps sexual fields in particular) are necessarily and always governed by hierarchy and struggle. In what follows, I make the case for framing questions about whether fields are constituted by attractive forces or hierarchical struggles as a matter of *empirical* inquiry—that is, to be determined on a case-by-case basis.

## Deliberate Domination and an Ethic of Care— Questioning Hierarchy in Sexual Fields

Are all fields structured by hierarchy? Are all sexual fields governed by, in Green's words, "tiers of desirability" (2008c, 32)? Much of the extant literature on sexual fields seems to suggest as much, based as it is on the implicit logic of the field of struggle model. This particular emphasis is understandable, given the origin of field theory in the work of Pierre Bourdieu (1977, 1990b). Although by the end of his career he was clearly expanding his application of capital, habitus, and field to gender, Bourdieu (1998/2001) developed these theoretical tools from empirical data directly referencing social class. Since class relations are inherently conflictual, it is perhaps not surprising that his strong emphasis on the struggle for distinction, status, and the achievement of a sense of one's place within a hierarchically ordered system has been transferred unproblematically in some recent applications of his work. In this section, I argue the need to more carefully examine this move, especially with respect to sexual field theory, by enlisting evidence challenging the notion that sexual fields are necessarily fields of struggle.

Analytically speaking, what happens to the concept *field* when you reformulate it without struggle and stratification? Can it still be called a field?[5] If one adheres to a strictly Bourdieusian approach, the answer to this last question is almost certainly no. Without Bourdieu's specific emphasis on struggle and status attainment within sexual fields, one might argue that, once you remove these elements, what you are left with might more accurately be described as a *scene* or a *subculture*. However, I would argue that there is much to be gained by relaxing the conceptual reins a bit here.[6] Part of Bourdieu's continuing relevance is the enormous fecundity of his conceptual triptych (habitus, capital, and field) and the many innovative applications scholars have made of these, often in the spirit but not always to the exact letter of Bourdieu's own approach. In light of this, some scholars have noted that strict adherence to Bourdieusian orthodoxy may unnecessarily limit the use value of habitus, capital, and field. As Richard Jenkins has observed, highlighting the practical utility of his concepts, Bourdieu is "enormously good to think with" (1992, 11).

Regarding subcultures, one might inquire about the extent to which scholars currently use Bourdieu in thinking about subcultures. To my knowledge, most of the prominent scholarship in this area has emphasized the interpretive meanings of subcultural style (Hebdige 1979; Muggleton 2000). The most extensive application of Bourdieu to subcultures is Thornton's (1996), but her approach is limited to a Bourdieusian analysis of subcultural capital. Thus, it may be that a distinction between subcultures and fields derives largely from theoretical habit; we tend not to view subcultures as fields. Perhaps they are (although obviously not all fields are subcultures).

As I think with Bourdieu in analyzing the bear community, I encounter questions that seem to justify a more liberal interpretation of field. What happens when a community (like the bears) fosters an explicit refusal of dominance and hierarchies and incorporates that into its foundational narrative? If you substitute warmth, openness, and conviviality for more traditional ways of judging attractiveness and status, can what results be called a *hierarchy*? If so, is it still a *sexual* hierarchy?[7]

Moreover, the concept of field explicitly addresses what holds a subculture together and what shapes the behavior of those operating within it. It can, in addition, specify a hierarchy, but perhaps it need not. Along the lines of the field of struggle metaphor, might it be permissible to view this as an empirical question to be answered over the course of the analysis, rather than hold sexual field theory to the more orthodox requirement that all actors subscribe to the logic of stratification? The bear community is especially illustrative of this last point as one of its curious features is the use of a fairly detailed taxonomy of bear types, based on identifications with real bears. A *grizzly* is usually understood as a middle-aged, larger, sexually dominant man, while *cub* denotes a submissive, usually younger man. Other bear types seem explicitly crafted to include men who are routinely stigmatized in other sexual fields (e.g., *polar bears* designates a place for older men in this community). Furthermore, the typology even extends to men who do not fit the typical physical profile of a bear, thereby effectively including the nonbear other in the community, provided of course these individuals identify as "bear admirers" (e.g., *otters* are thin-framed smooth men, while *wolves* are thin-framed hairy men).

But, even as bear culture fosters this elaborate typology, there is little detectable effort devoted to *ranking* these types. Such a ranking is simply not important to these men. On this line of thinking, a shared sense of what is important can be distinguished from shared values in that (in the bear and leather cases and presumably others) the power of this consensus is generated by shared life-historical experiences (in many cases, of rejection) and what Raymond Williams (1977) might call a shared *structure of feeling* accompanying this history. To be sure, status distinctions exist within the bear community, but on the basis of my field work I would argue that they do not align with any agreed-on hierarchy. For example, observations like, "He's the sweetest little cub," or "the hottest grizzly bear," or "just about the perfect otter," do not indicate a place in any hierarchy, as cubs, grizzlies, and otters are themselves not ranked. Obviously, even a shared sense of what is important might create a hierarchy (those who question the consensus will be deemed inferior to those who embrace it), but in this case the stratification is epiphenomenal rather than constitutive. All these fine-grained distinctions are missed if we understand communities like the bears as subcultures or if we impose a more restrictive sense of field on the analysis.

Furthermore, even if you concede the idea that the bear community is at some level stratified, it remains true that, as Green (chapter 1 in this volume) observes, collective valuations of desirability may or may not reflect actors' real desires. One *can* reduce the choice of sexual partners to agreed-on indicators of sexual capital, but the question remains, What characteristics of the field determine whether a participant *will* define the situation in this way? Specifically, how much leeway is granted to individual taste in a given field, versus negative consequences doled out to those who do not follow the rules of the game for partner selection (however vaguely or precisely defined they may be)? Thus, even if it is true that all sexual fields are characterized by an implied or explicit sexual hierarchy, the conditions of its instantiation remain undertheorized, especially with respect to the empirical conditions that might make a field more or less contentious. Absent these considerations, any articulation of such hierarchies may prove to be of limited value. With their foundational emphasis on acceptance and conviviality, my sense is that bears are far less likely to question or condemn the sexual choices of their fellows, in sharp contrast to the more complex and exacting criteria informing the sexual culture of, for example, the sorority women studied by Armstrong (2010a).

Suggesting the possibility of nonhierarchical fields has provoked some spirited pushback from readers of earlier drafts of this chapter. Perhaps the most thought-provoking challenge goes something like this: Fields themselves are hierarchically organized as lower-status fields are nested within higher-status fields. Lower-status instantiations of field activity may *seem* uncompetitive and nonhierarchical, but they are defined by higher-status, overtly competitive instantiations of the same activity and are thus intimately informed by hierarchy. For example, an informal family football game may be less competitive than a professional game, but, in the abstract, football as a game remains competitive and hierarchically organized. In the abstract, it is the higher-status activity that defines the game of football, not the friendly just-for-fun game.[8]

This strikes me as an enormously helpful way of thinking about hi-

erarchy in fields, but I would respond with two observations about sexual fields. First, people do not seek sex or play football in the abstract.
They act in concrete, immediate contexts that they interpret on the basis
of personal experience. Furthermore, perceptions of high and low status
are always organized intersubjectively, with group consensus also based
on lived experience. Bears clearly think of competitive sexual cultures as
*lower* status, and most have arrived at this judgment after extensive experience playing more competitive sexual games in mainstream gay culture. In response, they have created a community wherein a devaluation
of mainstream gay culture is made possible. Of course, this move simply
reverses the status hierarchy. In my fieldwork, I discovered that this reversal typically manifests itself in the disparaging attitude that some (but
by no means all) bear men adopt toward the *twink*, that is, the hairless,
muscled young men whose sexual capital is so highly valued in mainstream gay culture (Hennen 2008, 117).

But this reversal exists alongside a more complicated and inclusive move. My time in the field clearly indicated that many bears real-
ize the contradiction involved in rejecting the twink body while at the
same time trying to cultivate an appreciation for a broader range of body
types. This tension is effectively resolved through the convention of the
bear admirer. A man fitting the physical description of the twink is welcome in the bear community provided that he identifies as a bear admirer, that is, he indicates that he shares the intersubjective consensus
about the inherent attraction of the heavier, hairier bear body. This *may*
be interpreted as evidence of a reverse hierarchy, but this clearly does
not hold for all bear men. In one telling case I encountered, a tautly muscled ex-gymnast with no body hair was welcomed into the heart of the
community because he widely advertised his preference for older bear
men (Hennan 2008, 119). His preference was immediately enlisted as evidence of the appeal of the bear body, without necessarily introducing an
alternative hierarchy stigmatizing his smooth, athletic frame.

My second observation has to do with the naturalizing narrative informing much of the work I have encountered on sexual fields. Most of
this work assumes at the outset an inherently competitive, hierarchical view of nature. Consequently, sexual fields always figure as fields of
struggle. I characterize this view of nature as *evolutionary* because it implies that only the fittest gain entrance to the most desired sexual arenas. I mean *fittest*, not in the narrow sense of a toned, physically fit body,
but rather in the sense of how an individual fares with respect to what-

ever physical, intellectual, or cultural criteria define the particular field of struggle. The evolutionary view further implies that there is an objective, empirical process at work that separates sexual winners from sexual losers. Bears draw on a radically different naturalizing narrative that I characterize as *romantic* because it emphasizes harmony, inclusivity, and a sense of benign mystery governing sexual attraction.[9] Because the evolutionary paradigm currently dominates, the nesting metaphor seems apt. However, it may be that the nesting argument simply extends the internal hierarchical logic of the evolutionary view to subsume behavior it cannot account for, thereby marking that behavior as lower status. Moreover, romantic views of nature are easily satirized and seen as distorting, while, from the evolutionary perspective, competition makes sense. The evolutionary narrative may seem more accurate because it is less forgiving; it declines to traffic in the misty-eyed nonsense of the romantic narrative. But the implied biologistic assumptions actually make little sense in most fields, where sexual activity is organized around the pursuit of pleasure rather than reproduction and survival. Granted, sexual competition may deliver limited pleasures through the attainment of status distinctions, but it is surely a mistake to limit the erotic universe to status pleasures alone. Indeed, the protean pleasures exhibited in a dizzying array of contemporary sexual fields (think feet, fat, food, flogging, furries, etc.) suggests that this less forgiving rubric may itself be a source of distortion, if what one is after is an accurate understanding of how *sexual* fields work.

All this obscures the fact that, at least with respect to sexual fields, there is an undecidability between evolutionary and romantic naturalizing narratives. The evolutionary view seems to promise empirical verification of its truth but cannot deliver it. Even if it could, a naturalizing narrative works, not because it is empirically true, but because it facilitates desire and satisfaction. Personal experience will lead individuals to strongly prefer one or the other of these narratives, so the fact that these contrasting views of nature may be arranged hierarchically (or nested within each other) is unsurprising and may be beside the point. Again, status judgments are always made intersubjectively. The point is that each of these naturalizing narratives is *effective*. The "better" narrative is determined by preference, preference largely shaped by divergent life experiences. This again underscores the empirical nature of the field of struggle metaphor and the potential that in some instances the metaphor may not apply. Of course, whether nested or not, all sexual fields are in-

timately related to other fields. Yes, the bear field is defined in relationship to other, more competitive sexual fields, but that relationship is consciously, deliberately, and fundamentally oppositional.

However, if sexual fields must of necessity include struggle and stratification, then at the very least we need to acknowledge the limited scope
conditions that this implies. Simply put, I believe that the more orthodox
sense of *field* effectively organizes out some significant aspects of human
sexual behavior. Again, the bear case proves instructive on this point as
my time in the field convinced me that it is precisely the dismantling of
an agreed-on stratification logic that enabled desire for many of my research subjects. Several of the men I encountered spoke of never feeling
like fully sexual beings until they encountered the bear community, and
these accounts were always advanced with reference to the self-esteem
they were able to develop in this more accepting community. Part of the
founding narrative of the bear field explicitly rejects the lookism, objectification, and body fascism found elsewhere in gay culture. In its place,
bears substitute a narrative of inclusiveness, emotional warmth, gregariousness, and the erotic valuation of larger, hairier, and in many cases
older bodies. One commentator was moved to suggest that bear culture fosters what feminists have identified as an "ethic of care" (Gilligan 1982) that effectively undermines many of the alienating and competitive aspects of hegemonic masculinity (Connell 1995). To be sure, the
picture here is a mixed one. There is significant slippage between the
ideological commitments governing the field and actual practice. However, this bear man's comment succinctly summarizes the sense of inclusiveness and acceptance that I observed during my fieldwork: "At
a typical bar or a circuit event, people see me as a short, balding guy
with a belly and a pronounced limp, using a cane. When I'm at a bear
event or a bear bar people see me as a man who is happy and secure with
himself. . . . At a bear event or a bear bar, I feel that sense of acceptance
from people who don't know me" (Williams 2002, 220).

Perhaps the best illustration of slippage between ideological commitment and actual practice derives from the controversial status of bear
"beauty contests." The first of these, staged in the late 1980s and early
1990s, were produced and consumed as deliberate parodies, both of traditional female beauty pageants, like Miss America, and of established
leather contests, like International Mr. Leather and Mr. Drummer.[10] But,
after only a few years, such pageants began to take on a different meaning: "The International Mr. Bear contest . . . evolved in its first three

years from poking somewhat self-conscious fun at traditional gay values to striving in an increasingly serious manner to project an image of a self confident Bear ideal" (Wright 1997b, 36–37).

This development provoked controversy, as some bear men wondered why they were now constructing an ideal bear type after they had so vehemently rejected the same kind of iconic imagery among leathermen. One critic wondered: "What are the psychological consequences of joining the bear community to feel included, only to turn around and feel as though somehow one does not measure up physically as a Bear" (Locke 1997, 133)? The bear historian and founding figure Les Wright suggests that this development was part of a larger threat to the original vision of bear inclusiveness: "I have seen Bear groups, clubs, and commercial ventures devolve into the same in-group/out-group wrangling and cynical sabotaging of the perceived competition" (Wright 2002, 116).

Although these developments would seem to endorse the fields of struggle model, at least three complicating points need to be considered. First, it is at least plausible that, serious or not, bear beauty contests serve a qualitatively different purpose for bear men than they do for leathermen or for other types of contestants: "My overriding sense is that, although there may be political or ego-driven sexual motives that compel a contestant to the stage, the basic drive is one that seeks to affirm the Bear's own self-esteem as well as strengthen his connection with the Bear community" (Suresha 2002, 190). Framed in this way, bear competitions become less about competition per se and more about acceptance and conviviality. Second, it remains clear that, although the purity of the original intent of sexual egalitarianism and inclusive camaraderie may have been diluted in fairly short order, the historical record clearly indicates that they were a powerful part of the initial attraction bear men felt toward this field. This dedication to inclusiveness and emotional warmth, only partially realized in practice, nevertheless remains a fundamental part of how bears themselves describe their culture; it remains a fundamental organizing principle of the field. Finally, among those disenchanted with the current turn of events (toward greater exclusivity and the cultivation of an iconic bear ideal), the egalitarianism and the noncompetitive atmosphere of the past are part of a lively nostalgia.

In the leather community, I find further empirical evidence that hierarchies (at least as traditionally recognized) are not essential to fields. For example, the way in which players in leather BDSM fields explicitly embrace, rationalize, ritualize, and fetishize domination and submission complicates ideas of struggle and competition as they are understood in Bourdieusian terms. The unmistakable emphasis on training and technique in the field of leather BDSM means that members understand (and are constantly reminded of) the radically constructed nature of their status in the field. Given the proper training and technique, any actor in this field might assume a variety of dominant or submissive roles, or as Edmund White observed: "Tonight's top is tomorrow's bottom" (1980, 268). Furthermore, the fact that the careful cultivation of a submissive attitude and the meticulous attention paid to the quality of the submissive's interactions with the top (the dominant partner in a leather scene) clearly indicate that submission can be constructed as a positive, even prized, attribute. This significantly disrupts the logic of domination and struggle that Bourdieu takes as a given in any field recognizable as such. Of course, the fact that dominant and submissive roles are freely chosen and deliberately cultivated does not mean that there is no inherent logic ordering the field, and it does not necessarily imply that there are no status differences. Rather, it means that the most prized sexual capital in leather BDSM (i.e., a sense of intense presence in the scene, complete investment in one's role) is understood as available to all. The highly rationalized nature of this field and its emphasis on technique means that the necessary skills can, at least hypothetically, be acquired by any of the participating players. This radically democratized access to the field's most prized forms of capital again suggests that a theoretical reconsideration of the fields of struggle model may be in order. It also suggests other nonsexual fields that provide similarly democratized access to field-specific forms of capital and that need to be taken into account (e.g., social movements governed by consensus, certain religious sects that promote spiritual humility, etc.).

To conclude this section, the evidence I have presented here suggests that, instead of adopting entrenched positions in an either/or battle about whether sexual fields are constituted by struggle or harmony among its players, theorists may be better served by framing the matter empirically on a case-by-case basis. Admitting a bit more conceptual flexibility here opens up some significant new questions: How do life histories and personal narratives (Maynes, Pierce, and Laslett 2008; Hammack and Cohler 2009) affect field formation? What are the extra-field elements that predispose a field in formation to adopt a dynamic of struggle verses a dynamic of democratic acceptance? How and why does the internal balance between competition and harmony within an established field change over time? In challenging the hegemony of the fields of struggle model, the bear and leather cases open the door to these and other promising lines of inquiry.

## When Fields Collide—an Anecdote

In this last section, I use a personal anecdote to illustrate how sophisticated and subtle are the everyday perceptions of sexual capital among field participants and how fine-tuned their understandings of the habitus/capital/field complex. That this awareness efficiently communicates what Bourdieu calls a *sense of one's place* (1979/1984, 466) is by now a commonplace observation. In this section, I extend this point to demonstrate that, even in a situation in which actors inhabit the same physical space, carrying nearly identical "currencies" of sexual capital (Green, chapter 1 in this volume) and exhibiting an apparently identical "erotic habitus" (Green 2008a), fine-grained differences are relatively easily discerned by field participants, although they typically operate below the level of conscious thought. This granular discernment is especially evident in encounters in which varying understandings of *field* are at stake. Furthermore, I suggest that, if researchers do not attend to this subtle level of perception between and within fields, their research subjects are not likely to report them. This is because, as effects of the erotic habitus, they are generated by field participants below the level of conscious thought. Consequently, participants will typically revert to naturalizing narratives in their explanations ("that's just the way it is/I am"), and important field effects may be obscured or ignored.

\* \* \*

Picture a summer evening at one of Milwaukee's most notorious gay leather bars, ca. 1981. It's a sultry night in early July as I take my place among approximately a dozen other gay men in leather, all of whom stake out various areas of the bar, some alone, some coupled. Feigning aloofness, we regard each other. Between occasional gulps of my Miller Lite, I take deep drags on my Marlboro Light, all the while hoping I'm not coming off as leather light. I strike a pose at the bar that I hope my compatriots will find menacing yet alluring. As I survey the scene before me, I observe that most of the others are similarly engaged in this deeply serious form of impression management. All the familiar forms of sexual capital are in evidence tonight and on display: leather jackets (despite the heat), leather vests, boots, caps, tight T-shirts, a stoic disposition, potent stares, and attention paid to bearing, including how one drinks, smokes, speaks, etc. On this particular evening, the bar is especially crowded as the city of Milwaukee, one of the most convivial and alcohol-friendly cities in the country, is hosting its best-known festival, the annual ten-day ritual known as Summerfest. The sizzling July air is heavy with the redolent sweat of Lake Michigan and the thousands of dead alewives tossed up on the shore, and traffic outside the bar is backed up all the way to the fairgrounds. Tonight's festivities include a tribute to Milwaukee-based Harley Davidson, and a number of hard core bikers are stuck in the immovable line of vehicles trying to make their way toward the fairgrounds. Those of us inside the bar remain largely oblivious as our hallowed cruising rituals continue unabated.

Suddenly the door swings open; in swaggers an interloper, a man everyone seems to immediately recognize as a *real* leather biker. He sports a mullet and an intricate diamond-shaped design on the back of his leather jacket, the design itself composed of smaller diamond-shaped silver studs. He makes his way toward the bar with an intentionality that would knock Edmund Husserl back on his heels. Clearly, this man needs a drink. I quickly surmise that he has grown weary of waiting in traffic, pulled his bike over, and stopped in for a quick nip. My second thought is of impending doom. This is a potentially dangerous situation. The other patrons seem to share my assessment as the bar falls silent; we all wait. My mind races to thoughts of flying fists, perhaps a weapon, the man's angry friends hovering just outside the bar. The fear seems palpable as all eyes follow the interloper as he makes his way to the bar. Suddenly, just as he reaches the bar, he has a Bourdieusian epiphany. We can all clearly see the exact moment when he acquires a sense of his place: without so much as a sideways glance, he pivots abruptly and makes a beeline for the door, exiting with the same stone-faced swagger with which he entered. As the door closes behind him, there is a moment of stunned silence, followed by a spontaneous explosion of raucous laughter.

Thirty years later, I remain fascinated by this incident. How (and in what sense) did the interloper register as *real* in this context? Why was he so easily recognized as an outsider? Why did the situation register as *dangerous*? How was he able, in such short order, to acquire an accurate sense of his place or, in this case, a sense of *misplacement* in the bar?

What was funny about the episode? More to the point, what does this anecdote suggest about the subtleties of field perceptions?

Green (chapter 1 in this volume, p. 49) observes that "clothing and accessories have different connotations from one body to another" and provides examples to illustrate this point: the same coat communicates something very different depending on whether it is worn by a man or a woman; similarly, race and gender may shape how we interpret adornments such as jewelry etc. These examples effectively make the point, but they also describe social differences that are fairly easy to detect. With respect to my anecdote, a much more exacting approach is needed if we are to address the question of how (and in what sense) the interloper registered as real. How in fact were the bar patrons able to attribute any degree of difference to the interloper given the fact that, to an outsider at least, his field-specific capital was nearly identical to their own? He wore a coat quite similar to ones they themselves were wearing, he was (like the majority of bar patrons) white, and he displayed a similar bearing and self-presentation.

I cannot say why my fellow patrons so easily recognized the man as an outsider; I can only recount the subtle field-specific cues that registered with me. Perhaps most important was the attitude he displayed on entering. While the typical gay leatherman may enjoy a drink (and perhaps more so in Milwaukee than elsewhere), it is in my experience hardly ever the primary reason he goes to a bar. Our visitor exhibited a purely instrumental purpose in entering the bar, with little detectable concern for the social and sexual opportunities that an evening in this room might offer. The rest of us were focused on precisely these prospects—an important difference in habitus. Second, with respect to field-specific capital, the interloper entered sporting a mullet. Even in the early 1980s, this was frowned on by most gay men. Third (and paradoxically), the design on his jacket struck me as a bit too fancy for a man whose presentation of self was based on a deliberate homage to the rules of masculinity. Rather, it struck me as a feminine embellishment that only a man secure in his masculinity could afford to display.[11] None of these observations considered separately would necessarily raise questions about the man's place in the bar, but taken together they managed to raise some reasonable doubts. Conversely, I am convinced that our guest's rapid assessment of the bar derived from two specific observations of the field— the pervasiveness of leather among the patrons and the absence of women. While the former might have served as a welcome surprise to the stranded biker, the latter's suggestion of homosexuality immediately foreclosed the possibility that he would feel comfortable in this space. In his world, men who dress as he does are relentlessly heterosexual.

A more theoretical account might elaborate on the performance of "realness" and how this distinguishes fields. Among the men present, a shared sense of the radically constructed nature of masculinity, and leather biker masculinity in particular, operated as a kind of taken-for-granted field-specific knowledge (part of the field's doxa). The pleasures of our casual gathering keyed off of this shared understanding and what we did with it—what might be termed a *fetishistic dedication* to the rules of leather masculinity. Returning to the notion of shared generational experience, such fetishization would be impossible were it not for the fact that, at some point in all our lives and proceeding from a problematic association between masculinity and homosexuality, every man in the bar (with the exception of our surprised visitor) had likely been forced into a deliberate consideration of the rules of the game with respect to masculinity as well as their more or less arbitrary nature. Our realness as gay leathermen is akin to the realness chronicled by Jennie Livingston (1990) in the world of drag balls—a gesture toward authenticity in self-presentation that is fully conscious of the constructed (and therefore at some level not real) nature of the identity being produced (Butler 1990). It is in this context that the interloper can be perceived as real, but, paradoxically, only in the sense that he lacked an ironic distance from his own quite deliberate efforts toward identity construction.

This in turn helps explain perceptions of danger. The interloper's presentation of self was recognized by everyone in the bar as every bit as constructed as what was already going on there (i.e., a *performance* of hypermasculinity), but with no conscious acknowledgment of it on the part of the interloper himself. In other words, the real biker man had completely naturalized his masculinity (as a part of *his* taken-for-granted assumptions about how masculinity works in *his* preferred field). On entering the bar, he was confronted by a radically different way of doing leather masculinity, with starkly different implications. The encounter threatened to reveal his own assumptions as arbitrary and constructed rather than natural.[12] He responded to this threat by simply exiting the bar, leaving the disturbing implications of the field behind him. Having safely exited the scene, I can imagine him putting the entire matter to rest in a way that left the narrative naturalizing his own masculinity untouched: "Gay leathermen are fakers; I'm the real deal."[13] His primary concern with physically removing himself from the bar emphasizes the fact that his sense of misplacement is *embodied*, to the extent that it effectively organizes out reflection and critical thought.

None of this, however, likely registered with the participants in this scene. Bar patrons gay or straight rarely devote this much effort to theorizing their experience in this way. The question emerges, Can either the interloper or the other patrons at the bar produce an account that explains why they perceived the situation as they did? I would argue that none of the parties involved were fully conscious of why they made their attributions, that in all probability none of them were aware of the visual cues to which they were responding. Instead, both the wayward stranger and the bar patrons likely felt that their mutual recognition of otherness was only natural in this situation. There is more than a hint of Bourdieusian misrecognition here,[14] but for my purposes what I want to emphasize is the idea that fields filter perceptions of others in consequential ways and that actors are often imbricated in fields on the basis of extremely subtle observations operating (for participants) below the level of conscious thought. To this day, as I reflect back on this scene, it occurs to me that I do not really *know* what the stranger was thinking, I do not know why he left the bar, I do not know what might have happened had he stayed. I do not even know whether he was heterosexual. This seems all the more peculiar because, at the time, I knew all of this. Or perhaps it would be more accurate to say that *we* knew all of it. As collaborators in the field, my leather compatriots and I produced this knowledge on the basis, in all likelihood, of a shared interpretation of some extremely subtle visual cues. It seems to me that a celebration of this successful collaboration explains the exuberant laughter that followed the biker's exit.

Given our problematic histories with masculinity and our heightened awareness of the many contradictions within it, celebrating the ironies of the situation seemed only natural, in precisely the same way that the intruder's relationship to his masculinity seems only natural to him. But in both cases the erotic habitus has done its work and effectively concealed the techniques of masculinity construction from consciousness. Thus, it is up to the fastidious researcher to observe, record, and analyze the subtle but often powerful field effects produced by the erotic habitus and to say what these might mean. Having survived our ordeal, my compatriots and I had but one thing to say on that summer night in Milwaukee. We lifted a glass together with the old German toast to health and happiness—"Prosit!"

## Notes

1. The gay leathermen I studied valued a hypermasculine presentation of self and participated to varying degrees in bondage, discipline, and sadomasochism (BDSM). Bears constitute a subculture of gay men who are generally heavier and hairier than the smooth, gym-toned body of the reigning gay ideal. While the exaggerated masculinity of gay leathermen allows them to see themselves as more masculine than heterosexual men, bears strive toward "regular guy" status. Bears repudiate stereotypes of effeminacy in a carefully strategized masculine presentation of self (eschewing both the effeminacy of the stereotypical "Nancy" and the hypermasculinity of the gay leatherman), in an attempt to claim an authentic masculinity despite their same-sex interests. With these strategies, both bears and leathermen simultaneously challenge and reproduce traditional norms of masculinity. Insofar as their rejection of effeminacy signals a broader devaluation of the feminine, bears and leathermen recuperate the misogyny central to the logic of hegemonic masculinity (Connell 1995). On the other hand, bears and leathermen also confidently celebrate their attraction to other men. Bears do this in part through an elaborate set of symbolic appeals to nature and through varying degrees of identification with real bears in a collectively imagined pristine state of nature. They also explicitly reject what they see as the rampant sexual objectification of the gay leatherman in favor of a sexual culture informed by gregariousness, emotional warmth, and an "ethic of care" (Gilligan 1982). My research on bears and leathermen involved extensive ethnographies of these two communities as well as a third community not addressed in this chapter, the Radical Faeries (Hennen 2008).

2. Broadly speaking, this conception of turning away and its relationship to libido is obviously informed by several earlier conceptions: that of Freud, insofar as he presents desire as a kind of turning away from the restraints of the superego by the id, Lacan's concept of *jouissance* as a form of resistance to the law, and, more sociologically, Jung's emphasis on the symbolic nature of libido.

3. As Wright observes: "The origin of homosexual men self-identifying as bears is obscure." I was unable to locate any detailed empirical evidence as to exactly how the substitution of teddy bears for colored hankies occurred. After indicating that the term *bear* was used occasionally among gay men during the 1960s and 1970s, Wright observes: "By 1980 individual gay men in San Francisco, New York, Miami, Toronto, and elsewhere, are reported to have taken to placing a small teddy bear in a shirt or hip pocket, some of them with the intent of refuting the clone colored-hanky code, to emphasize being into 'cuddling,' that is resisting being objectified and reduced to preferred sex acts" (1997b, 21). An anonymous reviewer poses a helpful question: "How do we know that the acts of turning away are in fact individual? Maybe people didn't turn away until the cultural symbol of the little teddy bears was broadly available." This sug-

gests that, in terms of the actors forming the new field, we may need to make a distinction between two groups—those who came up with the resistant symbolism and were the first to adopt it (the cliff jumpers, in the terms of the previous metaphor) and a second set of actors who inquire as to its meaning and respond sympathetically.

4. This is not to imply that all fields are necessarily collecting discontent or that field subdivision is inevitable. This is an empirical question that needs to be determined on a case-by-case basis. I also do not mean to imply that, when they are successful in establishing a new field, discontented actors are necessarily fully aware of the implications of their actions or that their actions are necessarily politically transformative. Bourdieu makes it clear that, even in those rare cases where there is a significant transformation in habitus, the new habitus retains fundamental characteristics of the original (Bourdieu and Wacquant 1992, 131). Here, I assume the same thing about fields. In the bear case, conscious resistance concerned how to do masculinity and gendered sexuality. At no point did the new field (bears) resist fundamental assumptions about masculinity; neither community seriously embraces the feminine.

5. My thanks to Adam Green and an anonymous scholar for bringing this argument to my attention.

6. Michèle Lamont (2010) describes her own rejection of a strict Bourdieusian orthodoxy, referencing some of the same concerns: "Because of my own life experience, I remain persuaded that pleasure, curiosity, and a need for community and recognition are powerful engines for human action, certainly as powerful as the quest for power and the maximization of one's position in fields of power that are privileged by Bourdieu. These essential meta-theoretical differences put me at odds in a fundamental way with his work and that of some of his followers. Thus, taking distance from Bourdieu was not simply a matter of drifting away or pursuing questions he had not considered. It meant proposing a different approach focused on boundary work which, if it did not supersede Bourdieu's, was fundamentally 'other': I took novel angles on new and different issues, and several of these angles required rejecting some of the keystones of Bourdieu's theoretical apparatus." Elsewhere, Rogers Brubaker critiques his own earlier reading of Bourdieu as "too literal, too logical, too theoretical, too sociologically naïve—too respectful, I would almost say, of the texts, endowing them with a dignity and a definitiveness that they were not intended to possess" (1993, 216–17).

7. If it is true, as I suggest in the prior section, that this type of substitution marks a refusal or turning away and that this is inherently freighted with erotic energy, then this complicates considerations of sexual capital considerably. It obscures the easily recognizable criteria that are essential to the effective stratification of a field. On this line of thinking, two people might be fully aware of the fact that they possess low sexual capital (however this is defined) yet maintain a frisky disposition that allows them to turn to each other and see opportunity

where others see only abjection: "Let's you and I have ugly sex!" There is at least a possibility that these participants might find more than humor in such a proposition. Indeed, they might then (hypothetically) proceed to enjoy sex that is actually *better* (by whatever standards might apply in their particular field, if it could be measured) than the sex experienced by those with even the highest amounts of sexual capital in that particular field. Such a possibility, however remote, is extremely disruptive to the logic of sexual capital as it directly challenges the taken-for-granted link between the valuation of sexual capital in a field and the expected quality of any sexual experience with its possessor. In the case I have detailed here, desire that runs counter to the field-specific rules of the game is fed by the very act of transgression itself, provided that it is shared with at least one other person (sorry, transgressive masturbation does not count).

8. My thanks to an anonymous reviewer for this insight.

9. Among other sexual cultures drawing on the romantic narrative I would include the free love movement of the 1960s, some open marriage advocates, some lesbian-feminist communities that seek to organize sexuality around an "ethic of care" (Gilligan 1982), and another of my case study communities, the Radical Faeries (Hennen 2008).

10. The International Mr. Leather contest has taken place every year since 1979 in Chicago and is the highlight of a popular conference held annually in May. The judges' criteria for selecting the new International Mr. Leather include a demonstration of skills, with a significant component based on appearance ("presence" and personality account for 40 percent in the preliminary round, and physical appearance counts for 20 percent in the final round). The less prestigious Mr. Drummer contest has been affiliated with San Francisco's Leather Pride Week and Folsom Street Fair, held annually in late September.

11. In an earlier article, I have referred to the addition of this kind of feminine flourish to an otherwise unassailably masculine presentation as *appended effeminacy.* In such cases, the feminine references (usually visual) actually enhance the overall impression of masculinity (Hennen 2001).

12. For one who has made significant identity investments in such assumptions, this is not welcome news. Leo Bersani (1995, 18) has made a similar observation with respect to the "danger" of allowing gay men to serve openly in the military—that, in the studied and deliberate adoption of a military masculinity, the gay man forces the realization that *identity is not serious.* The gay leathermen had on some level already recognized this (albeit perhaps not on a fully conscious level), while for the real biker it was imperative that the same realization be resolutely avoided.

13. I thank Adam Green for this suggestion.

14. For Bourdieu, misrecognition is the common tendency to see social sorting mechanisms that perpetuate inequalities as freely chosen rather than conditioned; thus, it is a process critical to the legitimation of power and class differ-

ences in a society. In this case, rather than feeling excluded or unfairly treated, the intruder interprets the situation as simply one of personal preference—"I don't care for that sort" etc. The meaning of the encounter is misrecognized in that none of the parties present (neither the biker nor the bar patrons) fully understand either what is at stake in this encounter or the fact that the outcome has been "institutionally organized and guaranteed" in advance (Bourdieu 1977, 171). In this case, the outcome of the exchange legitimates the idea that sexual orientation is a real and consequential social difference, but this is not necessarily intended on anyone's part. Rather, this work is done below the level of conscious thought: "Each agent, wittingly or unwittingly, willy nilly, is a producer and reproducer of objective meaning. . . . It is because subjects do not, strictly speaking, know what they are doing that what they do has more meaning than they know" (Bourdieu 1977, 79).

# CHAPTER FOUR

# Rejecting the Specifically Sexual

*Locating the Sexual Field in the Work
of Pierre Bourdieu*

Matt George, Hawaii Pacific University

When a group, whatever it may be, has to produce an opinion, it is important for it to know
that it first has to produce an opinion about the way to produce an opinion. — Pierre Bourdieu, *The Mystery of Ministry*

Pierre Bourdieu worried about the dilution of his project for a coherent field theory of the organization of social striving (Bourdieu and
Wacquant 1992, 100, 185–86). On the one hand, there is the potential for
unnecessary fragmentation by sociologists proliferating various and sun-
dry subfields without properly situating them as fractions of larger fields.
On the other hand, there is the possible trivialization brought on by non-
empirical armchair theorists who might "impose" fields for any and every kind of endeavor (Bourdieu and Wacquant 1992, 100, 104). Yet it has
become common for Bourdieusian scholars to propose analysis of virtu-
ally any activity as a kind of field. It seems to have been taken for granted
that one could do so without degradation of the underlying theory and
that the underlying coherence of social field theory is not challenged but,
if anything, implicitly strengthened if we can analyze the fields of spelling
bees, jet-ski racing, perhaps even dog shows. Unfortunately, researchers
interested in the theoretical hypothesis of a specifically sexual field (with
correspondences that might shed light on the contemporary experience
of sexual capital) do not offer such a friendly amendment to Bourdieu's

theory. Thinking through the rubric of a historically emergent, relatively autonomous *sexual field* poses fundamental questions about the bases of Bourdieusian thought. Nowhere is this more apparent than in the notion of gender, for, as we shall see, Bourdieu deliberately constructed his theory to deny the autonomy of the sexual field.

At first glance, this denial is quite surprising, for three reasons. First, Bourdieu's career happened to span the radical set of changes often referred to as the *sexual revolution*, changes that involved a distinct rise in the autonomy of sexual life (Giddens 1992) and the importance of non-reproductive intimacy in particular (Jamieson 1988; Laumann, Gagnon, Michael, and Michaels 1994). Second, the historical construction of *sex-itself* was a pivotal intellectual question in the French social sciences at the time of Bourdieu's work (Foucault 1980). Third, and most importantly, it seems that Bourdieu's own career was decisively shaped by his encounter with the changing matrimonial strategies that were part and parcel of this wrenching social change (Bourdieu 2002/2008; Bourdieu and Wacquant 1992, 164). Nevertheless, Bourdieu never sought to formalize the idea of an autonomous sexual field. Instead, he paradoxically built his theory of gender on the very premodern principles that he also claimed were being dissolved by the progressive differentiation of fields in late modernity. Only a reflexive Bourdieusian analysis is able to demonstrate how Bourdieu's own location in the intellectual field was involved in these distinctive and potentially troublesome analytic choices.

## Bourdieu's Fundamental "Intuition"

I assume general familiarity with Bourdieu's overall theory but will isolate and highlight two interrelated aspects for the analysis that follows. First, it is important to understand that the conception of field was not simply any terrain of mutual orientation and striving. Whether it was a good thing or a bad thing, Bourdieu assumes that a field had a greater degree of organization, one that involved the generation not simply of capitals that were used in the attainment of what was at stake in any field but also positions of authority that could determine what forms of capital were legitimate. The fact that these positions of authority were normally contested and in flux in no way implies that a field could exist without any such positions. Further, Bourdieu increasingly seems to have believed that there was a necessary heteronomy to almost all fields (certainly all weighty ones, such as scientific fields) by virtue of the state retaining the right of final nomination—to say, in the last analysis, which type of doctors are the true doctors and who are the true poets. This somewhat centrist orientation to fields is not shared by most of the contributors to this volume, who tend toward a more bottom-up understanding of fields, but we cannot re-create Bourdieu's logic if we fail to understand that, for Bourdieu, a field implies the emergence of experts who secure their own distinction through consecrating others. A field possesses more autonomy when such experts are able to reproduce themselves—to choose not only what constitutes good art, say, but also who will be the next generation of critics (e.g., Bourdieu 1992/1996, 217, 299). Thus, it is not simply that every field pursues its own object (perhaps artists pursue aesthetic force and physical chemists models of atomic relation), or that actors pursue the capital that allows them to achieve these goals (and thereby accumulate greater capital), but that there is a constant interchange—sometimes appearing as polite conversation, other times as vicious struggle—over the capacity to make the final determination over what the object is (what is truly art, say) and what capital is legitimate (what techniques constitute cheating, say). A sociological analysis of the production of ideas, judgments, and works by these experts turns on mapping such "position takings" to a space of field positions (Bourdieu 1992/1996, 231). Thus, our understanding of action requires that we understand the endogenous character of the standards used to determine what is success—and what standards can succeed.

Yet all is not strictly endogenous. Many fields are subject to state regulatory initiatives, leading to a fundamental heteronomy. Further, the status of professional fields vis-à-vis one another is also subject to regulation. And the relative power of fields—whose experts triumph in interstitial negotiation—determines how the state prioritizes opinion, whether, say, it is legal or scientific experts or layperson celebrities whose opinions are decisive at a particular point or who have the right to define—and even enact as law—vital designations such as citizenship, race, sanity, and perhaps even sex. Any field, therefore, has a particular degree of autonomy that varies according to the degree to which extraneous criteria influence the exercise of judgment in the field, that is, evaluations of quality and legitimacy.

In the more autonomous zones of a field, Bourdieu believes, experts compete to position themselves within the spectrum of ortho- and heterodoxy. Sensitized to the historicity of the field, these specialists strive to define its boundaries and its object or activity (Bourdieu and Wacquant 1992, 245).[1] In an ideal world, these definitions would be those that empower the definers—hence power holders tend to insist on orthodoxy, and challengers introduce heterodoxy. But things are not always so simple, for, to the extent that the field is compromised or heteronomous, the discourse of elite specialists is shaped by force relations exterior to the field and by how these relations influence processes of authorization and delegation in the field (Bourdieu 1992/1996, 217; Maton 2005). Applying these insights to the practice of sociology implies taking a position in defense of the scientific autonomy of the field, and Bourdieu is keen to position his arguments from within this perspective. As we shall see, this could lead to ambivalence when he had to analyze the forces that he believed threatened our own scientific autonomy.

A second key part of Bourdieu's project follows epistemologically from the ontological assumptions outlined so far. His signature stance holds that no social science can be objective without being reflexive. Reflexivity in social science, in his view, demands that explanations include an account of how each scientific field is positioned in the field of politics (bureaucracy, administration, and the state). Sociological reflexivity, for Bourdieu, then, is not merely ethically but epistemologically de rigueur. It is not a matter of politely handicapping oneself with inspired efforts at self-criticism but instead an empirical need to explain precisely how "power is concentrated in definite institutional sectors and in given zones of social space" (Wacquant 2005, 145). In any full-scale description of social phenomena, what is important is to establish how the play of capitals conserves (or not) the reproduction of dominant positions as heritage and patrimony.

In short, a reflexive social science calls for sociological analysis of the production of scientific knowledge and the degree to which it is enmeshed in institutional and political struggles for conserving the reproduction of the social order. The meaning of a social scientific statement is not reducible either to the explicit intentions of its author or to its literal or logical meaning. Rather, it is a move in a field with a particular historical configuration (Bourdieu 1997a, 116). This is not merely a concern for historians of science; it is recommended protocol for the analysis of empirical data in general. As Wacquant aptly emphasizes about Bourdieu's "quasi-monomaniacal" insistence on reflexivity, above all it is a matter of "constructing scientific objects differently" (Bourdieu and Wacquant 1992, 42). Rather than accepting prefabricated analytic objects, by including the historicity of the field as one dimension of the phenomena to be explained, one avoids confusing mere positioning within the field (prochoice vs. prolife positions) with the deeper play of dispositions that might explain the distribution of opinion in the first place.

Finally, Bourdieu understood his theory of fields (and his prescription for reflexivity) as justified by empirical analyses of the complex process of the historical differentiation of fields. His view of modernity focuses on the historically unprecedented emergence of bureaucracy and of a specific kind of public "interest" that decenters absolutism with a coordinated array of fields that vie for a monopoly of "legitimate symbolic violence" (Bourdieu in Wacquant 2005, 48). A secular shift in types of legitimate expertise topples traditional dominants in one field after another, or, perhaps more likely, carves out new fields from what were previously relatively undifferentiated arenas of action (Bourdieu 1983/1986, 50–51). It might be expected, then, that in the process of this enlargement of bureaucratization and specialization (much like how Bourdieu described the arts and the economic field emerging in the modern period) sexuality would become increasingly delegated away from traditional authorities and move into an independent sphere of action with the development of autonomous forms of expertise.

## The Problem of Libido

Psychoanalysis popularized the idea that such a professional approach to sex was possible. Claiming not only privileged access to the truths of sex but also that these truths underlay many other aspects of human life, Freud is rightly seen as one of the main progenitors of the modern professionalization of intimacy (Birken 1988; Foucault 1980). But Bourdieu responded to psychoanalysis's imperiously monocausal grasp of social rationality with a countersortie, adopting *libido* as a general term for the differentiated forms of desire generated by all fields. Similar to his rhetorical strategy of problematizing the economic idea of capital, by importing and generalizing terms in this way, Bourdieu sought to demystify the power of a threatening neighbor discipline to sociology and, in the same stroke, to effect the classic structuralist vision of a unification of sociology, economics, and psychology—but on his terms.

For classic psychoanalysis, libido was an instinctual, biophysical sex drive, one that was viewed as making its entrance at least initially *op-*

*posed* to social order. Bourdieu's recasting gives libido no a priori trans-historical nature, nothing that is counterposed to the social (Bourdieu 1990b, 88). Indeed, a proper socioanalytic notion of desire should be based on the fact that "social magic can constitute more or less anything as interesting, and establish it as an object of struggle," and that there are as many libidos as there are games (Bourdieu 1990b, 88, 110). To allow a "libidinal libido" would, however, force Bourdieu into a position in which there are no palatable answers. Would he have to deny that, for a specifically sexual field, there would be no connection between the actions of those "in the game" and the experts "in the know," which would highlight the awkwardly exceptional nature of such a case? Or would he have to argue that what we can call the *metasexual knowledge* of professionals such as psychoanalysts and sexologists is pursued in a way that is fundamentally consubstantial with that in which sexual desire drives actors? Would he have to give a special dispensation for the libidinal libido of a professional field of sexual expertise that makes it forever heteronomous, tied to other aspects of social life, while all other fields can, in principle, be compatible with an ideal typical autonomy? This might save his general arguments about the role of the family and sexuality in class reproduction, but at the cost of the consistency of his field theory. Or does he emphasize the historicity of metasexual expertise and claim that it is only social magic that makes a sexual object and aim legitimate in one context but not in another and thus perhaps end up reinforcing the Sadean implications that, as we shall see, he sought always to avoid?

Thus, recognizing the relative autonomy of the professional sexual field might undo this theoretical strategy, for it raises the question of a libidinal libido, one that might seek its own professional autonomy through institutions that seek to regulate the meanings of sexuality as a bodily event per se. Bourdieu turned a caustic and near blind eye to a competing professional field that vied for a monopoly on the legitimate definition of sex-itself and served to therapeutically render sexuality capable of the transformations that highly differentiated, legal-juridical, bureaucratic societies seemed to demand of it.

Bourdieu, then, was reluctant to posit a specifically sexual field and a libidinal libido, one that must be treated as potentially autonomous from other stratification orders. Yet he claims that his original sociological "intuition" was provoked by a rude encounter with the power of the modern transformation of intimacy (Bourdieu and Wacquant 1992, 164)—what we might well see as the stirrings of a sexual field in formation. In what follows, I enlarge the "mental photos" of this experience (photos that Bourdieu claims to have developed continuously over the course of his career [Bourdieu and Wacquant 1992, 205; Bourdieu 2012]). Certain details in the background of these memories seem to have been filtered or left out of the frame by unconscious effects of position and perhaps deliberate polemical strategies that, when examined in light of the narrative of the emergence of modern sexual thinking, help reflexively situate the place of sexuality in Bourdieu's analytic of social fields.

## Sex and the City

Reviewing his earliest publications, we can see that Bourdieu launched his career by analyzing the very cusp of the transition from traditional to early modern sexuality with his earliest study of matrimonial strategy. In *The Bachelor's Ball* (2002/2008), he republished his analyses of changes in courtship in his home region of Bearn. At the center of the narrative is the rejection of eldest sons at a rural country dance. These "inheritors" would have been the most desirable bachelors under the old peasant patrimonial system but were ignored by the girls at the dance, who chose instead the more urban affiliated, "citified," and educated men—those who in the old system possessed questionable masculinity but were tickets to upward mobility in the new. As the young Bourdieu (2002/2008, 185–86) witnessed how European modernity created an "open market" matrimonial regime of "free exchange" (and especially how this socially distributes the victims of an "interior defeat" caused by the fleeing of women to cities and the celibacy of rural men), he received his first intimations of the power of symbolic violence as a strategy of governmentality.[2]

Looking back over these events years later, Bourdieu observed how, historically, France was able to rid its countryside of peasants in three generations with the soft violence of modern sexualization, in contrast to the brutal physical violence used to accomplish the same thing in Russia (Bourdieu and Wacquant 1992, 167). Rural orders were undermined, not by forced collectivization, but by allowing free marital choice with its inherent individualizations. The effectiveness of an emerging market in intimacy appears to hinge on how "everyone must manage on his own and can count only on his own assets . . . his ability to dress, to dance, to present himself, to talk to girls" (Bourdieu and Wacquant 1992, 165).

These same themes appeared in the later analyses of the reconversion strategies of late 1960s French elites in the face of social change. Bourdieu considered the seismic shift in sexual attitudes of the 1970s as an example of "the 'social policy' of a dominant class which concedes the better to conserve" (Bourdieu 1979/1984, 371). He focuses on one extraordinary structural shift that he claims transformed wide swathes of cultural life after the 1970s: the increased access of elite women to the halls of higher education. Although this might be seen as merely the corrective of helping women break the glass ceiling in elite employment, it also had the effect of empowering the nouveau bourgeoisie to break with the old and abandon the reserve associated with the traditional *grande* ethos. Repressive efforts at controlling the social events and courtship opportunities of its daughters were given over to free market principles that were just as successful at ensuring class endogamy: "The new measures concerning, in no particular order, parental authority (replacing paternal authority), spousal equality in matrimonial matters, estate management, divorce, cohabitation, voluntary termination of pregnancy, etc., merely write into law a set of practices whose appearance in the new bourgeoisie had been either authorized, favored, or determined by the transformation of the mode of reproduction" (Bourdieu 1992/1996, 275).

For Bourdieu, the counterculture of the late 1960s (and May '68 in particular) was formed by this new permissive tack in elite strategy. This change in strategy in turn was a response to fundamental socioeconomic changes: the expansion of the educational system drew new entrants from the working class into the petit bourgeoisie, while declining elites allied with the arriviste urbanizing peasants to challenge both traditional authority and educational modes of reproduction. It is clear from his end-of-career reflections that it was from this heady mix of social change that Bourdieu both developed his theory of habitus (Bourdieu 1990b, 71) and later developed his analytic of fields, though with specific attention to the Parisian intellectual and artistic milieu (Bourdieu and Wacquant 1992, 193). With only slight exaggeration, we can say that his biographical trajectory and the particular contours of the theories he was developing were largely reactions to the autonomization of the sexual field.

## Sex in the Field of the State

As we have seen, Bourdieu was well aware of the liberalization of sexual and courtship norms that characterize a great deal of late modern transformations in sexual life. Yet he did not connect these changes with the emergence of new expert discourses about sexuality, those of psychoanalysis and sexology, because this would in effect confer legitimacy on those whom he considered to be spouting destructive nonsense about the realm of sexuality—even as he recognized that the threat they posed meant that one could not entirely ignore the connection between these expert discourses and lay behavior. In addition, he felt that humanist counterculture and the therapeutic ethos were undermining the politicization of the working class. That is, he did not *ignore* changes associated with the rise of the sexual field: he *combated* them. With respect to the sociosexual changes he observed around him, Bourdieu was a committed midmodern sociologist with little tolerance for the embrace of what we might now recognize as postmodern subjectivity. By the late 1960s, he writes in *Distinction*, an "ethical avant garde" had emerged that advanced what he excoriates as a "morality of pleasure as a duty." In contrast to the politicization that he might have hoped for with his own style of scientific activism, this kind of "moralization" and "psychologization" "transmutes a spuriously positive definition of the 'normal' into an imperative of 'normality'" (Bourdieu 1979/1984, 367–69).

What is fascinating is that this discussion of the cultural influence of psychoanalysis and sexology is embedded in an analysis of how cultural democratization in the late 1960s created what Bourdieu denounces as a professionalized cadre of "ethical prophets" rising out of the explosion in psychoanalytic and humanist sexological therapies. True to his epistemological vision, he does not attribute to psychoanalysis either scientific truth or ideological power but instead explains its rise to importance by pointing to both the feminization of labor and the "constitution of a corps of professionals" that brings together psychoanalysts, sexologists, counselors, psychologists, specialized journalists, etc., all competing for a monopoly on the "legitimate definition of legitimate pedagogic or sexual competence" (Bourdieu 1979/1984, 369). We cannot miss his heightened vigilance against the rise of metasexual expertise associated with disciplines that he considered suspect, pseudoscientific interlopers and his sense of their encroachment on what he saw as the rightful preserve of the legitimate academic scientific field.[3]

In this passage, Bourdieu does not hesitate to refer to this "production of goods and services" as a vocational field, but, when he does, he makes a curiously defensive comparison between the "competence demanded in such matters and *real* competence" (Bourdieu 1979/1984, 369 [emphasis added]). It is a strikingly stark opposition of the real and the false, rarely seen in his writing. He emphasizes that the members of the humanistic-sexological-therapeutic nexus of the 1960s sought (what he considers to be ill-gotten) profit from their involvement in the emergence of the modern sexual domain. Specifically, these ethical prophets found substitution and compensation "for the prestigious positions the labor market refused them in the interstices of the teaching profession and the medical profession" (Bourdieu 1979/1984, 369). Their success in doing this lay not in the scientific autonomy or truth of their scientific theories—it lay in the usefulness of this pseudoscience for legitimating the sexed changes rippling through the educational and matrimonial strategies of the elite bourgeoisie (Bourdieu 1989/1996, 275).

The arguments here are tied to a fundamental historical account of how late modern societies come to see sexuality as a fungible, transactional form of power—convertible and manipulable as if it were capital. For instance, Bourdieu argued that a "bogus science of mores" baked "a la Kinsey" had "introduc[ed] the deadly, rational accountancy of equivalences into the area of sexual exchanges" to create "a systematic answer to the problems of daily existence," treating the body like "the psychoanalyst does the soul" (Bourdieu 1979/1984, 367–68)—that is, something to be "liberated" through new expert management. He notes that this Kinsey-inspired axiom of the universality of all forms of sexual outlet (in Kinsey's counts, every ejaculation was the same as any other) and the corresponding duty of all citizens (in what he called "Erikson's 'utopia of full orgasmic reciprocity'") to give and receive equal numbers of physician-approved orgasms are in stark contrast to sexuality in the premodern world. Even more, the details of sexual exchange rationalized by humanist psychoanalytic and sexological therapies threaten the underlying sociodicies that link blood and land, for the management of sexual exchanges is "one of the last refuges of collective misrecognition" (Bourdieu 1979/1984, 368).[4] For Bourdieu (1979/1984, 367), such fundamental cosmological or mythic misrecognition is fundamental to the coherence and identification of tradition-bound groups—in this case, he seems to suggest that working-class identity was undermined by how transactional notions of reciprocity in pleasure interfered with the "naturalized" and eternalized cosmology of the traditional peasantry.[5] This new permissive bourgeois ideology was, then, not only scientifically compromised but also politically disenfranchising.

Not only were these changes associated in Bourdieu's mind with the pseudoscience and bogus rhetoric of liberation coming from sexology, but they also betokened what we might now call *neoliberalism*, namely, the spread of capitalist market relations into all domains. All the talk of free love, sexual revolution, and libidinal economy wafting about Paris in the early 1970s seemed suspiciously useful for "supplying the economy with the perfect consumer whom economic theory has always dreamed of" because this new ethic would weaken "collective defenses against the immediate impact of the market" (Bourdieu 1979/1984, 371). By the time of the publication of *Firing Back* (2001/2003), Bourdieu found these suspicions confirmed. Just as neoliberal policy erodes barriers to trade, extending markets into zones formerly off-limits, so too humanist counterculture, psychoanalysis, and sexology all brought new forms of reasoning—at the practical level as well as the theoretical—to domestic and, especially, sexual life. Thus, his analysis of the changes in sexuality flirted with the functionalist Marxism of critical theory, but Bourdieu held back from any serious engagement. And this seems to be explicable only by consideration of his relations to a different analyst of the functional changes in sexuality, namely, Michel Foucault.

## Sex and the State of the Field

While Bourdieu was polemically distancing himself from the experts associated with the break of intimacy from familial norms and the development of new, unmoored forms of sexuality, Foucault was theorizing this as a crucial aspect of modern capitalism, one rooted, albeit paradoxically, in the bourgeois family itself. Foucault famously argued that, since the mid-1850s, "the family was the crystal in the deployment of sexuality" and that late modern "family values" only masked the intensifying role of intimacy in the formation and arrangement of class bodies beyond the nuclear family's circumference. The family and the familialist vision of antiquity are, in Foucault's view, the origins of this rupture in the mid-nineteenth century and "seemed to be the source of a sexuality which it actually only reflected and diffracted" (Foucault 1980, 111). Foucault went on to analyze the way the professionalization of intimacy was instrumental to the expansion of the state into domestic matters and how eugenicism gave conceptual support for the usefulness of these strategies in the governance of populations.

To understand these developments, Foucault argued, we will have to return to "formulations that have long been disparaged" and accept that "there is a bourgeois sexuality and that there are class sexualities." And, of course, what his narrative of sexual stratification underlined was that "sexuality is originally, historically bourgeois, and that, in its successive shifts and transpositions, it induces specific class effects" (Foucault 1980, 127). Foucault's history centered on the ways in which intimacy became something increasingly autonomous from reproduction, marriage, and the traditional familialist values of patrimony—those mechanisms emphasized by Bourdieu in *Masculine Domination*.

Importantly, Foucault stressed that the role of sexuality in late modern political hegemony did not arise directly out of labor relations but instead was connected to a transformation of the social symbolics of the sexual body, "because of what the 'cultivation' of its own body could represent politically, economically and historically for the present and future of the bourgeoisie" (Foucault 1980, 125). Foucault's view of the political utility of new forms of understanding erotic habitus is close to Bourdieu's idea in *Distinction* that the new liberatory sexual ethic is indeed a form of "enlightened conservatism." This is the same conservatism that Foucault denounced as a "garrulous sexuality" expressing an "arrogant political affirmation" that "the proletariat long refused to accept, since it was foisted on them for the purpose of subjugation" (Foucault 1980, 127).

Foucault's (1980, 118) exploration of the biopolitical foundations of neoliberal capitalism led him to point to a eugenic "'orthopedics' specific to sex" in early sexology as symbolically efficacious in how sexuality became "the source of an entire capital for the species to draw from." Such "capitalization" of the sexual body is more than a mere rhetorical trope. Moving through the fits and starts of the emergence of the modern sexual field, one encounters the increasing emergence of instrumental, calculative transactionality that distinguishes intimacy (the deployment of sexuality) from familialism (the deployment of alliance) by literally "distributing the living in the domain of value and utility. Such a power has to qualify, measure, appraise and hierarchize" (Foucault 1980, 112).[6] To restate this in Bourdieusian terms, one could say that Foucault was drawing a portrait of how, by taking orientation from imperialist and eugenic fixations on the social ordering of bodies, statist public capital at the highest levels of social administration used sexological discourses in new strategies of legitimation and of how this gave impetus to the development of a relatively autonomous field. Foucault's thesis of the deployment of sexuality coincides with Bourdieu's assessments of psychoanalysis and humanist sexology as advancing to prominence, not by dint of scientific rigor or even intellectual coherence, but because of how this pseudoscientific discourse on sex served to naturalize and eternalize new strategies of dominance and stratification.

Given the obvious relevance of Foucault's arguments for his own work, why did Bourdieu reject Foucault's arguments without reservation? Fortunately for us, he (2004/2008) attempted to write what he described as an objectivistic "nonobituary" (in other words, a nonpsychological, field theoretical analysis) of the similarities and differences of positions and dispositions between the two thinkers. His appraisal of Foucault's legacy focused primarily on the difference in political and social status between the fields of philosophy and sociology. It is a pained reflection when he notes: "Depending on whether it comes from a sociologist or a philosopher, the same action . . . may appear as the grossness of a Philistine or audacious and refined transgression of an aesthete" (Bourdieu 2004/2008, 82).

Although it may perhaps strain the normal tactfulness of appreciative critique, we should recognize the relevance of a set of linked binaries that seem to be invoked in Bourdieu's reaction to Foucault both as person and as intellectual:

> philosophy : sociology :: refined : crude :: upper-class : working-class :: homosexual : heterosexual.

Bourdieu acknowledged his and Foucault's many political concordances and dialogues, and even their friendship, but remained fundamentally dismissive of what he considered Foucault's trajectory in the intellectual field, one that began from points of social and intellectual privilege and sought the profits of philosophical grand theory: Foucault on the one hand provoking young people to romanticize revolt by stylizing himself as an avant-garde artist and on the other making broad empirical claims without paying the hard dues of becoming an empirical scientist.

Beyond the personal judgments, Bourdieu associated the sexual emphasis in French philosophy with the prestige of psychoanalysis and Jacques Lacan in particular. "What is certain," he wrote, "is that psychoanalysis, at least in 1970s France, was lodged among the noblest and purest intellectual activities." Sociology, he continues, was at the very antipode (Bourdieu 2004/2008, 17). It is also significant that he opens his autobiography admitting how much his refusals, although barely conscious, nonetheless revealed themselves in antipathies like his "fairly deep revulsion for the cult of Sade . . . or the vision of sexuality associated with Georges Bataille or Pierre Klossowski" (Bourdieu 2004/2008, 2). Nothing so classifies us as does how we classify, and it seemed that the Marquis de Sade was a signal figure in dividing the French intellectual field into camps, Foucault firmly in one, Bourdieu unshakably in the other.

The interplay of disposition and position here resulted in the fact that it was not Bourdieu, but actually Foucault who described the emergence of sex-itself as an autonomous realm, took seriously the role of new forms of expertise therein, and connected this to historical changes in class relations. Further, Foucault's account of this latter dimension emphasized the transition from landed property to the "special character of the elite body" as the key to the support of modern stratification systems. Thus, Foucault was the one who proffered a detailed historiography for tracing what Bourdieu (1979/1984, 367) called "the rationalization of sexual exchanges" that might underlie changes in political modes of legitimacy and subjection and shed light on late modern "class racism." In Bourdieusian terms, it was actually Foucault who was the first to propose that the *embodied social capital* had emerged as a new mode for establishing political legitimacy.

Further, although we may associate Foucault with a loose claim that sexuality is a discursive construction, we should bear in mind that the central role of professional expertise in the development of an autonomous field, especially in the conditions of modern bureaucratic society, follows naturally from Bourdieu's principles.[7] The first step, in the analysis of a field, is to situate the development of the field (and, thus, its autonomization) "vis-à-vis the field of power" (Bourdieu and Wacquant 1992, 104). This seems quite in keeping with Foucault's key historical argument—that the concept of sex-itself and the attendant categorizations it made possible were central to historical and cultural changes called for by new biopolitical strategies for the governability of populations.

Yet Bourdieu would have none of it.


## The Missing Sexual Field

Despite continuous engagement with parallel themes, Bourdieu never allowed that there could have developed a proper sexual field with its own autonomy, its own socially defined and contested libidinal libido, and its own aficionados and experts' experts. For example, his explanation of gendering in *Masculine Domination* has no sustained elaboration of the effect of institutional fields on sexual habitus. In *Distinction*, he makes defensive mention, but no intrinsic use, of the relevance of a metasexual institutional field. In *The State Nobility*, he offers a relatively monocausal account that attributes to 1970s humanist counterculture a new flexibility and permissiveness required by the rise of women in higher education. Because of his reluctance to reflexively situate his own positions on sexuality as vying for metasexual authority with those of psychoanalysis and sexology, he resisted exploring in field theoretic terms the possible source of changes in the political significance of sexuality in modern society. Even when he did refer to these transformations, he mentioned them only to highlight how they obscured the frame he was trying to draw around the social efficacy of familialism in *traditional* society.

In his early ethnographic work—on a traditional Algerian society (though one being forcefully modernized)—Bourdieu argued that our late modern sensibility risked misunderstanding how the cosmologies of Kabylia functioned by utilizing the modern category of "the sexual in itself" because "sexuality is not constituted as such" in Kabylian society (Bourdieu 1998/2001, 7).[8] Implicitly agreeing with Foucault that the aggregation of a set of aspects of human life into the *sexual as such* was a relatively recent phenomenon, he emphasized an embedding of the sexual in wider structures of society at the heart of Mediterranean civilization, "the sexualized cosmology that is rooted in a sexualized topology of the socialized body" (Bourdieu 1998/2001, 7).

In such societies, then, sexuality was integrated—rather than being some kind of wild card that perpetually threatens to upset stratification regimes (Goode 1959). The androcentric cosmology, which Bourdieu claims underlies all Mediterranean societies, treated social rank and erotic rank as naturally synchronized. Further, the sexual division of labor and the division of sexual labor are intimately related; property in women cannot be understood apart from the transmission of patrimonial property *through* women. But the modern transformation of intimacy introduces transactional and economistic values that threaten this synchronization of social and erotic rank (Bourdieu 1992/1996, 170), as Bourdieu himself had discovered at the bachelor's ball. As we have seen, he did not deny the significant changes in sex and gender that accompanied modernization, yet he insisted on developing his theory by taking the traditional as his point of reference, focusing on change as something that subtracted from this orderliness (as opposed to investigating the new principles of orderliness on their own terms), and emphasizing that less had changed than one might suspect.

In order for us to think sex in itself, Bourdieu writes, a "progressive dissociation of mythic reason" had to take place. By this, he meant that the very idea of sex as such is a historical invention, one that is connected to the emergence and differentiation of spheres that define the process of modernization. Specifically, in the case of sexuality, he points to the emergence of a set of fields such as the religious, legal, and bureaucratic that were able to "impose definitions in practices, particularly through families and the familialist vision" (Bourdieu 1998/2001, 104). Yet, even with these transformations, he emphasized the persistence of the role of property relations in sexual life: "The legitimate exercise of sexuality . . . remains ordered by and subordinated to the transmission of the patrimony" (Bourdieu 1998/2001, 96). The hegemony of ruling families over sexual norms, here, as elsewhere in Bourdieu's vision, functions as a default or "primordial political belief" grounded in the efficacy of inheritance for the conservation of both economic and social capital.[9] Although he is perhaps best known in North America for his argument that such conservation is supported (or indicated) by cultural judgment and attendant symbolic violence, Bourdieu (1992/1996, 170) argues that the "paradigmatic form of symbolic violence" is gender domination, which is imposed as a "universal viewpoint," a naturalized sociodicy of the familialist worldview. Sex supports gender, gender supports the family, the family supports property. And not all families are equal. The hands that rock the cradle most likely to rule the world are those with the most properties—economic, cultural, and psychological—to transmit to heirs apparent.

## Property, Sex, and Gender

Despite his sidelong glances at the social changes *undermining* this patrimonial gender system, Bourdieu used patrimony as the crucial lens for viewing contemporary sex and gender; thus, his attempt to develop a theory of sex and sexualization was deliberately grounded in the social relations of a premodern society (and one in which patriarchal clan relations are unusually simple and clear) in which sexual action had not yet been differentiated from male property ownership in land. Focusing on the historical continuity of the androcentric worldview, he remarks on the "extraordinary" independence of sexual structures from economic structures, "of modes of reproduction [from] modes of production"— that is, the fact that the same basic sexual sociosymbolic system is seen across place and time (Bourdieu 1998/2001, 81). Although he acknowledges that the legal system has taken the place of the mythico-ritual system in terms of consecrating and ratifying the established order (Bourdieu 1998/2001, 8; Bourdieu 1989/1996, 274), he insists that the ancient cosmologies of gender still persist in the "modern" world as Virginia Woolf confronted it in the 1920s, for example, in "a partial and, as it were, exploded state, in our cognitive structures and social structures" (Bourdieu 1998/2001, 6).

*Masculine Domination* amplifies the analyses presented first in *Distinction* and detailed later in *The State Nobility*, arguing that, even with the popular decline of marriage, "the legitimate exercise of sexuality" is still defined by elite "transmission of the patrimony, through marriage," because this remains a legitimate means for the transfer and conservation of wealth (Bourdieu 1998/2001, 96). If Bourdieu accused Foucault of inspiring bottom-up views of power (Wacquant 2005, 45), there is no doubt here why: in matters sexual, Bourdieu held a strictly top-down view of the imposition of norms. The "shift from the duty to the fun ethic" was part of that sort of "restructuring of the system of investment strategies" (Bourdieu 1992/1996, 277) that follows social change. Although in *Distinction* Bourdieu accused sexologists and humanist therapists of "creating their own market," implying the uselessness of their services, he also suggests that they succeeded in providing the symbolic weapons used by new-guard elite liberals to define themselves against the old-school conservatives.

The argument here relies on a careful distinction that is more subtle than it might seem. Polemically, Bourdieu was concerned to stress how the semiological-structuralist interpretation of kinship and of culture (encouraged by Lévi-Strauss) ignores how the reproduction of symbolic capital figures in strategies of the political conservation of power. At the heart of Bourdieu's understanding of habitus as a political stake are women—women whom he saw, not merely as gifts of sexual access in relays of exchange between clans, but as strategically stratified habitus inculcators. This is literally his term: to *inculcate* is to transfer schemas and models through eroticized and eroticizing interactional rituals of parenting and schooling. And this suggests part of the change Bourdieu was noticing: in traditional patrimonial society, property passes from man to man through woman's body as she generates a new generation of males; to the Kabylia (at least the men), the woman's role is a passive one like that of the earth to the plowing farmer (Bourdieu 1977, 64, 138). More generally, in traditional societies, women were controlled so that their movement in social space would "reproduce the conditions of access to social reproduction and not only to sexuality" (Bourdieu 1998/2001, 45). In the contemporary world, however, class position is passed down with women choosing the current, and shaping the next, generation of dominant men. Thus, female sexual agency becomes a major political stake when a woman may choose precisely as an isolated individual freed from the control of her lineage—in the back seat of her suitor's car rather than on the front porch of her family's household, to borrow Beth Bailey's (1988) historical contrast.

The social management of cultural inculcation is a strikingly different explanation than what is usually implied by the patriarchal domination of women thesis (that women are disempowered simply because of their sexual difference or that men seek to especially dominate women qua women for some reason that serves men as a category). The position of women has changed, but the connection between sexuality and social reproduction remains, leading to the remarkable persistence of the premodern gender metaphors in early to midmodern sexuality.

Various indices of modern sexuality (including divorce, premarital sex, declining fertility, enhanced contraception and abortion, the institutionalization of feminism, and increasing acceptance of alternative sexual identities) are widely claimed to have challenged the symbolic efficacy of the heteronormative order. To one who assumed that only heteronormative familism is compatible with class reproduction, this would imply a revolutionary destabilization of stratification systems. But Bourdieu's own work suggests that the decline of hegemonic familism, and the divergence of intimacy and reproduction, might be a workable basis for a renewed transmission of social patrimony, now held in the body, not the land. Sexuality pursued for its own sake, whether subversively removed in love from the metaphors of dominance and submission or ironically hyperrealized in play as literal power exchange itself, appears as a threat to patrimonial fantasies of gender. But this is occluded when, with Bourdieu, we might yoke social and sexual reproduction so tightly in our explanations of desiring that the actual empirical dynamics of emotional intimacy fall out as little more than small change in the understanding of erotic life.

## Conclusions

We have seen that, despite his attention to changes associated with the freeing of intimacy from traditional forms of class reproduction, Bourdieu refused to theorize a specifically sexual field. This would not only threaten to put sexuality in a privileged place as the only field with a libidinal libido but also seem to steer dangerously close to intellectual currents in France that Bourdieu found intellectually compromised, politically infantile, and personally objectionable—and that were associated with his greatest rival for the position of heresiarchal social thinker, namely, Michel Foucault. As a result, his theory of gender was based on premodern constellations of sexuality. Thus, changing his theory of sex requires changing his theory of gender, and changing his theory of gender requires changing his theory of social order, for Bourdieu argued: "The principle of the inferiority and exclusion of women, which the mythico-ritual system ratifies and amplifies, to making it the principle of the whole universe, is nothing other than the fundamental dissymmetry, that of subject and object, agent and instrument, which set up between men and women in the domain of symbolic exchanges, the relations of production and reproduction of symbolic capital, the central device of which is the matrimonial market, and which are *the foundation of the whole social order*" (Bourdieu 1998/2001, 42 [emphasis added]).

Although he did not formulate a key role for an autonomous sexual field, Bourdieu recognized many of the characteristics of its emergence, most notably, the rise of a professionalized field of metasexual opinion and therapy in the late nineteenth century. Like Foucault, he understood this rise as fundamentally political. Rather than reflecting economic conditions or having created a commodification of sexuality, both psychoanalysis and sexology provided causal narratives that highlighted what it is about the body (its linguistic, emotional, and corporeal aspects) that can be converted via sexual interaction into other forms of social power. More importantly, by focusing ever more increasingly on sexual difference as it is expressed in anatomy (with theories of phalluses and castration, on the one hand, and empirical study of organs and orgasms, on the other), these twin pseudosciences of sex-itself located the truth of sex more or less in the baseball strike zone—somewhere between the shoulders and the knees.

These changes in elite discourses may well have been matched by parallel changes in countercultural strategies that connect with a general view of sex as a purely biological or psychological matter and quite possibly derive from more specific psychoanalytic doctrines that sexual desire can be explained by sexual history. It is not only feminist theories influenced by psychoanalysis but also a wider world of critical-political discourses ("make love, not war") that seem related to the new conception of sexuality. To the extent that therapeutic ideas were adopted into 1970s counterculture, new notions of political action arose that sought to work first on the inculcation of habitus—changes in child rearing and courtship, in cohabitation and alliance, for example—in order to change the social order. It is a question, not of evaluating the effectiveness of these strategies, but of highlighting how the professionalization of intimacy may have encouraged desynchronization of the division of sexual labor from the sexual division of labor in certain ways. The expanding scope of female sexual agency thus enlarges the significance of emotional and bodily properties for both personal and political identity (Illouz 2007) and for the experience of gender (Giddens 1992).

In advanced, highly differentiated societies, the field of metasexual authority might be seen to act as do the economic or cultural fields and help constitute and regulate a fundamental form of capital (Martin and George 2006). That is, what Bourdieu attempted to oppose seems to have triumphed and to have proved the accuracy of his theoretical approach, against his own wishes. Erotic experience has been increasingly defined and managed by a professional matrix of metasexual—and often quasi-scientific—authority. Biologists, psychologists, sexologists, therapists, ethicists, media ratings boards, humanists, feminists, and LGBT activists all compete with religious and political authority to shape the legitimate exercise of sexuality and thereby profoundly shape the experience of sexual judgment, both in terms of expert codified regulations such as law and in terms of popular opinion.[10] The point is not to take an outside perspective on the play of expert opinion involved. The force of Bourdieu's sense of reflexivity and Foucault's deconstruction of sexual authority should direct us to place our own opinion squarely on the map of sexual opinion and paint ourselves into the room as objectively as we can. The first step is recognizing that we are already in an advanced state of the field of metasexual authority when these thoughts arise.

## Notes

1. "Ideologies owe their structure . . . to the functions they fulfill first for the specialists competing for the monopoly of the competence in question and secondarily and incidentally for the non-specialists" (Bourdieu and Wacquant 1992, 106).

2. Interestingly, Bourdieu footnoted in this early publication his difference from Foucault and a desire to stress the differences between his own conception of field and "Foucault's theory of domination as discipline or 'drilling'" (Bourdieu and Wacquant 1992, 167).

3. Writing elsewhere about the relation of professionals to laypersons, Bourdieu outlines, almost to a point, the exact positioning he enacts here: "Over and above everything which sets them against one another, specialists agree at least in laying claim to a monopoly of legitimate competence which defines them as such and in reminding people of the frontier that separates professionals from the profane. The professional tends to 'hate the common layman' who negates his professional status by doing without his services: he is quick to denounce all forms of 'spontaneism' (political, religious, philosophical, artistic) that will dispossess him of the monopoly of the legitimate production of goods and services. Those in possession of legitimate competence are ready to mobilize against everything that might favour popular self-help (magic, 'popular medicine,' self-medication, etc.)" (Bourdieu 1990a, 150–51).

4. It is important to bear in mind that, while Bourdieu uses his theory of misrecognition in a critical way, allowing us to comprehend the "bad faith" in various forms of domination masked as integration, he does not prefer the "good faith" of a shameless and unmitigated domination or a blatant tit-for-tat economism.

5. This traditional cosmology is the same one Bourdieu discovered in the Kabylian concept of *nif*, which signifies "sexual potency inseparable from social potency" and through the attendant definitions of maleness and femaleness imposes "a political mythology which governs all bodily experiences, not least sexual experiences themselves" (Bourdieu 1977, 93). The task proposed here is to explore how it is that the professionalization of intimacy weakens, displaces, or even conserves this cosmological, and thus misrecognized, power schema.

6. This form of administrative dissemination of power began, for Foucault, with Freudian prefigures like Charcot, who in their quest for metasexual authority "sought to detach the sphere of sexuality from the system of alliance, in order to deal with it directly through a medical practice whose technicity and autonomy were guaranteed by the neurological model" (Foucault 1980, 112).

7. In the tradition of philosophically oriented intellectual history, Foucault focused on such elites. With no institutional account for how canonical works accrue their status and no theorization of what happens on the ground level of experts engaged in professional disputation, the archaeology of discourse remains

in the vacuous causality of what Bourdieu associated with the semiological tradition in anthropology. But Foucault's initial forays, as impressionistic and canonically unreflexive as they may have been, have been greatly expanded and nuanced in their relevance to the history of state regulation of sexuality in the US context (Canaday 2009; Carter 2007; Chauncey 1994; Halperin 2002).

8. It is clear from where, at least in the French intellectual field, Bourdieu thought this idea of sex-itself had come from: "Psychoanalysis . . . too easily obscures the fact that one's own body and other people's bodies are always perceived through categories of perception which it would be naïve to treat as sexual" (Bourdieu 1990b, 77).

9. "It follows that the transmission of cultural capital is no doubt the best hidden form of hereditary transmission of capital, and it therefore receives proportionately greater weight in the system of reproduction strategies, as the direct, visible forms of transmission tend to be more strongly censored and controlled" (Bourdieu 1983/1986, 245–46).

10. If we look only at how sexual harassment law codifies certain norms and expectations and imposes them (albeit variably) across different fields, we can see how the state consecrates and elevates some quadrants of the metasexual field and disavows and denies others.

# CHAPTER FIVE

# Circuits and the Social Organization of Sexual Fields

Barry D. Adam, Windsor University
Adam Isaiah Green, University of Toronto

A growing literature in the sociology of sexuality has drawn from Bourdieu's (1977) theory of practice to conceptualize sexual sociality in field theoretic terms (Farrer 2010a; Green 2008a, 2008c; Martin and George 2006; Weinberg and Williams 2009). In this emerging approach, collective sexual life is understood to be organized, in part, by sexual fields that stratify sexual actors in hierarchies of desirability. Conceived as socially structured contexts composed of situated agents, institutionalized practices, and one logic of desirability (or more), sexual fields materialize in physical and virtual *sites* (Green 2008c) where actors congregate for social and sexual connection to others. But, while actors who inhabit a particular site often share social or sexual interests, these interests may not exhaust patterns of connection among them. In fact, in collective sexual life, there exist patterns of connection—or what we refer to here as *circuits*—that represent assemblages of actors who are linked to the extent that they rub elbows in some of the same sexual sites over time, but without the ties of interdependency normally associated with social networks (Adam, Husbands, Murray, and Maxwell 2008a). To be sure, such circuits may spawn intimate dyads, friendship ties, and other network structures (Bearman, Moody, and Stovel 2004), but their analytic significance should not be reduced to these potentialities.

In this chapter, we draw from a survey of men attending Toronto Pride in 2005 along with four years of fieldwork between 2005 and 2009 in To-

ronto's Gay Village to develop the concept of the circuit in relationship
to the sexual fields framework and to consider its significance for the social organization of sexual life. Taken together, these data suggest the
presence of more and less distinct circuits that can be distinguished by
patterns of participation at particular sites (e.g., bars, dance clubs, special events, Web sites, washrooms, bathhouses, and parks) and by atti-
tudinal measures, including attitudes toward condom use during anal
intercourse and beliefs about personal responsibility during sexual encounters (Adam, Husbands, Murray, and Maxwell 2008a), among others.
These data, in turn, suggest that circuits may be critical to a field theoretic approach to sexual life insofar as they map onto and distinguish sexual fields across sexual sites. Importantly, circuits provide the assemblage
of bodies from which interaction-based perceptions of sexual stratification, including the distribution of sexual capital within a given site and
self-attributions of one's own capital relative to others, are extrapolated.

Below, we consider some theoretical issues related to the composition
of a sexual field and establish the conceptual groundwork for an analysis of circuits. Two subsequent sections present quantitative and qualitative data to demonstrate the presence of circuits among Toronto gay, bisexual, and other men who have sex with men and their consequences for
actors' perceptions of the sexual field and social interaction more generally. A discussion section summarizes our findings and offers a theoretical discussion that integrates the concept of the circuit with the sexual
fields framework. Here, we offer suggestions for future research into circuits across sexual fields and consider the analytic promise of the concept for sexuality research more broadly.

## The Sexual Fields Framework

Recently, scholars of sexuality have turned their attention to the phenomenon of sexual stratification, conceiving of collective sexual life as
a composite of sexual fields (Farrer 2010a; Green 2008c; Martin and
George 2006; Weinberg and Williams 2009). Reflecting decades of
scholarship that document the presence of sexual hierarchies as an organizing principle of sexual social life (Armstrong, Hamilton, and Sweeney
2006; Bech 1997; Bersani 1987; Fitzgerald 1986; Levine 1998; Murray
and Adam 2001; Prieur 1998; Tewksbury 2002; Weinberg and Williams

1975b), this latest body of work has sought to theorize the social organization of sexuality in systematic terms. Drawing from a Bourdieusian field theoretic, including the tripartite model of practice—that is, field, capital, and habitus—sexual fields research begins with the axiom that transpersonal valuations of sexual desirability serve as a principle of stratification in erotic worlds as each world is organized by its own particular status order and institutionalized practices.

Fields are relatively autonomous configurations insofar as the logic of action is internally constituted rather than externally compelled. In the context of collective sexual life, fields are dynamic yet structured social spaces where actors vie for intimate partnership and social significance alongside other pursuits such as socializing with friends and seeking entertainment. Irrespective of individual motivations, actors are subject to evaluation by others and, in turn, become part of the field's sexual status structure. In this sense, whether or not they choose to play the game, actors in a sexual field are obliged to take account of the reigning currencies of sexual capital that define a given field and to assess their own sexual capital in relationship to both the field's structure of desire and the distribution of sexual capital among field players (Green 2008c, 2011). That actors themselves may arrive at somewhat different accounts regarding both may be less important than the fact that they nonetheless recognize the sexual status hierarchy and their location within it (see Green, chapter 1 in this volume).

To date, the sexual fields framework provides a broad outline of the characteristics of a sexual field but has not explicitly theorized the structural configurations of field participants, be they in the form of networks or, as we show below, circuits. These configurations are likely to be critical for understanding the social organization of a sexual field for at least two reasons. First, networks and circuits provide two kinds of participant profiles that reveal the social characteristics of field inhabitants from which a global portrait of fields and their relationships to one another can be assembled. Second, both networks and circuits are crucial sources from which actors deduce a conception of the sexual status order and, in turn, negotiate their own field participation.

While others have examined how networks can influence sexual norms and practices (Adam, Husbands, Murray, and Maxwell 2008a; Kelly et al. 1992; Laumann, Gagnon, Michael, and Michaels 1994; Thornton 2008), few have examined the presence and effects of circuit configurations (but see Adam, Husbands, Murray, and Maxwell 2008a). Yet circuits are likely to be consequential for field phenomenology and practice because so much of participation in collective sexual life revolves around the individual-level experience of one's self in relation to other actors with whom one has little personal knowledge or direct association. Even in Web sites on the Internet, actors are hard-pressed not to make observations and intersubjective assessments with reference to one's personal location in social space relative to others (Green 2011). Such actors constitute an assemblage of bodies (real and virtual) against which one theorizes a sexual status order and one's location within it. To the extent that this assemblage is not randomly distributed across sites but, rather, represents a patterned, recurring configuration of players, actors experience a more or less stable range of occupants of a given sexual field. Put differently, circuits may provide the practical basis on which subjective attributions regarding a field's sexual status structure and one's own sexual capital take form. In this regard, we might say that circuits offer a critical meso-level, structural feature of a field from which microlevel processes associated with individual-level, meaning-making procedures and strategies of action are configured.

Below, we turn our attention to two sets of data—the first, survey data drawn from the participants of the Toronto Pride celebration in 2005 and, the second, in-depth interviews and fieldwork in the Gay Village of Toronto between 2005 and 2009. We use the survey data in order to show patterns in sexual sociality that reveal the presence of circuits and how they are organized inside and across a set of sexual fields in Toronto. We use the in-depth interviews and fieldwork to show how individuals can draw on such circuits to arrive at a sense of a field's sexual status order, its structure of desire, and their particular placement within the field's tiers of desirability.

## Toronto Pride Survey

The survey drew on men attending Toronto Pride, one of the largest festivals of LGTB communities in North America, reputed to have an attendance of between 500,000 and one million people a year. Men were asked to indicate the venues, scenes, and Web sites they had frequented during the preceding month, as part of a larger project to ascertain the relationship between scenes and circuits with patterns of HIV risk (Adam, Husbands, Murray, and Maxwell 2008a). The survey succeeded in collecting 947 questionnaires with usable data. Men reporting both heterosexual identity and no sex with men within the past six months ($N = 25$; 2.6 percent) were removed from further consideration. This produced a sample of 922 men who had had sex with a man during the past six months or reported a gay identity.

Study participants filled out a questionnaire that explored two major areas among others: (*a*) bars, dance clubs, special events, bathhouses, gyms, sport groups, Web sites, phone lines, coffeeshops, parks, washrooms, and scenes frequented during the previous month and (*b*) demographic characteristics (education, ethnicity, employment, income, birth decade, serostatus, and postal code). An oblimin factor analysis (table 1) was performed on the venue list to discover commonalities among clientele and provide indicators of circuits.

The factor analysis revealed a set of circuits (listed in order of decreasing popularity):

1. A mainstream core circuit of nine bars, four dance clubs, four recurring special events, and one bathhouse. This circuit makes up a good part of the commercial venues of the Gay Village and is often considered to be *the* gay scene in the city in the press and the popular imagination. Bivariate analysis of this circuit with demographic variables shows that it is significantly more popular with men under the age of thirty-five. Around this circuit are a number of smaller circuits and, in terms of the factor analysis, a tail consisting of single venues of diminishing popularity.

2. The second circuit consists of a collection of quick sex sites: four washrooms, a park, and a phone line.

3. The third circuit includes four bars typically identified with the leather and denim scene. Two of the bars and the bathhouse are shared with the first circuit.

4. The fourth circuit is characterized by a bar, a dance club, and two special event recurrent parties. All these venues are known for their dance party atmosphere.

5. The fifth circuit is a popular Web site.

6. The sixth circuit includes this same Web site paired to another Web site popular for meeting up.

7. The seventh circuit consists of three parks and one special event.

8. The eighth circuit shares the one centrally located park in circuit 7 with a park located on the other side of the city from the parks in circuit 7.

**Oblimin Factor Analysis of Venues Attended in Past Month**

|  | Circuit | | | | | | | | | |
| Venues | 1 | 2 | 3 | 4 | 5 | 6 | 7 | 8 | 9 | 10 |
|---|---|---|---|---|---|---|---|---|---|---|
| Dance club 1 | .484 | -.240 | -.084 | -.144 | .145 | .030 | .086 | -.050 | .125 | -.204 |
| Bar 1 | .483 | -.289 | .272 | -.026 | .068 | -.006 | .023 | .047 | .046 | -.056 |
| Dance club 2 | .449 | -.310 | -.146 | -.117 | .178 | -.219 | .264 | -.111 | .172 | .005 |
| Bar 2 | .448 | -.353 | .098 | .041 | .001 | -.096 | -.067 | .102 | -.038 | .009 |
| Bar 3 | .380 | -.308 | .142 | -.096 | .003 | .029 | -.092 | .265 | -.133 | -.072 |
| Event 1 | .361 | -.036 | -.049 | -.152 | -.070 | .011 | -.046 | .138 | -.106 | -.128 |
| Bar 4 | .359 | -.326 | -.174 | -.028 | .178 | .104 | -.009 | .045 | -.052 | -.044 |
| Dance club 3 | .356 | .231 | -.297 | -.306 | -.253 | .109 | -.148 | -.125 | .063 | .080 |
| Event 2 | .330 | -.049 | -.212 | -.009 | -.001 | -.133 | .240 | -.175 | .235 | .217 |
| Bar 5 | .322 | -.229 | .177 | -.049 | -.057 | -.086 | .177 | -.185 | -.109 | .011 |
| Bar 6 | .307 | -.067 | .220 | -.019 | -.237 | -.041 | -.138 | -.300 | -.019 | -.043 |
| Washroom 1 | .256 | .406 | -.221 | .207 | .033 | -.163 | -.011 | -.128 | -.058 | -.152 |
| Event 3 | .329 | -.372 | -.159 | .104 | .130 | .096 | -.030 | -.018 | -.020 | -.136 |
| Washroom 2 | .210 | .354 | -.224 | -.071 | .016 | -.055 | -.154 | .009 | .258 | -.044 |
| Bath 1 | .210 | .307 | .140 | .131 | -.005 | .201 | -.054 | .128 | .306 | -.142 |
| Dance club 4 | .198 | .184 | .435 | -.323 | -.246 | .107 | -.192 | -.037 | .015 | .100 |
| Bar 7 | .237 | .099 | .413 | .133 | -.236 | .115 | -.156 | .075 | -.062 | -.062 |
| Event 4 | .326 | .293 | -.382 | -.130 | -.114 | -.084 | -.094 | .092 | -.058 | .083 |
| Dance club 5 | .319 | .167 | .365 | -.158 | -.106 | .117 | -.195 | .012 | .087 | -.113 |
| Bar 8 | .319 | .020 | .350 | -.049 | -.209 | .008 | -.112 | .196 | -.119 | -.004 |
| Bar 9 | .320 | -.024 | .334 | .033 | -.294 | -.066 | -.199 | .121 | -.210 | .056 |
| Dance club 6 | .256 | -.046 | -.323 | -.285 | -.061 | .024 | -.248 | -.067 | -.135 | .129 |
| Bath 2 | .305 | .076 | .314 | .030 | -.017 | .145 | .060 | -.086 | .052 | .236 |
| Bar 10 | .196 | -.121 | -.265 | .645 | -.156 | .097 | -.029 | -.013 | -.104 | .113 |
| Event 5 | .141 | -.173 | -.229 | .616 | -.091 | .106 | -.093 | -.011 | .013 | .131 |
| Dance club 7 | .268 | -.325 | -.166 | .354 | .048 | .066 | -.123 | .100 | -.026 | -.072 |

| Venues | Circuit | | | | | | | | | |
|---|---|---|---|---|---|---|---|---|---|---|
| | 1 | 2 | 3 | 4 | 5 | 6 | 7 | 8 | 9 | 10 |
| Bar 11 | .145 | .035 | .200 | -.008 | -.369 | -.003 | .035 | -.098 | -.065 | -.001 |
| Web site 1 | .240 | .172 | .121 | -.039 | .345 | .426 | -.001 | -.111 | -.059 | .049 |
| Washroom 3 | .234 | .312 | -.062 | .207 | .234 | -.390 | .054 | -.252 | -.095 | -.055 |
| Washroom 4 | .177 | .366 | .044 | .104 | .160 | -.387 | -.081 | .048 | -.025 | .055 |
| Washroom 5 | .107 | .296 | -.067 | .018 | .167 | .306 | -.134 | .188 | .122 | .172 |
| Web site 2 | .237 | .117 | .038 | -.078 | .296 | .172 | .050 | -.150 | .059 | .066 |
| Park 1 | .117 | .176 | -.186 | .026 | -.385 | .107 | .569 | .094 | -.139 | .043 |
| Park 2 | .014 | .154 | -.119 | .096 | -.210 | -.159 | .505 | .157 | -.171 | -.052 |
| Event 6 | .231 | -.264 | -.020 | -.073 | .169 | .056 | .362 | -.113 | .199 | -.106 |
| Park 3 | .179 | .320 | .002 | .027 | .016 | .027 | .356 | .303 | -.031 | -.073 |
| Bath 3 | .173 | .015 | .244 | .181 | -.060 | .031 | .103 | -.378 | .080 | .143 |
| Bath 4 | .143 | .146 | .198 | .056 | -.094 | -.021 | -.113 | .367 | .004 | -.017 |
| Bath 5 | .117 | .195 | .225 | .114 | -.165 | .108 | -.100 | .169 | .440 | -.087 |
| Bath 6 | .092 | .119 | .038 | .091 | -.045 | .116 | -.118 | -.063 | .399 | -.185 |
| Web site 3 | .246 | .320 | -.015 | .015 | .132 | .011 | -.050 | -.146 | -.398 | -.101 |
| Dance club 6 | .258 | -.010 | -.062 | -.253 | -.224 | .266 | .075 | -.122 | -.039 | .444 |
| Web site 4 | .007 | -.060 | -.014 | .144 | .180 | -.056 | -.006 | .057 | .046 | .433 |
| Bar 12 | .148 | -.040 | .128 | -.037 | -.120 | .295 | .000 | .203 | -.014 | .388 |
| Web site 5 | -.042 | .031 | .008 | .027 | .228 | .061 | .011 | -.036 | .044 | .380 |
| Park 4 | .073 | .170 | -.040 | .056 | .165 | .000 | .015 | .304 | .141 | .238 |
| Phone line 1 | .265 | .335 | .072 | .017 | .176 | .057 | .081 | -.046 | -.308 | -.009 |
| Event 7 | .153 | -.286 | -.116 | .326 | .049 | -.192 | -.083 | .087 | -.117 | -.021 |
| Bar 13 | .258 | -.094 | .303 | -.115 | -.075 | | .062 | .253 | .037 | .056 |

*Note:* Lighter shading indicates factors of greater than 3, i.e. stronger relationship to the circuit. Darker shading indicates factors of less than −3, i.e. least degree of relationship to the circuit.

9. The ninth is made up of three bathhouses.

10. The tenth brings together two Web sites, a dance club, and a bar.

The data from the Toronto Pride survey illustrate a pattern of circulation of common sets of gay men for which there is no single homogenous sexual field but, rather, circuits that express affinity groups of men who turn up with some regularity in a definable collection of venues. Analysis of the demographic variables shows that while a few venues are more popular with men of particular ethnocultural backgrounds—most notably special event parties organized specifically for East Asian or South Asian men—the circuits as a whole do not show statistically significant differentiation by ethnicity, at least in Toronto. Age is the one marker that defines the circuit structure, especially for circuit 1.

The circuits appear to be communities of taste with differentiated sexual status structures and markers of sexual capital. Their different spatial attributes—concentrated in Gay Village bars, parks often governed by the night, or the virtual space of men connecting via computer—suggest that their interactional dynamics may result in multiple and qualitatively diverse sexual fields. The ability of men to traverse these various circuits and play according to the game plans indigenous to various sexual fields points toward an array of actors moving through and across sexual fields. While some, no doubt, favor a single niche for sexual or romantic exploration, others may drop in, move through, or try out several circuits to discover their own affinities and achieve the connections with men they seek.

In the interest of fleshing out how circuits bear on the phenomenology of field participation, the following section reports on interview data focusing primarily on circuit 1, a circuit that exerts a strong centrifugal pull on men entering the gay world and the one that is the most publicly visible.

## The Subjective Consequences of Circuits

*The study*

The qualitative data reported here are based on a study of sexual life that was conducted by Adam Isaiah Green between 2005 and 2007 in Toronto and included seventy self-identified gay and bisexual men who responded to recruitment posters throughout the Gay Village area and online. The sample was selected to build in ethnocultural, class, and age variation, including men who self-identified as Aboriginal, Asian, Caucasian, black, poor, and over forty years of age, and a final subsample of men selected on the basis of reporting a history of high-risk sexual activities. Each subsample averaged approximately ten men. In-depth, semistructured interviews were conducted and audiotaped that sought to understand how (and whether) study participants cognized a sexual status order and with what effects on socialization and emotional and physical well-being. The names of study participants and the social sites they discuss have been changed in order to protect the privacy of these men and those who participate in gay life in the Village.

## The Interactional Basis of a Sexual Status Order

> You can see it. When you're there (at the bar), drinking, you notice guys who are checking whomever out. Yeah, it's pretty obvious. It's in the looks. A lot of the times it is blatant. It's like, straight up checking out the dude as he is walking by. Or staring at him and sizing him up. That kind of thing. — Glen, thirty-two years old, black

Sexual social life brings actors together in a bounded spatial or virtual domain for a wide range of reasons, including the search for a sex partner or a long-term relationship, socializing with old friends and, perhaps, meeting new ones, or just being among people. These varying motivations aside, the experience of a sexual field is, for many, the experience of entering a status order around which the most basic elements of interaction are organized. When sexual fields are tied to physical spaces like a bar or a nightclub, these elements may include eye contact such as glances, stares, or snubs and facial gestures that communicate interest, lust, intimidation, indifference, or ridicule.

> Just the way people glance. It's a two-second glance to sum people up. And that's all I take—a glance—and if you're really good looking, I'll pay more attention. If not, I'm gone. . . . It's like that one- or two-second assessment that we give each other on our looks. It's so age related as well, age dominated, age oriented. You're either young or beautiful or old and useless. — Ebert, forty years old, Native Canadian

Sexual status is also communicated via the spatial organization of bodies, including how they are grouped together (or not), the size of a given group configuration and the amount of space it takes up within a site, the location of individuals and groups within the site itself (e.g., by the doorway or at the core of the space), and the affect of individuals and groups, including the volume of the conversations between people, the energy of laughter and joke telling, or, by contrast, the discomfort of individuals standing by themselves, observing in isolation the busy action around them.

> Whenever you go to a gay bar, you can see all the unattractive people (I'm putting up quotes so the tape knows), like standing alone and no one's talking to them, and the attractive people always have like people coming after them. — Greg, twenty-one years old, white

As well, status distinctions are communicated via ritualized interactions, including who is bought drinks by whom (and who is not bought drinks at all), who waits on line for entrance to the club and who is granted immediate access, who is consistently engaged in conversation at the center of nodes of interaction, and who, by contrast, sits perpetually on the sidelines, staring at the video monitor or the cell phone or, when all else fails, into the head of his beer.

> Attractive men get into bars faster than the not so desirable men. They get drinks bought for them more than undesirable men. They get people wanting to talk to them all the time. You become a celebrity of sorts. — Glen, thirty-two years old, black

When sexual fields are tied to virtual worlds, a sexual status order is still discernible and, in some respects, even more readily. Many chat and dating sites attract users with domain names and representations that feature a given erotic theme or preferred demographic. For instance, consider Cougarlife.com, a Web site geared toward matching younger men and older women for sex and dating, or Bigmusclebear.com, a gay male Web site geared toward muscular and hairy men who are attracted to the same. These sites rely on domain names and representations that communicate a profile of desirability.

Moreover, personal profiles on chat and dating Web sites typically identify those characteristics that users find desirable in explicit terms—

characteristics that may draw on broad social categories such as age, race, and ethnicity or preferred body types.

> There's the race thing, the age thing, the weight thing. I see a lot of people sort of saying like "height/weight proportional" when you're looking for people on the net. So, you know, it's right away this thing that you know, you basically have to have a particular body size in order to even talk to somebody. — Geller, forty-nine years old, white

But even without these explicit markers of desirability, online users are able to surmise a sexual status order by sending and receiving "winks," "kisses," "hearts," or "pokes." Many such sites also enable users to see how many cyber compliments others have amassed. Moreover, Web sites of this kind may provide statistics regarding how many times a given profile has been viewed, how many times a given picture in a profile has been clicked on, and how many times a given picture or profile has been chosen as a favorite by other users. As well, Web sites that feature group chat rooms provide members with direct access to the evaluations of others via the published tweets in the dialogue box wherein a given profile or picture can be praised or damned. In this context, explicit evaluations of attractiveness or the lack thereof are quite common and may even escalate into pages of dialogue around the appearance of a given online member or members. To the extent that such sites generate sexual status orders through pictures and statistics, participants may become reflexive around the images they use to present themselves and, too, how to best represent themselves in descriptive statistics such as height, weight, and age.

As well, chat and dating sites generally feature messaging functions whereby one member can contact another either in a private dialogue box or via an internal email system. When participants rarely receive a message on the site's email system, and when favorable responses to their own e-solicitations are far and few between, they may develop a sense of a disadvantaged position in the field's status order. Conversely, participants with a steady influx of favorable messages and consistently favorable responses to their solicitations are likely to develop a very different, more positive, efficacious sense of their field position.

In either real-time or virtual contexts, while one can surely choose to tune out the interaction order and, thereby, refuse the terms of the game, most actors are unlikely to do so, not the least because, as Glen,

Greg, and Ebert observe above, the status order impinges on them at the most fundamental levels of interaction, if even only by locating them at the margins of the field. Put in different terms, one can choose to ignore the status hierarchy of a sexual field, but one *cannot* choose to opt out of its consequences, including the systems of evaluation and judgment to which one is subjected (Bersani 1987; Fitzgerald 1986; Levine 1998; Weinberg and Williams 1975b) and the interactional patterns that result (Green 2011). As a consequence, as Cecil remarks below, the interaction order in a sexual field encourages a reflexive stance with regard not only to how others view the self but also to how one views others.

> There's a lot of panopticism in homosexual culture. You're always be-
> ing looked at. You always feel like people are judging you. . . . And you
> are also judging them at the same time. . . . So you are in the bathhouse,
> you're looking at someone, you're judging how attractive they are. And so
> they are judging how attractive they are. So you are even judging how much
> value their attraction to you is worth because of how attracted to you they
> are. . . . [And] you always have to gauge how attractive you are in someone
> else's eyes. — Cecil, twenty-three years old, black

This reflexive stance, however, involves not only a calculation of one's worth in the eyes of others but also a self-assessment wherein one calcu- lates one's sexual capital by comparing the attractiveness of the self to the attractiveness of others—that is, one forms a theory of one's own sex- ual capital relative to the distribution of sexual capital in the field more generally.

> I guess you start comparing. You start looking around and looking at dif-
> ferent bodies and starting to wonder, whether or not, you know, do you look
> good enough? Have you been working out enough? Do you have enough—
> are you revved enough to kind of, you know . . . — Bill, thirty-seven years
> old, white

These evaluation schemes are not reformulated from scratch with each interaction. Quite the contrary, while actors on any given occa- sion are sure to tweak their self-assessments of sexual capital, these as- sessments have the tendency to cohere over time after successive expe- riences in the field. That is, repeated exposure to a given sexual status order has the effect of producing an enduring sense of one's field posi-

tion, which, in turn, has implications for how a given actor selects, negotiates, or, in some instances, avoids a given site or circuit.

> I don't tend to go to the saunas, because I don't have very much sex in the
> saunas, and I just find it hurts my ego. . . . I mean, I think I'm a relatively at-
> tractive-looking guy, and I find sometimes you're in the sauna, you're walk-
> ing up and down the aisle, just sort of looking in the room to see who's there,
> and I just find it, like, really old, fat ugly men will slam doors in my face,
> when I haven't even approached them. . . . And I just think that my ego is too
> fragile for something like that, so I just don't go. The few times I've been to
> some, I usually end up in my own room doing my own drugs and leave and go
> home. — Darren, forty-one years old, black

> You know, since I have a more attractive body than my face, I just know my
> assets, I just know that in a towel, I can be more successful, rather than in a
> bar, because in a bar, unless it's summer and you're wearing something tight,
> I know, I never get lucky in bars. — Ben, thirty-nine years old, Asian

In total, the accumulation of patterned interactions in the context of a
sexual site or set of sites encourages actors to become weekend social scientists who extrapolate a more or less stable sexual hierarchy from their
experience in the field, including an assessment of their position in the
field's tiers of desirability. These patterned interactions, too, underpin the
formulation of types of players and types of sexual fields. The typological
character of both, in turn, shapes how actors relate to and move through
collective sexual life. Below, we explore these ideas more fully.

## The Typological Character of Players and Fields

Having frequented a given site over time, actors are inclined to formulate a general sense of its social composition (or what we might call *social
circuitry*), including the demographic characteristics of its patrons, and,
in a somewhat related vein, a social typology of sexual types that typically inhabit the space. In the context of the specialized sexual fields that
arise within large urban centers, the process of discerning sexual types
is a fairly straightforward process. As Don notes below, sexual types are
a bit like a geographic identification whereby individuals are associated
with a particular region of sexual life.

Your twinks, your leathers, your bears, your athletes/athletics. That is the four I think. . . . It is the society, it is back to as the community gets larger, then you subset the community because I think people would say that they would have an easier time identifying with a subset of a community versus the entire community. . . . When you think of a gay individual, it is harder to think of a stereotypical gay individual nowadays that encompasses the breadth of choice or preference. . . . If you are from the west, you identify often as an Albertan before you identify as a Canadian. Or, you know, an Ontarian or a Torontonian. So you identify from where the region of the country. I would say this is exactly the same [in the sexual field]: the region of the sexuality, if you will, that I identify with. — Don, twenty-nine years old, white

Variations in the gendered affect of men, including "effeminate" and "straight acting," may serve a similar function, sorting players in a form of horizontal (and vertical) segregation that separates the acceptable from the unacceptable and distinguishes the sites in which these players socialize.

[At Pals] . . . you get a crowd of effeminate twinks. . . . And one thing I really like [is the] people, the major issue with the club scene right now is just, it's not easy being an effeminate gay male. . . . Some of these straight-acting queers don't want to associate with gay-acting queers or effeminate queers. . . . Like what I mean [by] straight acting, you know, they'll wear Diesel, they'll wear Abercrombie. They won't wear tight jeans, they won't wear tight, flared jeans. . . . It really divides the group. . . . There is a sect of the gay community that doesn't like effeminate-acting gay men. . . . Examples, you go online, you surf cruising sites . . . and you see the typical tag line, "No fats, no femmes, I want straight-acting guys only," "I'm not into the scene, I just want straight-acting guys." — Cody, twenty-one years old, white

Race, age, and class, too, sort social types in a pattern of segregation, distinguishing players within a given site and across them:

In the past, you'd have these clubs where everyone would be there, there'd be leathers, your bears, your twinks, you know? You had the twinks over by the pinball machines listening to Abba, hanging out with the trannies, you had leather men on the floor. . . . The Country House was like that. You had so many different types of people, fifty-year-olds and twenty-year-olds, and everyone partied together! . . . But as bars progressed and as more niche markets and more subcultures kind of took their own path, you don't see a twenty-year-old twink that's talking to a leatherman; you don't see a twink talking to a bear, you don't see some white twinks talking to an Asian person. . . . That's how this gay community has taken shape. And I think that's why we don't see many black people at Wings or Pals, y' know? — Cody, twenty-one years old, white

The formation of more or less distinct social circuits can become the basis on which one selects where and with whom to socialize:

Do you want rich here, do you want Player's? Do you want the upper class, or do you want this? . . . So you have a crowd. You don't fit into Player's, Bermuda's, and then you can go down the list. Or you can go down the other side. You got Celebrations, you got Boots, you have Train, then you have Buttons. where the two can intermingle. You know, the bars were all set up this way. It's the same even in the baths. Club Canada is sleazier and cheaper priced; the Basement attracts a lot of poor people. — Dennis, thirty-seven years old, Native Canadian

In reality, sexual types—be they determined by erotic preference, style, race, class, gender, age, or affect—are not mutually exclusive, and individuals can change their identification with a sexual type over time. Nevertheless, these sexual types are organized into distinct social groups of men insofar as their demographic characteristics, body types, self-presentations, and erotic preferences can be distinguished, as can the real-time and virtual sites in which they socialize (Levine 1998; Hennen 2008; Hennen, chapter 3 in this volume). In this sense, the typological character of player profiles across sexual fields reflects a form of horizontal segregation whereby sexual sites become associated with particular sexual scenes or "microcultures" (Adam 2005; Adam, Husbands, Murray, and Maxwell 2008a, 2008b).

The horizontal sorting of men by type across sexual sites does not, of course, preclude a form of vertical stratification within a given site or set of sites. Quite the contrary, to a greater and lesser degree, depending on the site, transpersonal valuations of attractiveness generate sexual status orders that distinguish those with sexual capital from those who lack it. To the extent that sites are associated with particular currencies of sexual capital, actors are inclined to formulate a schema regarding a field's structure of desire that includes bodily, affective, and presentational criteria against which the self can be ranked. In turn, any given site obtains the subjective character of a field through a distinct internal logic of sexual status and a set of institutionalized practices around sociality and self-presentation.

In the case below, for instance, Bart describes a highly disadvantaged position within a racialized sexual status orders attached to online dating sites and a particular bathhouse he frequented in the past.

> When you read those profiles online saying they're not attracted to Asian. . . . It kind of hurts. . . . Why are others so narrow-minded? They say, "Only White guys." . . . And especially even when you go somewhere like the Basement, for example, and you see like people making circles around you, you know, passing by, it doesn't feel good at all, you know, like, God, I'm not even interested in you first of all; second, even if I was, you know, there is always a way to say no; you don't have to, you know, do those things to say no. — Bart, thirty-nine years old, Asian

If Bart associates the Basement as a site with an inhospitable sexual field, Cecil feels similarly about bathhouses more generally, adding age into the mix of determinants of sexual capital:

> INTERVIEWER: What can you tell me about a pecking order at the bathhouse, if there is one?
>
> CECIL: It is definitely more toward the younger, attractive Caucasians. . . . But they can tell that they are at the top of the pecking order. They can tell and perform in a very specific way.
>
> INTERVIEWER: How do they do that?
>
> CECIL: They walk faster, refuse eye contact, they are in and out of sections a lot faster. And then it is different, sometimes they are willing to be performed on. . . . No, that would be the whole thing, they would just take if it someone was willing to perform fellatio. Otherwise, they are very specific, and they end up going to bed with whomever looks exactly like them. And if they can't find that twin, they just digress down the ladder to other people. — Cecil, twenty-three years old, black

In the present study, sites were associated with particular sexual status orders with great consistency. For instance, when asked to name the site wherein participants felt the least socially comfortable, the majority of respondents identified the venue Player's as the most hierarchically organized, looksist, "stand-and-model" site in the Village. Data from the Toronto Pride survey demonstrates that Player's is unusually heterogeneous insofar as it attracts multiple circuits of local men, catering at once to a core circuit of younger men along with "tourists" who circulate through the venue and then migrate outward to other sites within which they feel more comfortable.

For instance, Brian notes how oppressed he feels by the actors at Player's.

> If I was to say somewhere that makes you feel less attractive . . . it would have been Player's, again. They made me feel that way, years ago it was very intense like that, they would try to make you feel that way. And if you were weak minded, they would break you down. — Brian, thirty-six years old, black

Like Brian, Danny, too, feels uncomfortable at Player's, which he now avoids altogether.

> DANNY: Player's. . . . They're stuck up, and they don't interact. . . . They're, how shall I put it, unfriendly, and they clump together.
> INTERVIEWER: Do you feel like you're ignored at Player's?
> DANNY: Yeah . . . they just look at you—"Why are you here?" . . .
> INTERVIEWER: Is it a look, or do they say something?
> DANNY: Look, felt.
> INTERVIEWER: How does that look look?
> DANNY: Disgusting. — Danny, thirty-nine years old, Native Canadian

Andil expands on Brian's sentiments:

> ANDIL: The body language, the way they look at you. You're not welcome there. . . . I don't know, I just, I don't feel comfortable, I don't feel welcome. I don't feel like, feel good about that. . . . People don't talk there, even if I say hi, they just sometimes ignore me. It's like attitude, really.
> INTERVIEWER: How do you know that . . . is it a feeling? is it interactions you're having with men?
> ANDIL: It's intuition, you know. Every people have intuition. My intuition says it's not right place for me; I don't feel good, I don't feel good. It doesn't matter, you know, you can feel it inside, your guts tell you, OK? When you, when you not feel welcome, why you wanted to go? It's a good say-

ing in Sanskrit, say: "Don't even step the door of people who don't respect you." You're putting your self-esteem down, you know? I don't want
to put my self-esteem down for a bunch of idiots. I know I'm attractive
and good looking, I know. I've been with so many good-looking guys, they
find something in me. So why I should put myself down for this bunch of
losers? . . . They just want to put you down. — Andil, thirty-one years old,
South Asian

And, for Andrew, it is his class background that marginalizes him in the
sexual status order of Player's.

I would feel, perhaps, I'm a little less attractive to guys in Player's because I
don't have any money, and they can probably see that just by the way I dress.
I don't have brand new shoes; I've been wearing these shoes for a few years.
These pants are wearing out. They'd probably notice that right away, I would
think, and say—"Oh, he's not one of our crowd," you know? So I'm on a
lower rung a little bit to that crowd, whereas in Boots, I can be very attractive. — Andrew, forty-five years old, white

Indeed, my own participant observation confirmed these sentiments
insofar as there existed a distinct pecking order at Player's with a steady
weekend presence of top-tier, middle-class, athletic, muscular, affec-
tively masculine white men between twenty-five and forty years of age
who congregated in the back bar area with other similar-looking men.
Together, these men constituted what we might call a *core circuit* within
this venue. These men physically approximated pictures of men displayed on the lit placard outside Player's—muscular, white, masculine in
appearance, between twenty and thirty years of age, with rows of perfectly straight white teeth. Videos in the bar played soft and hard pornography with men of a similar appearance, and the bartenders, to the
last one, fit the profile.

Interestingly, the Toronto Pride data along with my own field observations suggest that Player's attracts one of the most diverse crowds compared to other venues in the Village, with a sizable customer base that
included women and visible minority men. Nevertheless, the contingent
of men with a great deal of sexual capital in the field appeared on a semi-
regular basis, forming a circuit of high-status participants against which
others would evaluate their own status. These kinds of *intersubjective assessments* require the actor to view himself or herself as an object in the

"looking glass" (Cooley 1902; Green 2011). In essence, when actors like Cecil and Bill work to discern their own sexual capital, be it through theorizing the attractiveness of the self in the eyes of others or through comparison processes to the sexual capital of others in the field, they do so in the context of a set of recurring bodies that they observe within a given field over a period of time—a set of circuits from which attributions of attractiveness, both self and other, are made. Thus, circuits provide the physical and interactional data on which a theory of the sexual status order and a theory of one's location within it are formulated.

## Discussion

This chapter advances the term *circuit* as a useful concept for understanding the social organization of collective sexual life and provides some illustrative examples of the perceptions of participants drawn primarily from circuit 1 of the Toronto gay scene. While other fields and circuits chare the characteristics of structured contexts composed of situated agents, institutionalized practices, and a logic of desirability, they can nevertheless show their own distinctive logics of desirability that distinguish them from the core circuit. Scenes like circuit 2, centered on quick sex environments like washrooms, have attracted some sociological attention (Desroches 1990; Hollister 2004), most notably Laud Humphreys's (1970/1975) classic *Tearoom Trade*. Circuit 3, located in the leather and bear scenes, values the masculinity of older men and larger body types compared to circuit 1. In circuits 7 and 8, located in parks, men encounter each other seriatim, typically under cover of darkness, and often disconnected from the downtown scene. Web sites over time develop reputations for attracting specific types of men and therefore draw men who increasingly fit that type or are attracted to it. They may differ in terms of the critical mass of participants who are younger or older, more romance or hookup oriented, more white or multicultural, more bisexual/heterosexually married or single, more suburban/ neighborhood or more downtown, and so on. All these circuits provide some variability in the standards of attractiveness and ease of making connection.

Though not yet networks, the circulation of a relatively common, if moving, "crowd" or "tribe" creates the territory for mutual recognition, dyadic connection, friendship, relationship, and networks that can develop from, and perhaps beyond, its origins in a circuit. These incipient linkages, connections, and networks can, over time, become the crucibles for microcultures, characterized by shared views on styles of masculinity, desirability, coolness, taste, and even norms of un/safe sexual practice. Actors can move through different circuits while looking for sex, buddies, and lovers, the circuits providing several possibilities for locating a social niche or a sense of being at home. At the same time, circuits no doubt affect sexual subjectivity, in some cases creating a star structure that elevates particular exemplars of beauty and desirability, generating particular currencies of sexual capital, and shaping the standards of attractiveness for circuit participants. They may as well generate a sense of abjection in those who are unable to embody the desirability of star players, at times amplifying the sense of rejection and abandonment that many gay men experience growing up in a heterosexist society, but this time the marginalization seemingly comes at the hands of fellow gay men. The circuits and sexual fields, which are enablers of sexual and emotional connection, are also implicated in the "body fascism" (Pronger 2002), eating disorders, social isolation, and depression (Green 2008a; Hospers, Molenaar, and Kok 1994; Martin and Knox 1997) experienced by some gay and bisexual men. In this way, circuits have an important role to play in organizing the subjective (but not random) perceptions of actors within collective sexual life, perceptions that can run the gamut from the availability of sexual partners and candidates for dating, to norms around self-presentation and sexual practice, to a reference group on which one cognizes a sexual status order and one's attendant location in social space.

# CHAPTER SIX

# Sexless in Shanghai

*Gendered Mobility Strategies*
*in a Transnational Sexual Field*

James Farrer, Sophia University
Sonja Dale, Sophia University

## Sexless in Shanghai: The Problem
## of Downward Sexual Mobility

Shanghai is sexy—but not for everyone. Along with a two-decade boom in overseas investment, trade, and tourism, Shanghai has attracted a population of over 200,000 international business migrants, language students, young interns, and other foreign sojourners (Farrer 2010b; Lu 2008). Concomitantly, its reputation as both a cosmopolitan and a sexually liberated city has been reborn (Farrer 2002; Gamble 2003). However, this reputation is gender specific. Shanghai is described as a "foreign adventurer's paradise," a place where Western men of any age can have casual affairs with young Chinese women (Farrer 2010a) or find an attractive and talented wife or even a wife–cum–business partner (Farrer 2008). As one British professional said of the Shanghai expat sexual scene:

> I think that a lot of guys who come here were not alpha males in their own country, but they become alpha males here. I see that the men are happier and they are more confident. If you measured it, I bet you would find that they probably have a higher level of testosterone. They are more outgoing.

They are always networking with other people. They are out in the nightlife at an age when they wouldn't be elsewhere. I can go out to a nightclub
here and feel welcome where back in the UK I would be seen as an old man.
I wouldn't even be let in the door, and maybe in some places might even be
beaten up. — Nick, forty

In other words, for Western men, China's global cities present an advantaged field for both short- and long-term interracial heterosexual relationships. At the same time, China is often described as sexual purgatory for Western women, as the following quotes from interviews
illustrate:

I think a lot of the guys who come here are like kids in a candy store, and I
think for a lot of women who come here it's a wasteland. — Mike, Chinese
American

Before I came to China I met some old male friends who were in Beijing
for four years. They told me, "China is heaven for western men, but hell for
western women." — White American woman, thirty-two (quoted in Zhang
2009, 84)

The perceptions and experiences of the sexual field by these transnational migrants are highly gendered and racialized. Many Western
women sojourning in China report feeling either pushed aside or sexually ignored (Willis and Yeoh 2002; see also Lan 2011 [for similar evidence on Taiwan]). In some senses, the downward sexual mobility of
Western women moving to Shanghai represents a paradox. Many of the
standard accounts of globalized beauty images and racial sexualization
do not readily apply. Sexy images of foreign white women grace bill-
boards and magazine covers in reform-era China (Erwin 1999; Schein
1997). Moreover, many white women who relocate to Shanghai experience *upward* economic and social mobility as their incomes increase
vis-à-vis their previous earnings (or the previous earnings of their working husbands), and they are able to enjoy luxuries such as nannies, driv-
ers, and prestigious addresses that would not be available at home. Thus,
many white women experience what could be described as *contradictory
racial mobility* in Shanghai, a rise in relative economic and social status and a decline in relative sexual status. Put more generally, mobility
across sexual fields requires its own independent analysis.

Applying the sexual fields framework to this ethnographic case study (Green 2008a, 2008b; Martin and George 2006), we explore the problem of sexual marginalization among white Western women in Shanghai and the decline in value of their sexual capital. Pushed to the margins of a sexual field and desexualized, these women experience a change in sexual status relative to their previous positions in what is best described as *downward sexual mobility*. Sexual status is shown to be context specific, that is, specific to certain sexual fields rather than constituted by a portfolio of portable personal attributes implied in some analysis of sexual (or erotic) capital (e.g., Hakim 2010; Michael 2004). Hence, men or women with high sexual capital in one field can easily find themselves marginalized or desexualized in a new one.

We suggest that the phenomenon of sexual mobility in the case of white Western women in Shanghai is fruitfully conceived as a process of socialization into a marginal position within the field. Accordingly, women who experience this downward sexual mobility develop patterned gendered and racialized strategies for coping with, overcoming, or escaping this unfavorable situation, a process we detail below. The present chapter contributes to the development of the sexual fields framework by providing a theoretical and empirical account of *sexual mobility* within and across fields, with special attention given to the increasingly common ethnosexual contact zones that emerge in the globalization of local communities. As well, it considers the ways in which sexual desire and desirability can be considered as sociological outcomes structured in the context of the sexual fields in which actors participate.

## Theoretical Problematics: Sexual Mobility and Ethnosexual Contact Zones

This case study engages with several general discussions about the social organization of sexual fields in the context of economic and social globalization.

1. *Globalization of sexual fields and the emergence of an interracial sexual field.* We can define a *sexual field* as a field of possible sexual relationships structured by social and political institutions as well as cultural and social boundaries to sexual contact. *Sexual capital* refers to the resources, competencies, and endowments of a person that provide status as a sexual agent within a field (Gonzales and Rolison 2005; Mar-

tin and George 2006; Michael 2004). Two rather different conceptions of sexual capital have been developed, a sociological definition based on the Pierre Bourdieu's idea of fields (Farrer 2010a; Gonzales and Rolison 2005; Green 2008a, 2011; Koshy 2004; Martin and George 2006) and an economistic definition based ultimately on the human capital theory of Gary Becker (Michael 2004), or a more naturalistic notion of erotic capital as a set of fungible personal assets (Hakim 2011). Both perspectives suggest that sexual status is not reducible to other forms of status and that a theory of sexual stratification must explain the distribution of sexual statuses as well as individual incentives to invest in sexual status. The economistic or rational choice approach, suggests how individuals rationally choose to invest in sexual capital (e.g., through paying more attention to their appearance or acquiring new sexual skills), particularly when expectations increase for higher returns on sexual capital (e.g., with the liberalization of the sexual regime or when moving to a new sexual environment) (Michael 2004). The field theory of Bourdieu has the advantage that it represents how notions of desirability and appropriate forms of desire are constructed within the sexual field as opposed to being naturally given outside of it (Green 2008a; Martin and George 2006). In this chapter, we emphasize that actors make strategic choices about utilizing and accumulating sexual capital or seeking out sexual fields with relatively higher returns on types of sexual capital while at the same time their erotic choices and preferences are shaped dynamically by experiences and socialization in a sexual field.

It becomes reasonable to speak of a separate field of sexual capital only when sex is an arena of life at least partly autonomous from other social fields (Green 2008a; Martin and George 2006; and the various chapters in this volume). In the West in the twentieth century, sexuality became a separate arena in which individuals could pursue relationships increasingly removed from economic and status concerns associated with marriage (Giddens 1992). The globalization of sexualities (Altman 2001) can be interpreted as the production of multiple transnational sexual fields. In China, the "opening up and reforms" since 1977 ushered in three decades of relative cultural pluralization, globalization, and liberalization of private life, including sexuality, allowing the development of multiple increasingly autonomous fields of sexual relations, an array of social spaces in which premarital, extramarital, casual sex, and same-sex sexual experiences are first imagined and then legitimated (Farrer 2002, 2006; Farrer and Sun 2003; Kong 2010; Pan 1993). The emergence of *a field of inter-*

*racial sexuality* in China's urban frontiers is one example of these transnational sexual fields. In this field, Western men have sexual capital that
is composed of their racial status, their association with sexual freedom,
their knowledge of nightlife cultures, their association with transnational
mobility, and (for some) their specialized knowledge of the Chinese language and Chinese culture (Farrer 2010a). This advantageous sexual
field of short-term affairs also produces gendered and racial advantages
in the field of long-term liaisons. During the thirty years since the "opening and reform" began, international marriages registered in Shanghai
have involved nearly ten times as many foreign men as foreign women.[1]

2. *Ethnosexual contact zones.* With the globalization of sexualities, we
must find a way of describing the processes in which such racially stratified sexual fields emerge. First, these interracial sexual fields are generally neither national in scope, like the systematic sexual stratification of
blacks and whites in the United States (Gonzales and Rolison 2005), nor
restricted to very local sexual worlds, such as the leather bars and other
scenes described by Green (2008a). We suggest that the transnational
sexual scene faced by Westerners in Asian global cities is best captured
in the term *sexual contact zone* (Tanaka 2007) or *ethnosexual contact
zone* (Farrer 2011; Nagel 2003). Mary Louise Pratt defines *contact zones*
as "social spaces where disparate cultures meet, clash, and grapple with
each other, often in highly asymmetrical relations of domination and
subordination—like colonialism, slavery, or their aftermaths as they are
lived out across the globe today" (Pratt 1992, 4). As this term indicates,
such sexual contact zones existed prior to what we today conceive of as
globalization, in the context of colonial cities or even earlier patterns of
trade and conquest. However, the current era of globalization—characterized by massive cross-border trade and investment, global human
rights discourses, and mass migrations—has created the conditions for a
new type of interracial contact zone based on at least nominal recognition of gender and racial equality and the rights of individuals to pursue
their sexual interests across political and ethnic boundaries. These new
globalized sexual contact zones are frequently concentrated in a single
area of a city, such as Roppongi in Tokyo or the Bund area in Shanghai,
but they are also simultaneously transnational in scope, such as the sexual scene between Western men and East Asian women that plays out
in designated urban zones around the Pacific Rim, ranging from Lank-
waifong in Hong Kong and Sanlitun in Beijing to Robertson/Clarke
Quay in Singapore (Farrer 2011). These ethnosexual contact zones are

spaces of complex social, economic, and cultural contact, conflict, and exchange, but they can also be studied more narrowly as stratified sexual fields in which new forms of racialized sexual capital are exploited and reconstructed in reaction to changing conditions.

3. *Geographic mobility and sexual mobility.* Ethnosexual contact zones are also spaces of sexual mobility. Some people may decide to migrate in order to maximize their sexual capital. Some people make cross-border moves in order to facilitate polygamous or extramarital relationships (Lang and Smart 2002; Liu-Farrer 2010) or seek a favorable environment for finding a marriage partner (Constable 2003). Others may venture to places where they have a racial advantage (Farrer 2010a; Lan 2011). But sexual mobility is not restricted to upward mobility. People may also experience sexual marginalization and desexualization when moving across sexual fields. This may even become a motive for further geographic mobility, as discussed below.

4. *The mobility of race and gender in sexual fields.* Finally, in addition to questions about geographic and sexual mobility, this case study points out racial and gendered mobility, or fluidity, within sexual fields. While race and gender generally can be considered stable categories when traveling across social boundaries, in the stories we discuss here people's gendered position may change on entry into an alien sexual field. For example, they may describe an experience of "feminization" or "masculinization," a kind of mobility from one gendered position to another. Gender status is closely associated with sexual status within a sexual field, and actors may experience an adjustment of gendered and racial position in a new social context. A woman who feels appropriately "feminine" in New York might find her behavior described as "masculine" in Shanghai. Similarly, a Chinese man may feel demasculinized in the West. Daniel Eng (2001) has referred to this process of emasculation of Asian American men in the United States as *racial castration*. Racial status is similarly mobile or malleable when crossing sexual fields. An Asian American may feel more Asian in the United States but more American in some Chinese contexts. In response to their gendered and racial mobility within a sexual field, actors may also consciously or unconsciously adjust their gendered and racial positions over time, for example, through a process of discovering a new racialized sexual affinity, acting more like a man (or a woman), or self-positioning closer to a preferred racial identity. Such gendered and racial mobility is an underexplored area of inquiry in the study of sexual fields.

## Data

This chapter is based on a larger study of foreign residents in Shanghai by James Farrer comprising a series of ethnographic interviews done with 250 foreigners living in Shanghai conducted between 2001 and 2010 as well as observations of the expatriate community in Shanghai. The period of residence in Shanghai of the respondents varied from one year to twenty-five, although there was an oversample of those who had been living in Shanghai for over five years. The majority of expatriates interviewed came from the United States (eighty-two), a fair number came from Japan (thirty-five), and the remaining others were primarily from Anglophone and European countries. Forty percent of the foreigners interviewed were women, and it is these interviews (with the exception of the Japanese as the Japanese experience differs considerably from that of Western expatriates) that will form the substance of this chapter. Related discussions on the Internet provide additional data for the project. All names used are pseudonyms.

Most of the women interviewed were in their late twenties to late forties, with the majority (over half) falling into the twenty-six- to thirty-five-year-old age bracket. They also stemmed from a variety of occupational backgrounds, and although some (ten women in this sample) were housewives who had come over as trailing spouses, most were professionals working in the arts (journalism, freelance writing, etc.), education (school principals, teachers, and so on), food and hospitality (restaurant/bar managers), and such other fields as business, marketing, and the commercial sphere.

For the purpose of this chapter, a thematic analysis of the interview transcripts was conducted using NVIVo8, a qualitative data-analysis software that allowed us to find and code themes related to sexual desire, interracial relationships, and related topics in the interview transcripts. Sonja Dale was responsible for much of the analysis for this part of the project.

*Note on racial terms in China.* Race is an underexplored feature of Chinese sexuality. Shanghainese (and foreigners in Shanghai) typically use the term *laowai* (old foreigner) or more formally *waiguoren* (foreigner) to describe white foreigners in the city. The term *heiren* (black people) is often used to describe people of African origin, regardless of nationality. Such terms are less often used to describe people of Chinese ancestry with foreign passports—who could be referred to as *ABCs* (American-born Chinese) or *huaqiao* (overseas Chinese) or more recently as *huayi* (Chinese origin). *Foreigner* is also the term most often used in English by Westerners themselves. We will generally use the English term *Westerner* to represent the local category of *waiguoren/laowai*, noting, however, that all these terms are used in multiple ways in social interactions.

## Marginalization, Desexualization, and Masculinization as a Process of Socialization into an Alien Sexual Field

As we note above, the expatriate sexual scene does not present the rosiest of prospects for white Western woman, yet this is the erotic world in which most heterosexual Western women saw themselves participating in Shanghai. Many reported a sense of desexualization or sexual marginalization and also described themselves as *masculinized* in sexual relations. *Desexualization* in this case refers to being perceived as and feeling sexually undesirable, whereas *masculinization* refers to being described (by oneself or others) as behaving like a man, primarily with regards to sexual conduct. While not all women go through these stages (as will be outlined below, women exercise various strategies of acceptance, resistance, and mobility), Western women on the whole are masculinized in four intersubjectively defined stages of socialization into a marginal position in the field of expatriate sexual relationships in Shanghai:

1. *Sexual marginalization*: perceiving a lack of sexual opportunities and a lack interest from men;
2. *Desexualization*: feeling less desired;
3. *Disorientation*: perceiving a lack of moral restraints on sexuality; and
4. *Gender mobility*: being treated as one of the guys or acting like a man.

As described in the introductory section, non-Asian Western women often perceive themselves as sexually undesired in the eyes of foreign men, who are seen as preferring the Chinese women who participate in the same dating/nightlife scenes. As Teresa, a white Canadian in her thirties, says: "A lot of Western guys are just not interested in foreign women because they can get Chinese girls. And then Chinese guys aren't interested in us." Mary, a white American also in her early thirties, notes the difficulty in fitting into this sexual scene:

> It is very hard to walk into a group of white men and Chinese women and be accepted by either one. It depends obviously on the group, but, if you're talking about a disco, let's talk about a random cheesy disco night with a group of drinking-buddy-type friends. That's what you walk into. Plus the Chinese women are often young, relatively speaking, and wearing a lot fewer clothing that I can get away with—ever could or ever would.

The problems brought forth by Teresa and Mary are, first, the belief that Chinese men are not interested in foreign women and, second, the belief that Western men can get a Chinese woman easier than a Western one and often a younger and sexier one at that. In both cases, it would seem that the Western woman is the one who loses out in the end as no one is willing to pick her up. In the worst case, women feel desexualized or completely excluded from the sexual field. However, even if a Western woman is perceived as attractive (i.e., having sexual capital), she may be the focus of less attention in a crowded sexual field, that is, sexually marginalized in an expatriate sexual scene favoring interactions between Western men and Chinese women.

At the same time, most Western women do not seek out relationships with Chinese men. Many informants professed to not having dated a Chinese man, often because they had not been approached by one. Others said that they are not particularly attracted to Chinese men. Shanghai Academy of Social Sciences psychologist Zhang Jiehai (2009) has devoted a book to exploring this phenomenon. As one of his interviewees (a twenty-five-year-old French woman who had been living in Shanghai for three and a half years) says:

> Honestly, I am not at all attracted to Chinese men. I have found that they don't pay enough attention to their appearance. This includes their grooming, hairstyle, and bearing. So, all in all, they don't move me to get closer to them. . . . And often Chinese men give you the impression they are not very clean. Like, they have long fingernails—it's disgusting—and spitting on the street. For Western people spitting on the street is a really terrible habit. . . . Other than appearance, Chinese men also give me the impression that they do not pay enough attention to women, they do not dote on them. (93–94)

In a survey of a small convenience sample of Western women in Shanghai, Zhang finds that most Western women attribute the relatively small number of white female–Chinese male partnerships to Western women's lack of interest in Chinese men—60.7 percent, compared to 21.4 percent who attribute this trend to Chinese men's shyness and 7.1 percent who attribute it to Chinese men's lack of interest in foreign women (Zhang 2009, 138). Women interviewed for this study showed similar responses, often describing little interest in dating Chinese men.

In response to this situation, there has been a spate of blogs and personal online reflections among Western women in Shanghai, with some suggesting that one should give Chinese men a chance. As a Western woman who admits to *not* finding Chinese men attractive concludes in her article: "It clearly pays to keep an open mind about dating, in every respect. Who knows—your perfect guy might be just around the corner, and he may be Chinese."[2] On *Speaking of China*, a blog written by a Western woman married to a Chinese man, one can even find a listing of blogs written by women with an interest in (or in a relationship with) Chinese men.[3] Although there seems to be increasing support for such relationships in the online expatriate culture, at the same time it is still assumed that they are much more unusual than those involving white men and Chinese women.

Some women identified dating Chinese men as a form of masculinization or gender shift, akin to taking the male role in dating and relationships. One American informant who married a Chinese man described her perception of reversed gender roles:

> Talking to my girlfriends who date Chinese guys, I think we all have a tendency to take on the male role. Like at the beginning you end up chasing the guys because they will not go after you. And later we end up taking on more of the male role in the relationship and in the marriage. These are not the typical male-female dynamics.

The sense that Chinese men were more feminized or passive in relationships was particularly associated with Shanghai men, she explained, pointing to a common stereotype about their softer masculinity compared to the more macho reputation of men from Beijing and North China in general.

Although most of our Western female informants had no experience dating Chinese men, they did come into frequent social contact with

Chinese women interested in Western men. In interviews and online discussions, many women expressed derogatory attitudes toward their Chinese female competitors. In online discussion of the expat dating scene in Shanghai, the level of malice toward Chinese women is readily evident, with, for example, one description of them as "local talent" that "has ruined a perfectly good evening with their benign dribble, giggles, ooohs & aaahhhs."[4] Although in these discussions the Chinese woman was often looked at as a threat to the Western woman, it was not in the sense that she was morally or intellectually superior; the Chinese woman was rather looked down on for her obsequiousness toward the Western man, in contrast with the presumed independence and moral integrity of the Western woman.

The common belief among the foreign women interviewed as well as among the online discussions was that foreign women lose out to their Chinese competitors owing to their unwillingness to throw themselves at men in the same manner. However, other interviewees suggested that some foreign men are simply *not interested* in foreign women. That is to say, foreign women simply do not exist within the sexual field of vision of these expatriate men who are absorbed in the interracial sexual field (Farrer 2010a). The following statements demonstrate this notion:

> I'm not really interested in them [Caucasian women] any more . . . so that's one [thing] and then all the other ones I see are moms—because of the kids—all the expat moms—and with some of them I get along really well and they tell me things they shouldn't sometimes. — Bert, twenty-seven, white Belgian

In Bert's case, Western women exist as desexualized mothers who divulge their secrets to him. As such, rather than being taken as sexual objects, the Western women he meets are seen as desexualized comrades. According to Ewan (thirty-three, African American), Western women are simply not "interesting":

> I typically don't date foreign women. Just because I've dated foreign [white] girls before in the US, and again you want to experience what China has to offer.

In other words, the desexualization of Western women is partly a result of their structural position in a sexual field in which many of the male participants—both Western men and Chinese men—have invested in sexual capital, including a linguistic and cultural repertoire, specifically oriented toward encounters with Chinese women. Some Western men who lived in China for several years reported no longer finding Western women attractive or expressed discomfort with Western-style rituals of courtship or flirtation. Western men's adaptations to the interracial sexual field in Shanghai thus further disadvantaged Western women.

Women themselves adapted to this situation in different ways. Their responses to desexualization and marginalization in the sexual field may involve a process of moral reorientation. Both male and female informants suggest that her marginality in the expat sexual scene results in the foreign woman having to "lower her standards" (and "act like a man"). Another man, Norbert, a twenty-five-year-old white American, shares his opinion:

> Some of the foreigners that I've dated, they're, I'll say a little crazier, a little more open, a little wilder . . . because they're here, and for them, there aren't many options for guys. Because Chinese are all over the place and those foreign girls aren't necessarily attracted to the Chinese men. And the foreign men are all going after the Chinese girls, at least the majority of them. So for them, it's a little more of a desperate situation. So as a result, though, their character changes a little bit, they become more, I wouldn't say more open, but a little more crazy. I've seen some [of the] wildness of the foreign girls here.

Many informants ascribe this sexual "wildness" to the lack of ethics and morals in the Shanghai expat dating scene, a view that expats are "on vacation" and thus not beholden to the rules governing "at home." This is a view common to other expatriate subcultures, such as the one studied in Dubai by Katie Walsh, in which women also face a culture dominated by short-term relationships (Walsh 2007). Similarly, one informant, Nancy (thirty-eight, Asian Canadian) stated about Shanghai: "Back home I would be considered promiscuous, but here I think it's completely normal." This in turn leads to women (and men) being more sexually open, active, and experimental than they would be in their home country. One informant related the story of a (female) friend who had slept with the "United Nations of Men" and similar stories of a "loosening" or even "losing" of morals were common.

In sum, socialization into this new sexual scene leads to a sense of moral reorientation—in that one has to adjust one's beliefs—for many participants. For some women, this liberation in sexual perspectives is perceived positively. As one thirty-five-year-old European woman said:

> The good thing about Shanghai is you come here and you learn you can have sex like a man. Maybe at home you have all your parents' education about the importance of sex and love and all that, but here you lose that. Or maybe it is just age. After all, all the women I came over here with are the same age as me. — Sabrina

Or it can also be viewed negatively, as a twenty-eight-year-old woman from New Zealand said:

> So with the European women. They tend to try to be like men, to fit in. That's the obvious thing I'm saying. They are too aggressive in terms of trying to win the boys. And how much beer I can drink. — Nicole

It is noteworthy that this sexual aggressiveness is linked to becoming more manlike, either by adopting male sexual practices or becoming seen as unfeminine (one of the boys) without any change in actual behavior. This process of masculinization shows that gendered subjectivity is fluid within a sexual field. Some women may become more like men in order to compensate for their loss of feminized sexual capital (while taking advantage of the economic and social capital associated with being white and Western or foreign). Other women may simply see themselves as less feminine with no sexual advantages. Their experience mirrors the "racial castration" described by Eng among Asian American men in the United States (Eng 2001).

Many single Western women feel that they must leave the expatriate sexual scene in Shanghai in order to find a suitable partner. Sabrina says:

> I feel very comfortable being on my own, but lots of people I find need company. And then I find as a foreign woman—they want a partner, and it's not that easy to find a guy, and they're not into local guys, and so they leave. I knew a few like that. They said I can't find a partner here, and they want to get married, and they leave. Whereas for guys it's easier, a lot that stay longer have a local Chinese girlfriend or wife, so they would have settled down and have kids here.

For many single women, the problem of marginalization was not so much the inability to find a date (or, rather, "getting laid"), as finding, or keeping, a suitable partner. As Nicole says: "I get a hard time. I don't think that's fair. It's great to have decent conversation, stimulating conversation, instead of sprees of sex or whatever."

The frustration of these women was described by Nick, a white male psychotherapist who has been working in the expatriate community:

> They are angry, the women who come here. . . . There is one thing unifying them: they have a really miserable time here, and they kind of have an asexual time here. They have real trouble finding boyfriends and getting dates because the guys are looking elsewhere.

Not only do single women experience sexual marginalization; married women do as well. This theme frequently emerged in conversations with "expat wives" (female trailing spouses) in Shanghai. One American woman who was a long-term trailing spouse described a specific case:

> I just had a friend call me while she was home. I got an email. She was home with her daughter, who was starting her senior year out here, and her son would be a junior in college. She went home for the summer. And her husband called her and said, Guess what, you're not coming back 'cause I have a twenty-six-year-old Thai that I'm now taken up with. That was the end of that. — Xandra

The sense of sexual threat conveyed in such anecdotes could lead not only to the greater monitoring of one's partner but also to a moral reorientation. Several women admitted to some degree of resignation to their husbands' possible affairs. One married woman said, for example:

> I think I've also changed slightly. I am a little bit more understanding than I was. I've seen these girls operate. At the end of the day, I've become a little more rational, it's only sex. . . . [For affairs] I think for once I could manage to understand, but twice, no. — Bertha, thirties, white British

In sum Western women in Shanghai's expatriate sexual scene are faced with a progressive sense of marginalization, desexualization, moral disorientation, and masculinization. Women perceive sexual marginalization (even within marriage) as a threat they must cope with either through resignation, increased resistance, or moving away. Some react to their prolonged marginal position in the sexual field by focusing on short-term affairs, joining what they perceive to be a morally loose atmosphere of the expat sexual scene. In this case, repositioning in a sexual field can lead to changes in sexual practices. Prolonged repositioning in a sexual field can lead to a change in moral orientation, for example, a greater tolerance for extramarital affairs. Many women experience their sexual transformation as a change in gendered positionality through a form of masculinization. Below, we turn to three specific cases of expatriate women in Shanghai to explore still other strategies of mobility that arise both within and outside the sexual field.

## Strategies of Mobility from a Marginalized Sexual Position

To explore alternative reactions to the marginalized position of Western expatriate women in Shanghai, we consider the cases of three professionals from different cultural backgrounds. Neelie is an Asian American, whereas Sabrina is a white European and Marriott a white American. Their experiences provide a greater understanding of how agents maneuver in a sexual field, depending on goals and variability in sexual capital.

*Neelie*

Neelie is an Asian American, that is to say, ethnically Asian (not Chinese), but culturally she identifies herself as American. At the age of thirty-five, she describes herself as being "midcareer." Her arrival in Shanghai marks a period of transition in her life. Prior to that, she gave up a stable career and comfortable lifestyle and left the States without having made any plans, let alone the decision to come to Shanghai. She attributes her coming to China to "fate" and has lived in Shanghai for approximately three years. However, she acknowledges that China is but one stop among many and that she is here "to get the China experience." She describes herself as having a "Taoist philosophy to living" and regards her future with a certain air of indifference, in that she will go "where the wind blows."

Without prodding, the first thing that Neelie brings up in the interview is her distaste for the dating scene in Shanghai. Her experience as "a woman who looks like a local, is mistaken for a local, but is completely Western inside" has clearly shaped her perspective: "The shit that I have to deal with from a dating standpoint because of that."

Neelie's frustration may be surprising insofar as the typical foreign woman's dilemma arises as a consequence of the preferences of Western men for local Chinese women. Hence, being Asian in appearance would seem to preclude her facing this problem. As she herself says, getting sexual interest is hardly a problem: "I know I can sleep with anyone at any time, and there's power in that; because I know that, I hardly do it." As such, she frames her problem as a function not of a lack of sexual interest from men but as one of the attitudes of men socialized to the easy sexual opportunities within the expatriate sexual field.

Neelie is also a salesperson and uses sales metaphors in describing dating, seeing the two as having the same principles. As such, dating is essentially "a game" in which she partakes but one the quality of which she is dissatisfied with. She frames the Caucasian foreign woman's experience within this game metaphor:

> It's hard for them to get in the game. My Australian girlfriend is successful, tall, really good looking. She's got it, she's got it going on by Western standards. No dates here. She's been here thirteen months. Granted, she works a lot, she's not socializing as much as me, and she's tall. I don't know, you tell me.

Neelie's response implies that being Asian is a means of getting into the game, a game she goes on to suggest for which she has her own tactics when playing:

> How I deal with it is, I meet guys, but I don't take people seriously. I don't take anything that they tell me in terms of their feelings about me or the great things about me, it's all for fun, unless proven otherwise. So I play the game, and as a salesperson this is a problem. This is the part that I admittedly enjoy, the gamesmanship of it. And I will play that game because I am better than everyone at it.

The problem is that, as with all games, there are rules involved, and in this case the men Neelie encounters often fail to conform to her relatively conservative, Western cultural and moral standards:

I don't know, to me, it's just American dating; it's the same standards from home. Honesty, spending regular time together, good kisser—I'm not asking for anything more. But these guys, they're disqualifying themselves. I'm not the one pulling the trigger. They're the ones sending SMS [text messages] to the wrong people; they're the ones flirting in front of me.

Her standard of "American dating" is her benchmark, and she makes repeated references to how what occurs in Shanghai would not occur "back home" and how most people seem to lower their moral standards after coming to Shanghai:

And that's a thing with me, I think a lot of the people here will play in the gray area, and in Shanghai they will broaden their definition of what a gray area is. Me, I am black and white. Absolutely black and white. . . . I don't sink down to the other women's level. I actually go the opposite way. I'm going to be that woman who won't let them drop their standards or their expectations. And I'm firmer on crossing the line or even dabbling with the gray area more so here in Shanghai than at home because I know all the other women out there.

Beyond the fact that Neelie finds the standards of dating in Shanghai not to her liking, she also notes of the sexual field that her potential male partners are somewhat limited in number and quality. When asked about the possibility of going out with Chinese men, she replied that they were turned off by her independence and forthright style of communication:

What are they going to do with somebody like me? If I'm at a bar, they see that by the way I carry myself and the way I am interacting in a group. It comes across; I don't try to hide that. And actually, I've had Chinese women tell me that. They tell me. They might ask the same question, which is, "Oh, have you dated any of the local guys, and what are they like?" "Oh, they don't come to me." And I had one woman say, "Oh, well yeah, because you're not the type." And I said, "Oh." I knew what she was going to say, but I just asked the question for the hell of it. I said, "Oh, what do you mean by that?" "Because you're not the sweet innocent type." "You're right! You're right!"

Because of the perceived clash of gender expectations with Chinese men, Neelie defines her sexual chances as lying entirely within the field of Western expatriate men. Within the expatriate sexual scene, however, she attributes her relatively marginal position, not to a lack of sex appeal, but to the mismatch of expat sexual mores with her own more authentic American erotic habitus or the rules of American dating culture. Her primary strategy for dealing with the objectionable practices of the expatriate sexual field is one of resistance. On the other hand, she freely admits that resisting the sexual culture of the expat scene is difficult in Shanghai and that she is contemplating leaving the city. (She left Shanghai a year after our interview.)

*Sabrina*

Sabrina has been in China for over five years and has had a long-standing interest in Chinese culture and language, studying at a prestigious local university. She works in marketing for an international company, and, although her work life is conducted primarily in English, she is adept at the Chinese language. She describes great satisfaction with her life in Shanghai and enjoys the whirl of social activities. She likes the dynamism and chaos of the city, which she sees in contrast to the seeming stagnation of Europe. When it comes to socializing, she sticks mainly within the expatriate circles and frequents events held by the Shanghai expatriate associations. This is also reflected in her dating choices, as she has never dated a Chinese man and expresses a clear aversion to doing so:

> INTERVIEWER: Did you ever date the Chinese guys here?
>
> SABRINA: No, never. It's just, I guess it's different for a woman. For a Chinese woman, they look very feminine—I can imagine for a guy, but the guys don't look very manly, you know? It's not really what I would be looking for in a guy.
>
> INTERVIEWER: Is it mostly looks or the culture?
>
> SABRINA: No, well looks have something to do with it, I guess, although I have to say if I look for a guy I'm not really into looks—its more their mind I guess, but there's also, I mean, they would be tinier than I am, and it's not something I find very attractive. . . . I don't meet that many, like when I go out, I have quite a lot of Chinese friends, but most of them are female friends. I don't know how that happened.

Sabrina's aversion to dating Chinese men is based partly on height, but it also included other factors such as difficulties making acquaintance or sustaining a conversation. As such, Chinese men have no sexual capital for her: "[They simply] do not excite me." Despite her lack of interest in Chinese men, she has had sexual relations with Chinese women, both in "threesomes" with Western men and one-to-one. For her, Chinese women are not desexualized in the same way as Chinese men. Nevertheless, most of her relationships have been with Western men, both those living in Shanghai and those traveling through. She prefers to keep an open mind toward the issues of sexual fidelity and monogamy, and this goes along with being more "manlike" in her sexuality:

> I think the same goes for women—they feel immediately threatened if a guy has another affair with a woman, even if it's purely physical. So many women take it as an emotional problem, but I guess maybe since I've been here a long time since many people say you become more like a man, but I think you can definitely separate the emotional from the physical part, so I can really understand that the guy can still be really in love with his wife but sleep with another woman. . . . It's also both parties . . . if you look at it from a different perspective and see that it doesn't necessarily mean that he loves you less or respects you less, it would make it easier as well.

Sabrina's strategy can be described as adjusting to the sexual scene through gender mobility—or accepting a more masculine sexual standard. Although never sexually conservative, even when living in Europe, Sabrina explained that Shanghai "encourages promiscuity" and allowed her to be more experimental and active in a way that she was not permitted before. In her own words:

> The good thing about Shanghai is you come here and you learn you can have sex like a man. Maybe at home you have all your parents' education about the importance of sex and love and all that, but here you lose that.

Sabrina seems to chastise the expatriate women who do not advocate a more masculine stance and who refrain from adapting to the "Shanghai scene." However, as she says, one has to enjoy living alone in order to like Shanghai as a foreign woman. (Three years after these interviews, Sabrina married a European man she met while traveling and left Shanghai.)

*Marriott*

Marriott has been in China for over ten years and can be considered a settler. By profession, she is a researcher and writer, and, with her advanced Chinese ability and interest in the local culture, she is integrated into the local Shanghai cultural scene. She describes herself as having "gone native" and dates non-English-speaking local men and socializes with local Chinese as well. She has had several Chinese boyfriends but at the time of the interview was single. She confesses an aesthetic preference for Chinese men but is not closed off to dating Western men either.

> MARRIOTT: The foreign guy contingent here, not very promising.
> INTERVIEWER: Why is that?
> MARRIOTT: There's a lot of 2–10-ers. The guys who are 2 in their homeland and come here and they're 10. They think they're really hot stuff, but they're not. . . . Personally, I find Asian guys aesthetically more attractive. It's like the top 20 percent of Asian guys versus the top 2 percent of white guys.

Marriott's disdain for Western men is apparent, but it is a disdain that extends to those Chinese women who would condescend to associate with them:

> Not all, but there are Chinese guys with foreign fetishes. But with Chinese guys with foreign fetishes are one to ten out of all the Chinese girls with foreign fetishes. You know what type of girls . . . they'll date a foreigner after foreigner after foreigner. And eventually marry one. We go to a lot of parties—house parties or whatever, the only Chinese people there are the serial foreign dating chicks. They don't want to speak Chinese because they want to practice their English. Normal Chinese people will feel uncomfortable being around girls like this. You know, they're just slutting it up and trying to hit on all the foreign guys. . . . Maybe it's just the people that I hang out with now. It's been such a long time since I've last gone to one of those house parties where it's all skanky Chinese with foreign guys or skanky guys with Chinese girlfriends. Actually what it is, is that most of the people I know like that have gotten married and have stopped going out anyways.

Despite her deep affinities to the local culture, Marriott projects her integrity as a Western woman by contrasting herself to the Chinese woman: as such, the Western woman is not being rejected by the Western man; rather, she is just *too good* for the types of men that Chinese women are pursuing. On the other hand, she also has to deal with the problem of racial fetishization with Chinese men:

> Chinese guys are like, "Oh, exotic white person." The problem is that I find that they have the foreign fetish thing and they want a foreign girlfriend for the exotic factor. . . . They want to go abroad, and they want to practice their English. They find there's something that's aesthetically fascinating.

For Marriott, being open-minded and accepting of her independent nature is an important aspect in romantic relationships. For her, most of the interesting Chinese men are involved in the arts:

> [It's] the artsy Chinese guys who are more open-minded, more interesting, better to hold a conversation with. It's a horrible thing to say, but the bulk of the Chinese people, whether women or men, are just incredibly boring. They don't have many interests, or they're so caught up in the rat race of buying a house, buying a car, getting married, having a kid, and finding a mistress. It's such a competitive environment. It's kind of has to be because it's at the bottleneck of development. So few people have anything to talk about.

For Marriott, the strategy of coping with sexual marginalization was a kind of racial mobility or "going local," embracing an identity as a Shanghainese, dating local men, and speaking the Shanghainese dialect. Nonetheless, assuming even a local identity involves making distinctions with Chinese women who date foreign men and also the vast majority of Chinese who lack cultural capital or interest in the arts. Her strategy of racial mobility thus does not negate race but rather accepts certain aspects of racialization as inevitable (such as sexual fetishes). Like some other Western women who dated Chinese men, she also claims a more assertive or proactive position in her pursuit of local men, preferring in her case to date men considerably younger than herself. She thus situates herself in a constructed hierarchy of gendered and racialized distinctions in which she occupies a privileged position, herself being an artsy Western woman with local knowledge and ties and a pragmatic, manlike attitude toward pursuing sexual relations. (As of the writing, Marriott is still single, living in Shanghai.)

## Conclusions: Strategies of Mobility in a
## Transnational Sexual Field

Economic and cultural globalization has resulted in a proliferation of transnational sexual fields that constitute a variety of sexual opportunities for mobile individuals. People may experience upward or downward sexual mobility within the "ethnosexual contact zones" of sexual globalization (Nagel 2003). In the transnational sexual scene of expatriate Shanghai, many Western women experience a downward sexual mobility that is discordant with their general upward social mobility as members of the "transnational capitalist class" (Sklair 2001). In other words, mobility across sexual fields does not always result in an advantaged new position; it may involve, as in this case, learning to cope with a marginalized position. The cases detailed above outline different strategies women take with regard to their marginalized status in a transnational and interracial sexual field. These can be outlined as follows:

- *resignation*: accepting a marginal or weaker position;
- *resistance*: demanding alternative standards of sexual practice;
- *geographic mobility*: leaving permanently (or temporarily to find partners);
- *gender fluidity*: becoming more man-like in sexual practices; and
- *racial adaptability*: becoming "Chinese"/dating Chinese men.

Both *resignation* and *resistance* can be described as psychological responses to perceived downward mobility in the sexual field. Resignation is the most common strategy in response to marginalization in a sexual field. To some extent, in this study, most female informants admitted resigning themselves to a marginal or weaker position in the sexual field in Shanghai, lowering their aesthetic or moral standards for sex partners, or lowering previously held standards for their own sexual conduct. Resistance is another common reaction. In some cases, resistance may be symbolic. In this study, women used online discussions to condemn the behavior of Western men or Chinese women or to uphold home country sexual customs. Resistance also may involve relationship strategies, such as expressing jealousy or monitoring the activities of partners. In either case, it may not have much impact on standards within the larger sexual field.

*Geographic mobility* is another individual-level response to sexual marginalization, but also one with important sociological consequences. In short, onward migration can be a sexual strategy for some people. Even when staying within the larger field of global expatriate enclaves, some Western female informants described feeling more sexually valued in expatriate locales such as Kuwait or Dubai, whereas Western men did not have access to a large pool of local women (Walsh 2007). Geographic mobility does not have to take the form of a permanent move. As in many male sojourner societies in the past, Western women with sufficient income in Shanghai can travel to meet partners either in their home countries or elsewhere or engage in short-term affairs with men in spaces that carried a reputation as sexually favorable environments for white Western women (such as Italy, Jamaica, Morocco, and Bali). These latter instances constitute a kind of sex tourism in which some of our more wealthy female informants participated. Put simply, sociologists should be mindful of the role that sexual fields can play as a factor in migration decisions.

*Gender fluidity* is more directly an effect of position within the sexual field, rather than a property of individual decisionmaking. As Green (chapter 1 in this volume) suggests, sexual capital is a property not only of the individual but also of relations within the field. Similarly, gender identity, as produced and expressed in sexual relationships, is, in part, an effect of position within a sexual field. Although gender fluidity might be best described as a field effect, it is one in which individuals exercise some tactical control. As we note above, when women are pushed to the margins of a sexual field, they may experience not only a challenge to their sexual subjectivity (desexualization) but also a challenge to their gender identity (masculinization). However, gender shifting is not simply passively received; it can also be understood as a strategy of adjustment within a sexual and social field. Having sex like a man may be a conscious choice. For example, acting like a man through casual sex may be a way of recovering position in the sexual field, by redefining goals (lowering moral or aesthetic standards), and getting back in the game as a liberated (though masculinized) Western woman. Similarly, some Western female informants who described themselves as assuming a more assertive role in pursuing Chinese men perceived themselves as masculinized but also as pragmatically adapting to a sexual scene in which Chinese men did not usually approach Western women.

*Racial adaptability* is another tactical response to a diminished position within a sexual field. Racial realignment may involve identifying

more closely with one racial status or another or attempting to strategically align oneself within racial hierarchies. And, moreover, in the context of interracial sexual fields, racial realignment and gender fluidity
are not mutually exclusive phenomena but must be considered in more
complex terms. While becoming one of the guys is often directly associated with a sense of desexualization and loss of sexual status, this gender
positioning can also be interpreted as a strategy of racial alliance. Put
simply, some Western women would rather identify with white/West-
ern privilege than place themselves in a gendered category with Chinese
women. Becoming a man (with connotations of autonomy and aggressiveness) distinguishes the masculinized white female subject from the
frequently denigrated character of the hyperfeminized Chinese woman
who chases Western men. Gender fluidity thus may be a strategy of recovering or claiming both racial and sexual status.

In contrast, going local represents a break with the racial homogamy among Western women in China. While not as common as becoming one of the guys, it seems increasingly common for Western women
to discover an interest in Asian men. More broadly, this sort of flexible
interracial desire is now the normative sexual strategy within the new
global expatriate class, in which biracial and bicultural marriages are
constructed as economic and cultural assets (Farrer 2008). In online discussions, at least, many Western women also seem to acknowledge the
desirability or at least normalcy of interracial parings. Racial adaptability and even racial ambiguity (e.g., accentuating one's own personal ethnic and cultural diversity) are accepted strategies of sexual capital investment within ethnosexual contact zones.

## The Meanings of Race in Defining and Contesting Sexual Fields

Although a full discussion is beyond the scope of this chapter, it is important to consider the larger historical contexts in which these multiracial
sexual fields emerge. Clearly, sexual fields are the outcome of macrolevel
historical processes and not merely emergent at the level of social interactions. For example, it is impossible to explain the persisting gender gap
in interracial dating in Shanghai without some reference to colonial racial legacies, in particular racial hierarchies of masculinity and femininity. Other scholars document a lingering postcolonial association of the
West with masculinity and of Asia with femininity that structures no-

tions of racial sexual desirability (Ho and Tsang 2000; Kelsky 2001; Koshy 2004). In particular, we cannot deny the longer-term historical processes that have produced a devaluation of Asian masculinity in Western
societies (Eng 2001). The reluctance of many informants to even consider dating Chinese men could reflect these historical prejudices.

As described above, relatively few white women in this study expressed an active interest in dating Chinese men, for example, citing
the difference in physical stature (Chinese men being "too small") as
an obstacle to attraction. Popular discussions of racial sexual preferences usually focus on this level of individual preferences or on generalized cultural stereotypes. We take a different approach. More sociologically, we argue that these patterns of individual desire (or lack of desire)
are structured at the level of the sexual field. In short, there is a well-
developed set of social institutions—bars, nightclubs, and Web sites—
promoting interactions between mobile Western men and a new group
of highly mobile urban Chinese women (Farrer 2010a, 2011). A similar sexual scene has not developed in which Western women easily meet
upwardly mobile Chinese men. It is not so much that individual foreign
women are not attractive to individual Chinese men at a physical level,
or vice versa, but rather that attraction, flirtation, and sexual come-ons
are all socially organized forms of interaction that must be learned and
practiced in culturally specific ways and in relatively organized settings
(see Green, chapter 1 in this volume).

The socially structured space of a sexual field shapes the relative competitive advantages of actors, which in turn can systematically shape decisions to invest in sexual capital (Michael 2004) and the formation of
erotic habitus (Green 2008a, 2008b). In China's coastal cities, thousands
of karaoke nightclubs and other venues exclusively cater to but also shape
the erotic habitus of wealthy Chinese men (Zheng 2009). This commer-
cialization of China's nightlife as a space of sexual consumption for elite
Chinese men structures these men's sexual choices and habits and partly
explains why Chinese men show relatively lower levels of overt sexual interest in Western women. Although socially mobile Chinese men do participate in Western-style social activities such as bars and clubs in Shanghai, they tend to focus on the far more numerous and accessible Chinese
women in such settings, often women who are themselves paid compan-
ions. Thus, in contrast to the relatively large number of Chinese women
interested in foreign men, far fewer Chinese men invest in the (costly
and specialized) cultural and linguistic skills specific to dating foreign

women. Without a socially organized sexual scene of some scale, it is difficult for this attraction to develop. In other words, attraction is to some extent a socially learned and socially organized behavior. As a result, most Western women did not find in Shanghai an organized social space in which to learn to interact with Chinese men, whereas many Western men did find a ready-made scene involving Chinese women with linguistic and cultural skills attuned to Western men.

It would be too simple, in other words, to label our informants as simple dupes of colonial racial stereotypes, though such stereotypes are reproduced in their conversations about their sexual dilemmas. Rather than colonial history, therefore, we suggest that racial patterns of sexual interaction, and the political uses of racial discourse within this sphere, can be more precisely understood as a reaction to the immediate contexts of the ethnosexual contact zones of contemporary global cities and the transnational and interracial sexual fields that emerge within these zones. In particular, the sexual strategies of Western women in Shanghai can be understood as reactions to their marginal positions in an interracial *sexual field*, as an attempt to define a better position within the field and also to define or defend its boundaries. While none of our informants advocated an explicitly *racial* boundary to the expatriate sexual scene, many implicitly advocated boundaries based on linguistic and cultural competence that would exclude most Chinese women without international experience and good English skills. (Many Chinese women active in this scene also advocated their own boundaries, such as a Shanghainese prejudice against women from other provinces.) Generally, the erotic worlds of global cities are dynamic and changing, and the situation described here is undoubtedly no exception. Hence, the present case underscores the more general point that the boundaries of sexual fields are continually contested and defended by participants. On the other hand, sexual strategies and preferences (or erotic habitus) are also shaped through participation in these fields. Western women in Shanghai find themselves adapting to the expatriate sexual scene even as they attempt to reshape its boundaries.

In conclusion, we should conceptualize sexual fields as sites of both mobility and social contestation. It is not enough simply to identify the hierarchies of sexual value within a field as though they are the arbitrary rules of a sexual game. Sexual fields in global cities are produced within ethnosexual contact zones that are sites of struggle for status and recognition among different racial, ethnic, and gender groups. Within these sexual worlds, marginalized actors seek strategies for mobility and thus play with the boundary conditions of their (de)sexualization, including gender, race, and place, hoping to change the conditions of participation or define the criteria of admission to the game. Historical legacies, such as colonial racial categories, provide cultural material for these contemporary local processes, but the meanings of these interactions are best understood as adjustments to changing positions in existing sexual fields and attempts to acquire and maintain forms of sexual capital therein.

## Notes

1. According to official government statistics, out of 826 Chinese-foreign marriages that took place in 1985, 733 involved a Chinese woman, i.e., a foreign male partner, which equates to about 89 percent of all marriages. In 2006, the number of marriages involving a Chinese national and a foreigner stood at 2,943, with about 82 percent of cases involving a foreign male partner. Statistics from the *Statistical Abstracts of Shanghai* (2011).

2. http://news.echinacities.com/detail/4012-Boys-Boys-Boys-Dating-Chinese -Guys.

3. http://www.speakingofchina.com/china-articles/china-blogs-western-women -love-chinese-men.

4. http://www.shanghaiexpat.com/phpbbforum/where-s-all-the-western-women -in-shanghai-t105691.html.

# CHAPTER SEVEN

# The Crucial Place of Sexual Judgment for Field Theoretic Inquiries

John Levi Martin, University of Chicago

## Nature of Field Theory

The chapters collected here represent a line of inquiry suggesting that field theory can be of use for an examination of the organization of sexual experience; here, I want to note that examinations of the organization of sexual experience may be of use for the development of field theory. If indeed field theory has the potential to cut through the intellectual knots of current thinking in the social sciences, it comes not merely from what it does *not* do (for avoiding various forms of current sociological thought crime such as dualism, external impulsion, and so on can be handled simply by refusing to think much), but from how it anchors human action in the organized experience of a field. Pursuing this suggests that no phenomenon is more theoretically central for this approach than sexual attraction. I first discuss the nature of field theory, then distill its key elements, then map them onto the arena of sexual decisionmaking, and then suggest what we need to know about the sexual field.

Orthodox Bourdieusians often make the error of imagining that Bourdieu's great accomplishment was to manufacture, through sheer effort of will, an idiothesis, a particular structure of thought, and that all subsequent investigations need to be checked against particular statements that he did or did not make. This is like those sorts of Marxists who treat Marx's works as a text to be snipped apart and turned into watchwords, theorems, spells, and mantras. But the glory of Marx was that he, more than anyone else, perfectly understood the core nature of dialectical materialism. So too the brilliance of Bourdieu was to hit on the key elements of a consistent field theoretic approach.

These are habitus and field. I am going to briefly rederive these from the earlier approach to field theory developed by the gestalt theorists, relying in particular on the wonderful work of Wolfgang Köhler (esp. 1920, 1938, 1947).[1] What is a field—that is, in field theory most generally? Fields are organized sets of vectors. What are vectors? Vectors are combinations of directions and intensities—pushes or pulls of different strengths in one direction or another. Why do we apply field theory to social action? Because we know that such vectors exist in everyday life. That is, we have the phenomenological experience of being pushed and pulled in different directions—not physically, as in, say, when we are pulled by the force of gravity, but practically, anthropologically, that is, in-the-sense-of-those-about-to-act.

This is as much as to say, as Köhler (1938) emphasized, that things like "value" or "requiredness" are experienced by us as being in the world, as properties of objects or situations. In contrast, most current Western philosophy assumes that all such vectors, anything that points in one direction as opposed to another, must be inside our brains—the world contains just dull, cold, gray "is"-ness, and we subjectively (and indefensibly) add the color of "ought"-ness (see also Dewey 1929, 95–96, 264–65).

Now the puzzle is that we know, phenomenologically, that we *experience* the oughtness as in-dwelling in objects. That is, our qualitative experience of these objects involves "affordances"—the objects call out for us to do different things with them. For example, a doorknob says "grasp me," and a nettle says "don't grasp me." Yet we know that we cannot analytically demonstrate the oughtness of these objects to a hostile critic. We can establish intersubjective validity, at least in some cases, but we are not surprised where and when this intersubjective agreement ceases. For example, my experienced world includes in some way the American Republican Party, and I experience it as reprehensible.

Most of my friends and probably my readers share my qualitative experience of this party. But there are two things to note about this experience. The first is that the further we go from our own position in social space, the less likely we are to find this unanimity, this fellowship in judgment, and we find it impossible to convince others that our judgment is correct, just as we find it impossible to convince those who do not share our culinary or musical tastes. The second thing to note is that when I talk about the Republican Party, I have only a very vague idea of what I mean—I am not sure who this is and what its members do. We will need to return to this puzzle later—how I can be sure that I am correctly perceiving very vivid qualities of an object that remains in many ways obscure to my best (even if not very good) conceptual thought.

The first point, namely, our inability to convince others regarding our judgments, turns out to be crucial for understanding our relation to the qualities of objects in our worlds. That is, sometimes we can force others to agree that one object is heavier than another—we put two figurines, say, on the scale, and agree that the larger number indicates the heavier object. But there are other qualities that defeat our efforts at such proof. Interestingly, these are the qualities that we tend to see as most qualitative. We may agree as to which figurine is more beautiful, but, if we disagree, we lack a beaut-o-meter to settle the dispute. As we pursue the nature of these qualities, we find that they are predicates that we attach to objects, predicates that lack some sort of objectivity. And, indeed, we find that they are not attributes of *things* so much as *relations*—that is, they are themselves *vectors*, pushes and pulls.

The best exposition here is Kant's (1790/1987) *Critique of Judgment*, and it was this that led to Bourdieu's single greatest work, namely, *Distinction* (1979/1984), which is a deliberate attempt to sociologize the Kantian approach in a critical way. It is quite straightforward to derive both the importance of field theory and the importance of attention to sexual fields from a serious engagement with Kant. In brief (for less brief, see Martin 2011), consider what Kant called *reflexive judgments*, those that we cannot prove with concepts. He emphasized that at least some of these, aesthetic judgments, are treated as legitimately demanding intersubjective agreement—we understand that not everyone will agree with us, but we are unhappy if no one does. Let us, like Kant, take as our case the question of how we judge something—or someone—beautiful. Kant argued that what we are investigating here is how our capacity to react with pleasure to the world can give us insight into the lawfulness of this world. We must determine how, say, our individual reactions of pleasure to the presentation of beauty in the form of other people are correlative to some sort of transindividual regularity. From there, it's just a hop, skip, and a jump to a theory of the sexual field.[2]

But there's a shorter way to start with the issue of judgment and proceed to the heart of field theory, one that Bourdieu also shows us. Here we focus not on how we *convince* others about our judgments but rather on how we *make* them in the first place—how we cognitively perform qualitative predication. That is, we know that people do not make all their judgments through linear, conscious reason. Although we can at least partially account for our reactions with such reason (e.g., noting that we generally find rotten corpses repulsive, or symmetry in faces pleasing), we do not do such a mental calculus in order to determine our reaction. We immediately see the disgusting nature of the rotting corpse, the beautiful nature of the smiling face, and immediately are repelled or attracted. The repulsiveness or attractiveness is experienced as a quality *of* the experienced object, even though in both cases the qualities have to do with our *relation* to the object.

One of Bourdieu's most famous points is that this sort of immediate reaction is characteristic of much important human action. An executive who "knows how to live" can simply see, obviously, that garden gnomes are tacky (Bourdieu 1979/1984, 300). The lower-middle-class housewife who "gets it just about right" (347) can just see that this executive's furniture is cold and not for her. We have become so used to some of Bourdieu's verbal formulas, structuring structures, objective subjective, and so on that we may glaze over and not appreciate the fundamental point here: we can see the qualities in objects because we develop our sensory apparatus in a world with these precise objects and their kin. This is literally true for our visual system and everything else. We do not see anything *once*—we recognize it only when we have developed a sensitivity to its actual qualities. Put another way, *all* taste is cultivated taste; although some aspects of our sensory system develop in a nearly hardwired form, they are only the building blocks for a more complete sensory engagement in the world that arises via postnatal development of an organism in its environment.

This sort of repeated engagement that sensitizes and specializes our faculties for sensing and acting on the world is universally known as *habit*. And indeed this is a key aspect of Bourdieu's approach. *Habitus* of course is something broader, involving one's whole way of being, but we should not ignore the fundamental kinship between habit and habitus. Both involve dispositional familiarity crafted via repeat engagement with the regularities of the world.

Thus, it is no accident that an attention to fields requires a development of the idea of habitus. *Capital* is actually a less fundamental concept, though it is of inestimable practical importance. That is because there can be fields in which there is no capital other than that redundantly contained in habitus. This might be the case, for example, in a field such as wine criticism, and it may also be to some extent true of sexual fields.

## What Is a Sexual Field?

When Matt George first seriously proposed attention to the sexual field in his 1996 dissertation, it was as a "young Bourdieusian." As someone who summarized *Distinction* as "100 more reasons to hate the rich," George was primarily interested in the historical changes whereby a specifically sexual field could be said to emerge and the processes whereby this field *became* a field, that is, achieved autonomy. This is crucial, because I think that many later approaches to the sexual field have assumed a lack of autonomy as they look for evidence of the usual suspects in terms of various forms of inequality or naturalize sexual capital into cookbook formulas that are the equivalent of a superficially sociological version of "how to meet girls"/"how to catch a man."

The Bourdieusian approach, in contrast, had great potential to solve some of the paradoxes that were arising in other approaches to sexual decisionmaking. The most obvious (treated in some depth by Martin and George [2006]) is the difficulty in analytically separating aspects of persons that are seen *as* (or as causes *of*) sexual attractiveness from those that compensate for a *lack* of this attractiveness. Further, by assuming equal exchange, the market approach tended to generate shadow utilities such that disutilities (by calling forth a shadow balancing utility) were themselves seen as utilities. It is not that we cannot imagine that a person may seek to partner with someone of lower value in order to extract subservience; it is that, though initially appealing and seeming to possess wide explanatory potential, the market metaphors easily became contradictory when dealing with the complexities of a situation of pairing in which no products were exchanged. While in a true market atomization yields order, in the chaos of a mere forum for action, approaches that assume atomization may fail to see the order that is there.

Indeed, it may be that it is precisely the difference between the analyses of the field approach to sexual action (on the one hand) and the analyses of the conventional approach (on the other) that allows us to grasp the theoretical importance of the sexual field. That is, let us approach the sexual field in terms, not of the categories that immediately confront us, but of the abstracted position of an idealized person making an idealized choice—with whom to try to have sexual contact.[3] Thus, it is important that, in this narrow sense of the sexual field that I will use here, almost no sexual action takes place "in" the field, and perhaps most sexual choice does not actually happen in the field, just as most empirical acts of humans dancing do not take place in the field of dance. The field emerges only as sexual choice and sexual action are disembedded from other forms of social organization. But what does it mean to say that this sexual choice is a field effect?

It seems to say that we can understand A's choice of B only in terms of the phenomenologically attractive power of B—that is, the vector connecting B to A. This vector, in turn, must be understood in terms of the positions of A and B in some field, although we must recognize that what we mean by this position can vary from the tautological (the position is that which explains the observations, a reasonable methodological principle supporting data-reduction techniques like correspondence analysis) to the problematic (we define position on the basis of stable exogenous individual characteristics, thus belying our argument as to the importance of the field effect). So far, we merely have a promissory note that the vector *should* be explained by the positions of the actors. The dismissive "naturalist" response is to insist that sexual attraction, as an obvious, innate program, is not problematic and hence needs no such tortuous explanation. Surely all animals successfully reproduce, which means that all have some instinct to seek out members of the opposite sex and mate. It is hard to imagine (say) fish, which are extremely dim creatures, having a sense of attractiveness owing to position in a sexual field.

Yet at least some of them do. Lee Dugatkin (1996) found that female guppies were more likely to approach a male for mating if they saw a previous female do so than if not. We are of course free to say that she takes this as a cue for the increased fitness of the male and so on and so forth, which is presumably trivially true. But, whatever her extremely impoverished sexual sensibility is, all this biospeak translates to the male's increased attractiveness. This is, I propose, the very simplest form of a field effect. It is wholly quantitative, consisting of a single vertical dimension, with no horizontal differentiation. It is like a "popularity tournament" (Martin 2009), where everyone wants to be friends with the popular and one is popular if many people want to be one's friend. In some cases, there are clear explanations for popularity—we may like people who are wealthy, say (a common finding in studies of adolescents). But in a popularity tournament popularity *itself* is attractive. If a poor person manages to get a few choices, she will then receive more because of the choices garnered earlier. Indeed, even in a world in which there are *no* exogenous predictors for popularity at all, such popularity effects can lead to a strictly hierarchical structure—even though there are an infinite number of possible outcomes (Orléan 1988). Where such endogenous popularity effects are important, we are likely to see booms and busts—we all want what others want, but if they don't want it any more, then we don't either, unless they want it because we want it . . .

Interestingly, there have been many cases of sexual fields that have been described as having precisely this characteristic. But, even more interestingly, this barely provokes an eyebrow being raised in studies of sexual decisionmaking. Despite the common acceptance of the naturalist belief that attractiveness just *is*, we also accept (naturally?) the importance of endogenous popularity effects. But such effects are, I believe, the simplest case of how a social field effect works. That is, the key phenomenology whereby habitus responds to position is visible and accessible. And this vector is of the simplest form—toward the other or away from.

Of course, it might well be that a field analysis could still be of use were there no endogenous popularity effect. For example, if popularity were entirely explained by wealth, we would be able to use it as one measure of position in an economic field. But popularity itself would not be particularly enlightening for helping us develop an understanding of field effects, for pushing field theory forwards. Thus, when it comes to sexual action, if we are able to explain attractiveness by recourse to other individual characteristics, we are unlikely to find this a promising place for the development of field theory. It is the potential endogeneity of attractiveness—something pointed to by previous theorists (e.g., Waller 1937)—that makes the sexual arena so promising. Here we seem to have, sitting in a cage ready for observation, replicable instantiations of that fetishism whereby relations are perceived as qualities of social objects. If we cannot understand this, we cannot understand field theory beyond loose verbal formulations and data-reductive techniques. To make further inroads into the heart of field theory, we need to focus on the riddle of attractiveness.

## The Riddle of Attractiveness

My wife was viewing some Web page for a sociologist (I have forgotten the specifics) and reached the part where his "interests" were described: things like "aging," "quantitative methodology," and so on. "Huh," she drily commented. "I'm more interested in things that are more interesting." That's a funny joke because it seems to us totally redundant to say that we are interested in interesting things, because we imagine that there is nothing in the things themselves that makes them interesting; what makes things interesting is that we are interested in them. If someone views *our* list of interests and says that they are not interesting, we would probably think "not interesting to *you*" and not worry about it.

But, if we ask someone out on a date and are turned down with the explanation, "No, I'm more attracted to attractive people," we might not find it so simple to dismiss this as a mere mismatch. Yet the two situations are, at least formally, precisely parallel. Now one might attempt to justify the asymmetry of our reactions by appealing to evidence of physical bases for attractiveness—symmetry, averageness—and great inter-rater reliabilities, and hence claim that attractiveness is less subjective than interestingness. But interestingness also has suspected evolutionary bases and high reliabilities: people in general are interested in things that display purposive motion, that are sentient, that have eyes, that are light sources, that have imperfect regularity, that are novel, and so on. In fact, there are better evolutionary explanations of what we find interesting than there are of what we find attractive. And this even applies to fields of study. There are parts of the sociology of aging that are pretty interesting, and there are lots of parts that are important, but aging *is not* as interesting as sex, and even scholars of aging won't deny this.[4] If all government funding were to disappear tomorrow, there would be fewer people studying aging and probably more studying sex.

So we must not simply dismiss the riddle of attractiveness. That does not mean that we deny, or even ignore, the evidence of stable, physical bases of attractiveness. Rather, it means that we try to isolate and understand the field effect. So we do not need to worry about the fact that our female guppy passes by a truly deformed and downright ugly male without a second glance and that no amount of clever manipulations will change that. This fact may not require a field explanation, but it does not disprove one either. But, where we *do* see a field effect, we need to determine what changes for the female when she sees her rival approach another male.

The popularity tournament is, I have argued, perhaps the simplest example of a field that we have. This is because a field is, in many senses, a terrain of organized institutions, and a popularity tournament is the institutionalization of the fact of institutionalization. By *institutionalization*, we generally mean a regularization of expectations that leads to transpersonally valid interlocks between actions and meanings. Thus, holding out a hand "means" something because there "is" an institution of a handshake. The existence of such institutions can be understood as a collapse between first- and second-order statements. The former refer to our own relation to the world, for example: "Bill Cosby is a very funny fellow," or, "I am Soviet intelligence agent." The latter refer to *others'* relations, usually compiled, as in, "Most people find Bill Cosby very funny," or, "At work, they think I come from Idaho." In many cases, we can oppose these—"at work, they think I come from Idaho, but, in fact, I am Soviet intelligence agent." An institution, as I think David Bloor (1997) has said more elegantly than others, is when these two orders are inseparable, even coterminous. An example might be citizenship—to be a citizen is to be recognized as being a citizen. Bourdieu (e.g., 1994) was interested in this as an example of nomination, arguing that state power could be such as to have overwhelming effects on the process of institutionalization. But the key thing is this collapse—the inability to say, "No one recognizes that I am a citizen, but trust me, I am."

We cannot imagine it making any sense to say, "I am very popular indeed, but everybody thinks I'm not," because the popularity tournament is the process of an endogenous institutionalization. We must examine such systems—like the "rating and dating" system famously described by Willard Waller (1937)—not just in terms of their temporal development (which can be modeled as if it were the evolution of a set of choices), but also in terms of their synchronic phenomenology, for here we see the *experience* of institutionalization, which is not a diachronic pronouncement but a continuous living. Calling this a *reproduction* theory is to trivialize and in fact split apart the need to understand this phenomenological unity. That is, if the popularity tournament produces a field effect, actors will directly perceive the aggregated and organized perceptions of others, for the attractiveness of one for another incorporates (literally) this one's attractiveness to all others. They agree, not because they agree to agree, or because in a game theoretic fashion they choose to invest in what others seem to want, but because the set of relations leaves traces in their experience of social objects.

How do we understand this? Here, I would like to return to the writings of the greatest phenomenological field theorist, Wolfgang Köhler (1944/1971, 364; cf. Köhler 1938, 77; and Dewey 1929, 405). In the course of arguing that the qualities of objects had to be understood as being present in the objects—and hence that these were not subjective additions made by an arbitrary will of the perceiver—he used the example (typical for a male German scholar of his day) of men succumbing to the charms of women. Could it be said that the charms are really in the men, as would be implied by a conventional account that considered all values subjective? Obviously not, he concluded; therefore, the charms must be in the women.

Köhler thus made an opposition between (on the one hand) each man singly as perceiving subject and (on the other hand) each woman singly as perceived object. He discounted the possibility that the charms are in the men as organized aggregate, or in the entire ensemble of social relations. But that is more or less what Waller (1937) argued was the basis of the dating logic—that women desired by many men were desirable simply on account of their desirability. Building on the quite different logic of Lévi-Strauss (1949/1969), Gayle Rubin (1985) emphasized that it made perfect sense that women would serve as units to order relations between males.

Now Rubin was basically wrong in terms of her idea that you could take theories of the exchange of women developed from study of the kinship structure from some societies and apply them to very different societies (those of Europe, whose incest laws come not from exogamous marriage classes but from the entrepreneurial tendencies of the Catholic Church, which progressively extended the idea of "relatedness" as a revenue-generating scheme, as costly dispensations were increasingly necessary given the normal tangle of premodern communities). But, analytically, this is on the right track. That is, the one thing we know about so-called exchange structures is that women are *not* being exchanged as if they were objects. But women *are* objects, and indeed they are so *especially* where they are not exchanged. The problem is that we have misunderstood what it means to be an object, imagining (quite illogically) that an object cannot be a subject.

In the gestalt tradition, an object is a phenomenologically valid unity, even though its simple existence cannot be demonstrated through definitions using logical deduction. That is, we perceive a mountain as such even though it has no clear boundary lines. So, if we insisted on being axiomatic, we might have to admit there really is no "such thing" as "the mountain." But one person can say to another, "Meet me at the top of the mountain," and the two can end up in the same place. The Republican Party is an object, in that we have knowledge about it, we know what it has done, and what its qualities are; indeed, I know its relative position to me—off to the far, far right.

But, if an object is not a thing, what is it? An object is *a bundle of relations*—a set of relations *crystallized* to the extent that it can bear attributes. Köhler's women might be objects if their charms were in part the relations of desire that the men as organized set had to the females as a second set. They are objects because the qualities they bear—and that they bear perceivably—would vanish if the web of relations was destroyed. In a situation in which men's attractiveness was similarly defined, the men would identically be objects (and men are objects for and in other respects). This idea of mutual definition gets to the heart of the duality that Ronald Breiger (2000; also 1974) has shown to be intrinsic to Bourdieu's methodological approach. It is not at all that the objectification of women devalues them—it is on the contrary that it *values* them, with values that index the internal relations of members of an exogenous set (men). Anything unpleasant about this experience comes from the heteronomy inherent not in being worthless but in being worthful for another.[5] To return to the idea of endogenous popularity, it seems significant that in many American dating systems women's value seemed to be *more* endogenous than that of men; men's status was easier to predict on the basis of other attributes than was women's, women's status was more labile and easier to game, and there were institutions for men to demonstrate their evaluation of the worth of their date (e.g., the corsage [Bailey 1988])—none were needed for women, because women *were* the currency anchored to the male gold standards of parentage, salary, and football.

The objectification of women in this specific sense is a good template for objectification in general—the transmutation of a set of relationships into a sensible "thing" with attributes that index these relationships. It is this that Marx (1867/1906) saw as the fetishism of commodities—the fact that we can imagine that value is *in* a particular physical product, and in fact feel it, sense it, there. But the value is really in the set of relations around the object (also see Simmel 1907/1978). Like the Churinga discussed by Durkheim (1912/1954) in the *Elementary Forms*, the object glows with borrowed magic because it incarnates social relations. And *this* is the core phenomenological experience from which a field effect stems.

But it is not only this. It is that this field effect, the seemingly isolated perception of an object by a person, *itself* invokes the field as a whole—and not by fiat, in that "field theory always starts from the whole." Rather, this seemingly isolated perception itself can be studied, in itself, only by recourse to the field. And this is because, as we pursue the logic further, we find a strict duality between objects and positions—the two are related to one another as perception is to apperception, or what Bourdieu calls *a sense of one's place*.

Seen from the perspective of the men (as Köhler did), this set of relationships may appear incarnated as quality, but, seen from the perspective of the women, it may appear as position (in this case, perhaps a position of differential charmingness in a specifically sexual field). To understand the perception of attractiveness is to understand the "more" that can arise when social relations are aligned—when we produce a field.

## From Decisionmaking to Judgment

We began from the common way of speaking about *sexual decisionmaking*, which implies that we take the perspective of a generic actor who is attempting to use reason and foresight to secure the best results given his or her preexisting preferences and a changing situation partly out of his or her control. But the field approach reorients us to look, not at the choices made by the actor (actors do make choices, sometimes, but not all actions, even free ones, are best understood as choices), but at the intersubjectively valid qualities of the objects in the world that surround the actor. The crucial cognitive relation of the actor to these objects is not choice but *judgment*—the ability to perceive (or "intuit") the qualities of these objects.[6] The person running toward a cry for help may do so freely, but he does not choose this direction (say, in degrees, 275°) by arraying all 360 possible directions in degrees and selecting one. Rather, he responds to the affordance inherent in the environment, which perceptually changes as the cry is heard (Koffka 1935, 43).

Similarly, as health professionals can report (to their great frustration), many sex acts do not seem to be the result of any decision at all. Of course, some distinctly calculating types may make many decisions, but in many cases even where we believe as actors that we have made a choice, we have difficulty giving any accounting that does not start from the qualities of the object outside us—its compelling nature, the field that has drawn us in. This is theoretically plausible, agreeing with what the behavioral sciences have told us about people and their capacity to make rational choices (e.g., Wilson and Brekke 1994). But it complicates our avenues of plausible research. We must zero in on the experience actors have of the world and not be overly swayed by the seemingly rational post factum accountings that actors give. I close by considering how we can perhaps best accomplish the next steps.

## For the Future

Our basic problem is that the core issues are those of phenomenology, but most of our data are—and should be—behavioral. (Simply put, our own recollections of our experiences are suspect, and from other people we get behavior, not direct access to subjectivity.) We are likely to make the greatest progress if we turn our attention to cases in which sexual field effects are likely to be strong and "simple," and where we can get data that are as close to unprocessed experience as is possible.

Of course, perhaps nothing is "simple," but we can accept that field effects are clearest where fields are most autonomous, and so we must focus on cases of relative purity of the field, even though impurity is the rule and purity the exception. That is, we want to avoid situations in which the heteronomy of everyday life leads to *compromise*—where a person's action is in part attributable to the field effect and in part to something else. Most obviously, we want to avoid marriage, in which there are, even in "love" systems, widely recognized trade-offs (yes, he is attractive, but he is so poor). The evidence suggests that the more serious and permanent the relationship, the more social homogamy has a hand in predicting who will pair with whom (see, e.g., Laumann, Gagnon, Michael, and Michaels 1994, 255).[7] It might well be that there is an actual phenomenological effect here—that is, that some men or women are actually sexually desirable as spouses even though they are not desirable as one-night stands—but it will be hard to be sure before analytically more tractable cases are dealt with.

For, if we look at the simplest case of the field effect, the popularity tournament, and find that there actually *is no* inherent and autonomous field effect, I think we should be very happy to abandon field theory and move to some sort of classic action theory. That is, if our female guppy (or the human equivalent) does *not* perceive the male as any more attractive after the rival approaches, but instead *calculates*, "Well, he doesn't seem that hot to me, but maybe she knows something I don't," then we need not appeal to field theoretic processes for our explanation of this case. If her perception itself *does* change, the question is how and in precisely what ways. (Further, it is perhaps worth restating that, as not all sexual action takes place in the sexual field, we must be looking in the right place if we are to have a chance of finding a clear field effect.)

So we are looking for the phenomenological investigation of the perception of attractiveness largely in casual relationships or in the consideration of same. Second, we want to avoid confusing outcomes with inputs. We do want to make sure that we are not asking general, abstract questions, like, "What kinds of people are attractive to you?" and thereby invoking subjects' *theories*. But we also want to make sure that we understand that what people do is not always their first choice, and that a great deal of information can be gathered from asking people how they see others—both in yes/no checklist format and in richer detail.

Third, we may want to privilege investigations of same-sex desire. This is both because such relationships are more divorced from the homophilous tendencies of marriage and because they are of greater analytic tractability simply because (as George [1996] has said), since theories of sexual capitalization are themselves often moves within the field, a theory of the sexual field is an immediately useful club in the boy-girl wars. We know that not all men or women see things the same as others of their sex (and that there are structured divisions other than gender that are relevant), but our theories of the theories of the sexes too greatly inform our theories of the sex. Further, there is an obvious reason to focus on male same-sex desire because there have been and still are more male arenas of exclusively sexual organization that produce extremely strong field effects with high phenomenological recognizability. That has an obvious danger—we do not want a theory of sex that is a theory of only male sexuality. A focus on homosexual male fields might well lead to a huge bias in our understanding of sex but might still provide a serious improvement in our basic phenomenology of field theory.[8]

Fourth, we want to use a number of different methods, even those associated with banal or cruel research traditions. It is easy to confuse how people talk about how *others* are with how people talk about how *they* are with how people *are*, and hence we need to bring together data of many different sorts—not only in situ observation, but also in-depth interview data, survey data (especially relational data), Facebook™ data, and experimental data, though we want to avoid the premature conclusions as to ill-understood "effects" that have characterized this sort of work in many cases. And we even want, in the abstract, biological and bodily data (e.g., changes in blood flow, free hormone production, nasal and pupil dilation, and so forth). It seems that, for the near future, there will be serious limits to our ability to collect these data, although we have underexplored the possibility of using animals as coresearchers, given how sensitive dogs and chimps (say) are to our body language and scent production.[9]

Fifth, we need participant observation. Lynn Chancer (1998, 173) once tried to provoke sociology into a reflection as to why it was assumed that it would be impossible for a female field researcher to study prostitution via prostitution—to do what Loïc Wacquant (2004) has called a *carnal sociology*. We have not yet answered the questions she raised (see also Bernstein 2007). We cannot go forward if there is no room for the sort of trial and error that allows ethnographers to understand whether they have mastered a foreign culture.

But any such research has to use systematic research design and data collection if it is not to degenerate into lurid gossip or idiosyncratic reflection. And it has to be focused on answering key questions. These seem to me to involve the nature of sexual judgment, and not decisionmaking, or even patterns of stratification (which are, after all, really about the marginal distribution of a particular population under study). One question (mentioned above) has to do with whether there are attributes that are not seen as sexually attractive yet compensate for attractiveness—how are they perceived? Does the young attractive woman pursuing what Parsons (1942/1949, 225) called the *female glamour pattern* and catching a rich old man find his richness attractive? Not sexually attractive but compelling in some other way (a vector toward)? Or does she find him repugnant, but she holds her nose (a vector away from)? A second question has to do with types of relations (e.g., short-term vs. open-ended in duration). Do some people *appear* more attractive to those seeking certain types of relations (and not "certain types of relations-with"), the same way in which people's appearance tells us what to do with them? Gestalt theory focused on the fact that we can intuit the "affordances" of an object—that a shoe can be used for foot protection but also as a hammer.[10] This is a necessary place to start, though not to end. First, as Gibson (1979/1986, 143) pointed out: "When Koffka asserted that 'each thing says what it is,' he failed to mention that it may lie." Second, *we* may be wrong—the branch tells us that it can support our weight, but it cracks, and we fall to our deaths. But we cannot leave to pop psychology an investigation of how the way in which we look suggests to others what they should, or can, do with or to us. Any move away from a single vertical dimension of attractiveness that treats us all not simply as comparable but as quantitative will have to deal with the horizontal differentiation of Freud's (1938, 553) idea of what we "aim" to do with the "object" of desire—and the fact that there is no undifferentiated "we" here.

So, actually, the most relevant work would *not* be systematically having sex with people and recording the resulting data. Rather, it should be comparable to Brian Lande's (2010) study of the process of basic training for the police, and the development of a particular habitus, or Matt Desmond's (2007) work, or of course Wacquant's (2004). The best thing would be if we could delay puberty and go through it with a Bourdieusian ethnographer's eye. Another rare but theoretically crucial case would be a sex change operation on the part of the ethnographer, especially where sexual object choice changes as well (see, e.g., Schilt 2010, 67ff.), or perhaps something short of this but going beyond the Griffin (1961) approach of make-believe. But there may also be low-impact situations in which we can repeatedly expose ourselves to semiexperimental treatments and record our own conceptions and learning experiences.[11]

In sum, field theory is not simply a vocabulary that we can use to spice up an otherwise dull account of human interaction. It is the most promising way forward in having a systematic study of human interaction, our subject. It may turn out to be a dead end, but the only way to tell will be to go further. Right now, field theory seems to combine the rigor, systematicity, and reflexivity of any social science with the key to our humanness, namely, the qualitative experience of the world that is examined by phenomenology. I would like to end by quoting the words used by William James (1890/1950, 2:438) as he concluded his discussion of historical changes in sexual behavior as an example of the ways in which habit forms our sexual desires: "These details are a little unpleasant to dis-

cuss, but they show so beautifully the correctness of the general principles in the light of which our review has been made, that it was impossible to pass them over unremarked."

## Notes

1. This is a condensed version of an argument made with more specificity in
*The Explanation of Social Action* (Martin 2011).

2. Indeed, this was the puzzle that perhaps started this chain of theorizing.
Kant's key work on aesthetics had been preceded by his essay *Observations on
the Feeling of the Beautiful and the Sublime* (1763/1960), the title clearly a reference to Burke's earlier *A Philosophical Enquiry into the Origin of Our Ideas of
the Sublime and Beautiful.* There, Burke (1756/1937, 37–38), like Rousseau a year
earlier in his *Discourse* (1755/1967), emphasized that humans are different from
animals in having no periodicity to their sexual desire. This brought him to the
section "Of Beauty" in which he began by denying that animals' mating preferences were due to a sense of beauty (e.g., they find their own species more beautiful than others)—only man's love responses combine this physical aspect with
*social* qualities that "direct and heighten the appetite which he has in common
with other animals" (what Rousseau [1755/1967, 205] referred to as the "moral"
part of love "engendered by society, and cried up by the women with great care
and address in order to establish their empire, and secure command to that sex
which ought to obey"). Burke also noted that it was difficult to explain the results of our sense of beauty (preferring the company of other persons or even animals who inspire this feeling in us) in terms of utility (e.g., what we might now
consider fitness). Further, he specifically considered the vectoral nature of qualities when defining the nature of beauty: "By beauty I mean that [sensible] quality or those qualities in bodies, by which they cause love, or some passion similar to it. . . . I likewise distinguish love . . . from desire or lust; which is an energy
of the mind, that hurries us on to the possession of certain objects, that do not
affect us as they are beautiful, but by means altogether different. [For] we shall
have a strong desire for a woman of no remarkable beauty; whilst the greatest
beauty in men, or in other animals, though it causes love, yet excites nothing
at all of desire" (1756/1937, 75). Finally, Burke made an explicit comparison to
the field of gravity and castigated Newton for attempting a mechanical explanation. In his section on the "efficient cause" of beauty, Burke carefully noted that
he was not attempting to explain the ultimate cause: "This is all, I believe, we
can do. . . . When Newton first discovered the property of attraction, and settled
its laws, he found it served very well to explain several of the most remarkable
phenomena in nature; but yet, with reference to the general system of things, he
could consider attraction but as an effect, whose cause at that time he did not attempt to trace. But when he afterwards began to account for it by a subtle elas-

tic aether, this great man . . . seemed to have quitted his usual cautious manner of philosophizing [and left us no better off than before]" (1756/1937, 103).

3. What they try to do afterward may also be analyzed in field theoretic terms, but, for purposes of simplicity, I ignore that here.

4. Indeed, in English, we use the case of the visual observation of the aging of vegetation as an expression to indicate intense boredom; strangely, in German, to *hear* the grass grow means to believe that one is all-knowing.

5. "In so far as I am the object of values which come to qualify me without my being able to act on this qualification or even to know it, I am enslaved" (Sartre 1956, 267).

6. In hindsight, we see that George's (1996) original contribution made the same problematic turn that we see in Dilthey's (1883/1998) and Simmel's (1905/1977) contributions to the philosophy of history, namely, to believe that the model for their endeavors should be Kant's *first* critique, that of pure reason, and not his *third*, which turned on judgment.

7. The exception is that certain short-term relations are very homogamous.

8. It also might lead to an underestimation of the field effects if the way that men judge bodies is more easily reducible to a set of specified visual patterns. This then pushes back the problem to a more complex one of the development of the visual standards and their own dispersion and internal syntax. Although this development may ultimately be explainable in terms of the endogenous constitution of the set of relations constituting a sexual field (or, for some hegemonically enforced corporeal archetypes, e.g., "clones," a smaller "erotic world" in Green's [2008] terminology), the task becomes harder the less variation in attractiveness there is independent of body type.

9. There are potential downsides with this; I have noticed that, at least in movies, whenever a chimpanzee enters a bar, a brawl is sure to erupt.

10. Hannah Arendt (1963) considered this knowledge special to women, given that their heels work quite well as hammers, but I have seen a male professional builder, the owner of six hammers, attempt to pound in a nail with a sneaker he happened to be wearing because shoes announce their capacity for hammering.

11. Finally, and in special reference to the issue of how different people read different bodies, I have had a number of colleagues admit that this would be a good idea, although no one has been willing to write a proposal, but I think perhaps the single best way to proceed would be to combine a phone-sex line with a computer-assisted telephone interviewing system that could randomize various treatments and see how patrons responded. It would allow us to find out how at least some people understand the positions of different types of bodies in a sexual field, how they connect these to different scripts, and, indeed, what sorts of mismatches they intuit as inherently violating the logic of the field. It would also be self-funding.

# References

Adam, Barry. 1985. "Age, Structure, and Sexuality." *Journal of Homosexuality* 11:19–33.

———. 2005. "Constructing the Neoliberal Sexual Actor." *Culture, Health and Sexuality* 7, no. 4:333–46.

Adam, Barry D., Winston Husbands, James Murray, and John Maxwell. 2008a. "Circuits, Networks, and HIV Risk Management." *AIDS Education and Prevention* 20, no. 5:420–35.

———. 2008b. "Silence, Assent, and HIV Risk." *Culture, Health and Sexuality* 10, no. 8:759–72.

Adkins, L. 2002. *Revisions: Gender and Sexuality in Late Modernity*. Philadelphia: Open University Press.

Akers, Aletha Yvette, Cheryl P. Lynch, Melanie A. Gold, Judy Chia-Chi Chang, Willa Doswell, Harold C. Wiesenfeld, Wentao Feng, and James Bost. 2009. "Exploring the Relationship among Weight, Race, and Sexual Behaviors among Girls." *Pediatrics* 124, no. 5:913–20.

Altman, Dennis. 2001. *Global Sex*. Chicago: University of Chicago Press.

Arendt, Hannah. 1963. *Between Past and Future*. Cleveland: Meridian.

Armstrong, Elizabeth. 2010a. "Bringing Bourdieu to Sexual Life." Paper presented at the conference "Bringing Bourdieu to Sexual Life," University of Toronto, May 22.

———. 2010b. "Sluts." Paper presented at conference "Bringing Bourdieu to Sexual Life," University of Toronto, May 22.

Armstrong, Elizabeth, Laura Hamilton, and Brian Sweeney. 2006. "Sexual Assault on Campus: A Multilevel, Integrative Approach to Party Rape." *Social Problems* 53:483–99.

Bailey, Beth L. 1988. *From Front Porch to Back Seat*. Baltimore: Johns Hopkins University Press.

Bearman, Peter S., James Moody, and Katherine Stovel. 2004. "Chains of Affection: The Structure of Adolescent Romantic and Sexual Networks." *American Journal of Sociology* 110:44–91.

Bech, Henning. 1997. *When Men Meet: Homosexuality and Modernity.* Chicago: University of Chicago Press.

Benjamin, Jessica. 1988. *The Bonds of Love: Psychoanalysis, Feminism and the Problem of Domination.* New York: Pantheon.

Bernstein, Basil B. 1971. *Class, Codes and Control.* London: Routledge & Kegan Paul.

Bernstein, Elizabeth. 2007. *Temporarily Yours.* Chicago: University of Chicago Press.

Bersani, Leo. 1987. "Is the Rectum a Grave?" *AIDS: Cultural Analysis/Cultural Activism* 43:197–222.

———. 1995. *Homos.* Cambridge, MA: Harvard University Press.

Birken, L. 1988. *Consuming Desire: Sexual Science and the Emergence of a Culture of Abundance, 1871–1914.* Ithaca, NY: Cornell University Press.

Bloor, David. 1997. *Wittgenstein, Rules and Institutions.* London: Routledge

Bockting, Walter, Michael Miner, and B. R. Rosser. 2007. "Latino Men's Sexual Behavior with Transgender Persons." *Archives of Sexual Behavior* 36: 778–86.

Bourdieu, Pierre. 1977. *Outline of a Theory of Practice.* Cambridge: Cambridge University Press

———. 1979/1984. *Distinction: A Social Critique of the Judgment of Taste.* Translated by Richard Nice. Cambridge, MA: Harvard University Press.

———. 1983/1986. "The Forms of Capital." In *Handbook of Theory and Research for the Sociology of Education*, ed. J. G. Richardson, 241–58. New York: Greenwood.

———. 1989/1996. *The State Nobility.* Translated by L. C. Clough. Stanford, CA: Stanford University Press.

———. 1990a. *In Other Words.* Translated by M. Adamson. Stanford, CA: Stanford University Press.

———. 1990b. *The Logic of Practice.* Cambridge: Polity.

———. 1990c. *Reproduction: In Education, Society and Culture* London: Sage.

———. 1992/1996. *The Rules of Art.* Translated by Susan Emanuel. Stanford, CA: Stanford University Press.

———. 1994. "Rethinking the State: Genesis and Structure of the Bureaucratic Field." Translated by Loïc J. D. Wacquant and Samar Farage. *Sociological Theory* 12:1–18.

———. 1997a. *Pascalian Meditations.* Translated by R. Nice. Stanford, CA: Stanford University Press.

———. 1997b. *Pascalian Meditations.* Translated by Richard Nice. Cambridge: Polity.

———. 1998/2001. *Masculine Domination.* Translated by R. Nice. Stanford, CA: Stanford University Press.

———. 2001/2003. *Firing Back.* Translated by L. Wacquant. New York: New Press.

———. 2002/2008. *The Bachelor's Ball.* Translated by R. Nice. Chicago: University of Chicago Press.

———. 2004/2008. *Pierre Bourdieu: Sketch for a Self-Analysis.* Translated by R. Nice. Chicago: University of Chicago Press.

———. 2012. *Picturing Algeria.* Edited by Franz Schultheis and Christine Frisinghelli. New York: Columbia University Press.

Bourdieu, Pierre, and Loïc Wacquant. 1992. *Invitation to a Reflexive Sociology.* Chicago: University of Chicago Press.

Breiger, Ronald L. 1974. "The Duality of Persons and Groups." *Social Forces* 53:181–90.

———. 2000. "A Tool-Kit for Practice Theory." *Poetics* 27:91–115.

Brekhus, Wayne. 2003. *Peacocks, Chameleons, Centaurs: Gay Suburbia and the Grammar of Social Identity.* Chicago: University of Chicago Press.

Brubaker, Rogers. 1985. "Rethinking Classical Theory: The Sociological Vision of Pierre Bourdieu." *Theory and Society* 14:745–75.

———. 1993. "Social Theory as Habitus." In *Bourdieu: Critical Perspectives*, ed. C. Edward LiPuma and M. Postone, 212–234. Chicago: University of Chicago Press.

Burke, Edmund. 1756/1937. *Philosophical Inquiry into the Origin of Our Ideas of the Sublime and Beautiful.* New York: P. F. Collier & Son.

Buss, David M., Todd K. Shackelford, Lee A. Kirkpatrick, and Randy J. Larsen. 2001. "A Half Century of Mate Preferences: The Cultural Evolution of Values." *Journal of Marriage and Family* 63:491–503.

Butler, Judith. 1990. *Gender Trouble: Feminism and the Subversion of Identity.* London: Routledge.

Caceres, C. F., and J. I. Cortinas. 1996. "Fantasy Island: An Ethnography of Alcohol and Gender Roles in a Latino Gay Bar." *Journal of Drug Issues* 26:245–51.

Canaday, Margot. 2009. *The Straight State: Sexuality and Citizenship in Twentieth Century America.* Princeton, NJ: Princeton University Press.

Carter, Julian B. 2007. *The Heart of Whiteness: Normal Sexuality and Race in America, 1880–1940.* Durham, NC: Duke University Press.

Chancer, Lynn. 1998. *Reconcilable Differences.* Berkeley and Los Angeles: University of California Press.

Chauncey, G. 1994. *Gay New York: Gender, Urban Culture, and the Making of the Gay World, 1890–1940.* New York: Basic.

Chodorow, Nancy. 1994. *Femininities, Masculinities, Sexualities: Freud and Beyond.* Lexington: University Press of Kentucky.

Coan, Dara L., Willow Schrager, and Tracey Packer. 2005. "The Role of the Male Sexual Partners in HIV Infection among Male-to-Female Transgendered Individuals." *International Journal of Transgenderism*, 8:21–30.

Connell, R. W. 1995. *Masculinities*. Berkeley and Los Angeles: University of California Press.

Constable, Nicole. 2003. *Romance on a Global Stage: Pen Pals, Virtual Ethnography, and "Mail Order" Marriages*. Berkeley and Los Angeles: University of California Press.

Cooley, Charles H. 1902. *Human Nature and the Social Order*. New York: Scribner's.

D'Emilio, John. 1983. *Sexual Politics, Sexual Communities: The Making of a Homosexual Minority in the United States, 1940–1970*. Chicago: University of Chicago Press.

Desmond, Matt. 2007. *On the Fireline*. Chicago: University of Chicago Press.

Desroches, Frederick. 1990. "Tearoom Trade." *Qualitative Sociology* 13, no. 1:39–61.

Dewey, John. 1929. *Experience and Nature*. New York: Norton.

Dilthey, Wilhelm. 1883/1988. *Introduction to the Human Sciences*. Translated by Ramon J. Betanzos. Detroit: Wayne State University Press.

DiMaggio, Paul J., ed. 1987. *Nonprofit Enterprise in the Arts: Studies in Mission and Constraint*. Oxford: Oxford University Press.

Dor, Joël. 2001. *Structure and Perversions*. New York: Other.

Dugatkin, Lee Alan. 1996. "Interface between Culturally Based Preferences and Genetic Preferences: Female Mate Choice in *Poecilia reticulata*." *Proceedings of the National Academy of Sciences* 93:2770–73.

Durkheim, Emile. 1912/1954. *The Elementary Forms of Religious Life*. Translated by Joseph Ward Swain. Glencoe, IL: Free Press.

Eisenberg, Marla E., Dianne Neumark-Sztainer, and Katherine Lust. 2005. "Weight-Related Issues and High-Risk Sexual Behaviors among College Students." *Journal of American College Health* 54:95–101.

Emirbayer, Mustafa, and Victoria Johnson. 2008. "Bourdieu and Organizational Analysis." *Theory and Society* 37:1–44.

Eng, David. 2001. *Racial Castration: Managing Masculinity in Asian America*. Durham, NC: Duke University Press.

England, Paula, and Elizabeth Aura McClintock. 2009. "The Gendered Double Standard of Aging in US Marriage Markets." *Population and Development Review* 35:797–816.

Epstein, Steven. 1991. "Sexuality and Identity: The Contribution of Object Relations Theory to a Constructionist Sociology." *Theory and Society* 20:825–73.

Erwin, Kathleen. 1999. "White Women, Male Desires: A Televisual Fantasy of the Transnational Chinese Family." In *Spaces of Their Own: Women's Public*

*Sphere in Transnational China*, ed. M. M. Yang, 232–57. Minneapolis: University of Minnesota Press.

Farrer, James. 2002. *Opening Up: Youth Sex Culture and Market Reform in Shanghai.* Chicago: University of Chicago Press.

———. 2006. "Sexual Citizenship and the Politics of Sexual Storytelling among Chinese Youth." In *Sex and Sexuality China*, ed. Elaine Jeffries, 102–23. London: Routledge.

———. 2008. "From 'Passports' to 'Joint Ventures': Intermarriage between Chinese Nationals and Western Expatriates Residing in Shanghai." *Asian Studies Review* 32, no. 1:7–29.

———. 2010a. "A Foreign Adventurer's Paradise? Interracial Sexuality and Alien Sexual Capital in Reform Era Shanghai." *Sexualities* 13, no. 1:69–95.

———. 2010b. "New Shanghailanders or New Shanghainese? Narratives of Emplacement of Western Expatriate Settlers in Shanghai." *Journal of Ethnic and Migration Studies* 36, no. 6:1–18.

———. 2011. "Global Nightscapes in Shanghai as Ethnosexual Contact Zones." *Journal of Ethnic and Migration Studies* 37, no. 5:747–64.

Farrer, James, and Zhongxin Sun. 2003. "Extramarital Love in Shanghai." *China Journal* 50:1–36.

Ferguson, Priscilla Parkhurst. 1998. "A Cultural Field in the Making: Gastronomy in 19th Century France." *Journal of American Sociology* 104:597–641.

Fischer, Claude. 1975. "Toward a Subcultural Theory of Urbanism." *American Journal of Sociology* 80:1319–41.

———. 1976. *The Urban Experience.* New York: Harcourt Brace Jovanovich.

Fitzgerald, Frances. *Cities on a Hill.* 1986. New York: Simon & Schuster.

Fligstein, Neil. 2001. *The Architecture of Markets.* Princeton N.J.: Princeton University Press.

Foucault, Michel. 1975. *Discipline and Punish: The Birth of the Prison.* New York: Vintage.

———. 1980. *The History of Sexuality.* Vol. 1, *An Introduction.* New York: Vintage.

Freud, Sigmund. 1938. "Three Contributions to the Theory of Sex." In *The Basic Writings of Sigmund Freud*, trans. and ed. A. A. Brill, 553–629. New York: Modern Library.

———. 1961. *Civilization and Its Discontents.* In *The Standard Edition of the Complete Psychological Works of Sigmund Freud* (24 vols.), ed. James Strachey, 21:57–146. London: Hogarth.

———. 1962/2000. *Three Essays on the Theory of Sexuality.* New York: Basic.

Gamble, Jos. 2003. *Shanghai in Transition: Changing Perspectives and Social Contours of a Chinese Metropolis.* London: Routledge Curzon.

George, Matt C. 1996. "The Critique of Sexual Reason." PhD. diss., University of California, Berkeley.

Gibson, James J. 1979/1986. *The Ecological Approach to Visual Perception.* Hillsdale, NJ: Erlbaum.

Giddens, Anthony. 1986. *Constitution of Society: Outline of the Theory of Structuration.* Berkeley and Los Angeles: University of California Press.

———. 1991. *Modernity and Self Identity.* Stanford, CA: Stanford University Press.

———. 1992. *The Transformation of Intimacy: Sexuality, Love and Eroticism in Modern Societies.* Stanford, CA: Stanford University Press.

Gilligan, Carol. 1982. *In a Different Voice.* Cambridge, MA: Harvard University Press.

Glaeser, Andreas. 2010. Keynote address, twelfth annual Chicago Ethnography Conference, DePaul University (Loop Campus), March 6.

Gonzales, Alicia M., and Gary Rolison. 2005. "Social Oppression and Attitudes toward Sexual Practices." *Journal of Black Studies* 35, no. 6:715–29.

Goode, William J. 1959. "The Theoretical Importance of Love." *American Sociological Review* 24:38–47.

Gould, Terry. 1998. *The Lifestyle: A Look at the Erotic Rites of Swingers.* Toronto: Vintage.

Green, Adam Isaiah. 2007. "Queer Theory and Sociology: Locating the Subject and the Self in Sexuality Studies." *Sociological Theory* 25, no. 1:26–45.

———. 2008a. "Erotic Habitus: Toward a Sociology of Desire." *Theory and Society* 37:597–626.

———. 2008b. "Health and Sexual Status in an Urban Gay Enclave: An Application of the Stress Process Model." *Journal of Health and Social Behavior* 49:436–51.

———. 2008c. "The Social Organization of Desire: The Sexual Fields Approach." *Sociological Theory* 26, no. 1:25–50.

———. 2011. "Playing the (Sexual) Field: The Interactional Basis of Sexual Stratification." *Social Psychology Quarterly* 74:244–66.

———. 2013. "'Erotic Capital' and the Power of Desirability: Why 'Honey Money' Is a Bad Collective Strategy for Remedying Gender Inequality." *Sexualities* 16:137–58.

Green, Adam Isaiah, M. Follert, K. Osterlund, and J. Paquin. 2010. "Space, Place and Sexual Sociality: 'Toward an Atmospheric Analysis.'" *Gender, Work and Organization* 17:7–27.

Griffin, John Howard. 1961. *Black Like Me.* Boston: Houghton Mifflin.

Hakim, Catherine. 2010. "Erotic Capital." *European Sociological Review* 26:499–518.

———. 2011. *Honey Money: The Power of Erotic Capital.* London: Allen Lane.

Halperin, David. 1989. "Is There a History of Sexuality?" *History and Theory* 28:252–74.

———. 1993. "Is There a History of Sexuality?" In *The Lesbian and Gay Studies Reader*, ed. Henry Abelove, Michele Aina Barale, and David Halperin, 416–31. London: Routledge.

———. 1997. *Saint Foucault: Towards a Gay Hagiography*. Oxford: Oxford University Press.

———. 2002. *How To Do the History of Homosexuality*. Chicago: University of Chicago Press.

Hamilton, Laura, and Elizabeth Armstrong. 2009. "Gendered Sexuality in Young Adulthood: Double Binds and Flawed Options." *Gender and Society* 23:589–616.

Hammack, Phillip L., and Bertram J. Cohler. 2009. "Narrative Engagement and Stories of Sexual Identity." In *The Story of Sexual Identity*, ed. Phillip L. Hammack and Bertram J. Cohler, 3–48. Oxford: Oxford University Press.

Hebdige, Dick. 1979. *Subculture: The Meaning of Style*. London: Routledge.

Hennen, Peter. 2001. "Powder, Pomp, Power: Toward a Typology and Genealogy of Effeminacies." *Social Thought and Research* 24, nos. 1–2:121–44.

———. 2008. *Faeries, Bears, and Leathermen: Gay Men in Community Queering the Masculine*. Chicago: University of Chicago Press.

Herdt, Gilbert, and Andrew Boxer. 1992. *Gay Culture in America*. Boston: Beacon.

Heritage, John. *Garfinkel and Ethnomethodology*. Cambridge: Polity, 1984.

Ho, Petula S. Y., and A. K. T. Tsang. 2000. "Negotiating Anal Intercourse in Inter-Racial Gay Relationships in Hong Kong." *Sexualities* 3, no. 3:299–323.

Hollister, John. 2004. "Beyond the Interaction Membrane." *International Journal of Sociology and Social Policy* 24, nos. 3–5:73–94.

Hospers, Harm, Sjaak Molenaar, and Gerjo Kok. 1994. "Focus Group Interviews with Risk-Taking Gay Men." *Patient Education and Counseling* 24:299–306.

Humphreys, Laud. 1970/1975. *Tearoom Trade: Impersonal Sex in Public Places*. Expanded ed. Chicago: Aldine.

Illouz, E. 2007. *Cold Intimacies: The Making of Emotional Capitalism*, Cambridge: Polity.

Jackson, S., and S. Scott. 2007. "Faking Like a Woman? Towards an Interpretive Theorization of Sexual Pleasure." *Body and Society* 13:95–98.

James, William. 1890/1950. *The Principles of Psychology*. 4 vols. New York: Dover.

Jamieson, L. 1988. *Intimacy: Personal Relationships in Modern Societies*. Cambridge: Polity.

Jenkins, Richard. 1992. *Pierre Bourdieu*. London: Routledge.

Kalish, Rachel, and Michael Kimmel. 2011. "Hooking Up: Hot Hetero Sex, or the New Numb?" *Australian Feminist Studies* 26:137–51.

Kant, Immanuel. 1763/1960. *Observations on the Feeling of the Beautiful and the Sublime*. Translated by John T. Goldthwait. Berkeley: University of California Press.

———. 1790/1987. *Critique of Judgment*. Translated by Werner S. Pluhar. Indianapolis: Hackett.

Kelly, Jeffrey A., Janet S. St. Lawrence, L. Yvonne Stevenson, Allan C. Hauth, Seth C. Kalichman, Yolanda E. Diaz, Ted L. Brasfield, Jeffrey J. Koob, and Michael G. Morgan. 1992. "Community AIDS/HIV Risk Reduction: The Effects of Endorsements by Popular People in Three Cities." *American Journal of Public Health* 82:1483–89.

Kelsky, Karen. 2001. *Women on the Verge: Japanese Women, Western Dreams*. Durham, NC: Duke University Press.

Kennedy, Elizabeth Lapovsky, and Madeline D. Davis. 1993. *Boots of Leather, Slippers of Gold: The History of a Lesbian Community*. New York: Penguin.

Kimmel, Michael. 2008. *Guyland: The Perilous World Where Boys Become Men*. New York: HarperCollins.

Koffka, K. 1935. *Principles of Gestalt Psychology*. New York: Harcourt, Brace.

Köhler, Wolfgang. 1920. *Die physichen Gestalten in Ruhe und im stationären Zustand*. Braunschweig: Friedr. Vieweg & Sohn.

———. 1938. *The Place of Values in a World of Fact*. New York: Liveright.

———. 1944/1971. "Value and Fact." In *The Selected Papers of Wolfgang Köhler*, ed. Mary Henle, 356–75. New York: Liveright.

———. 1947. *Gestalt Psychology*. New York: Liveright.

Kong, Travis. 2010. *Chinese Male Homosexualities: Memba, Tongzhi, and Golden Boy*. London: Routledge.

Koshy, Susan. 2004. *Sexual Naturalization: Asian Americans and Miscegenation*. Stanford, CA: Stanford University Press.

Lamont, Michèle. 2010 "Looking Back at Bourdieu." In *Cultural Analysis Bourdieu's Legacy: Settling Accounts and Developing Alternatives*, ed. E. Silva and A. Warde, 138–39. London: Routledge.

Lan, Pei-Chia. 2011. "White Privilege, Language Capital, and Cultural Ghettoization: Western High-Skilled Migrants in Taiwan." *Journal of Ethnic and Migration Studies* 37, no. 10:1669–93.

Lande, Brian. 2010. "Bodies of Force: Observations of a Sociologist-Cop on Becoming a Deputy Sheriff." PhD. diss., University of California at Berkeley, Department of Sociology.

Lang, Graeme, and Josephine Smart. 2002. "Migration and the 'Second Wife' in South China: Toward Cross-Border Polygyny." *International Migration Review* 36, no. 2:546–69.

Laumann, Edward O., Stephen Ellingston, Jenna Mahay, Anthony Palk, and Yoosik Youm, eds. 2004. *The Sexual Organization of the City*. Chicago: University of Chicago Press.

Laumann, Edward O., John H. Gagnon, Robert T. Michael, and Stuart Mi-
  chaels. 1994. *The Social Organization of Sexuality: Sexual Practices in the
  United States.* Chicago: University of Chicago Press.
Levine, Martin. 1979. *Gay Men: The Sociology of Male Homosexuality.* New
  York: Harper & Row.
———. 1998. *Gay Macho.* New York: New York University Press.
Lévi-Strauss, Claude. 1949/1969. *The Elementary Structures of Kinship.* Trans-
  lated by James Harle Bell, John Richard von Sturmer, and Rodney Need-
  ham. Boston: Beacon.
Lindau, Stacy Tessler, Philip Schumm, Edward O. Laumann, Wendy Levinson,
  Colm A. O'Muircheartaigh, and Linda J. Waite. 2007. "A National Study of
  Sexuality and Health among Older Adults in the U.S." *New England Journal
  of Medicine* 357, no. 8:762–74.
Liu-Farrer, Gracia. 2010. "The Absent Spouses: Gender, Sex, Race and the Ex-
  tramarital Sexuality among Chinese Migrants in Japan." *Sexualities* 13, no. 1:
  97–121.
Livingston, Jennie. 1990. *Paris Is Burning.* Miramax Studios.
Lizardo, Omar. 2004. "The Cognitive Origins of Bourdieu's Habitus." *Journal
  for the Theory of Social Behavior* 34:375–401.
Locke, Philip. 1997. "Male Images in the Gay Mass Media and Bear-Oriented
  Magazines: Analysis and Contrast." In *The Bear Book: Readings in the His-
  tory and Evolution of a Gay Male Subculture*, ed. Les K. Wright, 103–40.
  New York: Harrington Park.
Lovell, T. 2000. "Thinking Feminism with and against Bourdieu." In *Reading
  Bourdieu on Society and Culture*, ed. B. Fowler, 11–32. Oxford: Blackwell.
Lu, Hanlong, ed. 2008. *Zhuanbianzhongde shanghaishimin* (Shanghai urban
  citizens in transition). Shanghai: Shanghai Academy of Social Sciences.
Magister, Thom. 1991/2001. "One among Many: The Seduction and Training of a
  Leatherman." In *Leatherfolk: Radical Sex, People, Politics and Practice*, ed.
  Mark Thompson, 91–105. Los Angeles: Alyson.
Martin, James, and Jo Knox. 1997. "Loneliness and Sexual Risk Behavior in Gay
  Men." *Psychological Reports* 81:815–25.
Martin, John Levi. 2003. "What Is Field Theory?" *American Journal of Sociol-
  ogy* 109:1–49.
———. 2005. "Is Power Sexy?" *American Journal of Sociology* 111:408–46.
———. 2009. *Social Structures.* Princeton, NJ: Princeton University Press.
———. 2010. Keynote address presented at the conference "Bringing Bourdieu to
  Sexual Life: A Conference on Sexuality and the Sexual Field," University of
  Toronto, May 22.
———. 2011. *The Explanation of Social Action.* New York: Oxford University
  Press.
Martin, John Levi, and Matt George. 2006. "Theories of Sexual Stratification:

Toward an Analytics of the Sexual Field and a Theory of Sexual Capital." *Sociological Theory* 24, no. 2:107–32.

Marx, Karl. 1867/1906. *Capital*. Vol. 1. Edited by Frederick Engels. Translated from the 3rd German ed. by Samuel Moore and Edward Aveling. Chicago: Charles H. Kerr.

Maton, Karl. 2005. "A Question of Autonomy: Bourdieu's Field Approach and Higher Education Policy." *Journal of Education Policy* 20:687–704.

Mauk, D. 2008. *Stigmatized Desires: An Ethnography of Men in New York City Who Have Sex with Non-Operative Transgender Women*. New York: Doctor of Public Health Dissertation, Mailman School of Public Health, Columbia University.

Maynes, Mary Jo, Jennifer L. Pierce, and Barbara Laslett. 2008. *Telling Stories: The Use of Personal Narratives in the Social Sciences and History*. Ithaca, NY: Cornell University Press.

McClintock, Anne. 1995. *Imperial Leather: Race, Gender and Sexuality in the Colonial Contest*. New York: Routledge.

McIntosh, Mary. 1968. "The Homosexual Role." *Social Problems* 16, no. 2: 182–92.

Mead, George Herbert. 1934. *Mind, Self, and Society*. Chicago: University of Chicago Press.

Michael, Robert T. 2004. "Sexual Capital: An Extension of Grossman's Concept of Health Capital." *Journal of Health Economics* 23:643–52.

Muggleton, David. 2000. *Inside Subculture: The Postmodern Meaning of Style*. Oxford: Berg.

Murray, James, and Barry D. Adam. 2001. "Aging, Sexuality, and HIV Issues among Older Gay Men." *Canadian Journal of Human Sexuality* 10, nos. 3–4:75–90.

Nagel, Joan. 2003. *Race, Ethnicity and Sexuality: Intimate Intersections, Forbidden Fruits*. New York: Oxford University Press.

Nash, Roy. 2010. *Explaining Inequalities in School Achievement*. London: Ashgate.

Orléan, André. 1988. "Money and Mimetic Speculation." In *Violence and Truth*, ed. Paul Dumouchel, trans. Mark R. Anspach, 101–12. London: Athlone.

Padgug, Robert. 1989. "Gay Villain, Gay Hero: Homosexuality and the Social Construction of AIDS." In *Passion and Power: Sexuality in History*, ed. Kathy Peiss and Christina Simmons, 293–316. Philadelphia: Temple University Press.

Pan, Suiming. 1993. "A Sex Revolution in Current China." *Journal of Psychology and Human Sexuality* 6, no. 2:1–14.

Parsons, Talcott. 1937. *The Structure of Social Action*. Glencoe, IL: Free Press.

———. 1942/1949. "Age and Sex in the Social Structure of the United States." In

*Essays in Sociological Theory, Pure and Applied*, 217–32. Glencoe, IL: Free Press.

Paul, Jay P., George Ayayla, and Kyung-Hee Choi. 2010. "Internet Sex Ads for MSM and Partner Selection Criteria: The Potency of Race/Ethnicity Online." *Journal of Sex Research* 47, no. 6:528–38.

Poon, Maurice Kwong-Lai, and Peter Trung-Thu Ho. 2008. "Negotiating Social Stigma among Gay Asian Men." *Sexualities* 11:245–68.

Pratt, Mary Louise. 1992. *Imperial Eyes: Travel Writing and Transculturation*. New York: Routledge.

Prieur, Annick. 1998. *Mema's House, Mexico City: On Transvestites, Queens, and Machos*. Chicago: University of Chicago Press.

Pronger, Brian. 2002. *Body Fascism*. Toronto: University of Toronto Press.

Reback, C., and S. Larkins. 2006. *Once in a Blue Moon: Toward a Better Understanding of Heterosexually Identified Men Who Have Sex with Men and/or Preoperative Transgender Women*. Contract C-102523. Los Angeles: City of Los Angeles, AIDS Coordinator.

Rosch, Eleanor. 1978. "Principles of Categorization." In *Cognition and Categorization*, ed. E. Rosch and B. Lloyd, 27–48. Hillsdale, NJ: Erlbaum.

Rousseau, Jean-Jacques. 1755/1967. *Discourse on the Origin of Inequality*. Edited by Lester G. Crocker. New York: Washington Square.

Rubin, Gayle. 1985. "The Traffic in Women: Notes on the 'Political Economy' of Sex." In *Toward an Anthropology of Women*, ed. Reyna Reiter, 157–210. New York: Monthly Review Press.

Rupp, Leila J. 2012. "Sexual Fluidity before Sex." *Signs* 37:849–56.

Rupp, Leila J., and Verta Taylor. 2004. *Drag Queens at the 801 Cabaret*. Chicago: University of Chicago Press.

Sanday, Peggy. 1990. *Fraternity Gang Rape: Sex, Brotherhood, and Privilege on Campus*. New York: New York University Press.

Sartre, Jean-Paul. 1956. *Being and Nothingness*. Translated by Hazel E. Barnes. New York: Philosophical Library.

Sausa, Lydia A., JoAnne Keatley, and Don Operario. 2007. "Perceived Risks and Benefits of Sex Work among Transgender Women of Color in San Francisco." *Archives of Sexual Behavior* 36:768–77.

Schein, Louisa. 1997. "The Consumption of Color and the Politics of White Skin in Post-Mao China." In *The Gender/Sexuality Reader*, ed. Roger N. Lancaster and Micheala Di Leonardo, 473–86. London: Routledge.

Schilt, Kristen. 2010. *Just One of the Guys?* Chicago: University of Chicago Press.

Schilt, Kristen, and Laurel Westbrook. 2009. "Doing Gender, Doing Heteronormativity: 'Gender Normals,' Transgender People, and the Social Maintenance of Heterosexuality." *Gender and Society* 23:440–64.

Seidman, Steven. 1996. *Queer Theory/Sociology*. London: Blackwell.

Silver, Daniel. In press. *Setting the Scene*. Chicago: University of Chicago Press.

Silver, Daniel, and Terry Clark. n.d. "Scenes: The Spirit of Place and the Character of Communities." University of Toronto/University of Chicago. Typescript.

Simmel, Georg. 1905/1977. *The Problems of the Philosophy of History: An Epistemological Essay*. Translated and edited by Guy Oakes. New York: Free Press.

———. 1907/1978. *The Philosophy of Money*. Translated by Tom Bottomore and David Frisby. London: Routledge & Kegan Paul.

Simon, W., and D. K. Whittier. 2001. "The Fuzzy Matrix of 'My Type' in Intrapsychic Sexual Scripting." *Sexualities* 4, no. 2:139–65.

Sklair, Leslie. 2001. *The Transnational Capitalist Class*. Oxford: Blackwell.

Sontag, Susan. 1979. "The Double Standard of Aging." In *Psychology of Women*, ed. J. Williams, 462–78. New York: Norton.

*Statistical Abstracts of Shanghai*. 2011. Shanghai Academy of Social Sciences. http://www.stats-sh.gov.cn/tjnj/nje11.htm?d1=2011tjnje/E0213.htm.

Stein, Arlene. 1989. "Three Models of Sexuality: Drives, Identities, and Practices." *Sociological Theory* 7:1–13.

Stoller, Robert. 1985. *Observing the Erotic Imagination*. New Haven, CT: Yale University Press.

Stryker, Sheldon. 2008. "From Mead to Structural Symbolic Interactionism and Beyond." *Annual Review of Sociology* 3:15–31.

Suresha, Ron Jackson. 2002. "Bear Beauty and the Affirmation of Bear Contests." In *Bears on Bears: Interviews and Discussions*, 189–98. Los Angeles: Alyson.

Tanaka, Masakazu. 2007. "Kontakuto zonu no bunkajinruigaku he" (Toward a cultural anthropology of contact zones). *Contact Zone* 1, no. 1:31–43.

Tewksbury, R. 2002. "Bathhouse Intercourse: Structural and Behavioral Aspects of an Erotic Oasis." *Deviant Behavior* 23:75–112.

Thoits, Peggy. 1999. "Self, Identity, Stress and Mental Health." In *The Handbook of the Sociology of Mental Health*, ed. C. S. Aneshensel and J. C. Phelan, 345–68. New York: Kluwer/Plenum.

Thomas, William Isaac, and Dorothy Swaine Thomas. 1928. *The Child in America: Behavior Problems and Programs*. New York: Knopf.

Thornton, Robert J. 2008. *Unimagined Communities: Sex, Networks and AIDS in Uganda and South Africa*. Berkeley and Los Angeles: University of California Press.

Thornton, Sarah. 1996. *Club Culture: Music, Media, and Subcultural Capital*. Middletown, CT: Wesleyan University Press.

Vennix, Paul, Lucíe van Mens, Frank ten Horn, Dick Lavina, Meike van't Hof, and Ine Vanwesenbeek. 2000. *Klanten van Transgenders: HIV preventie, seksueel gedrag en seksuele Networken van klanten van transgenders op de tip-*

*pelzones van Amsterdam en Rotterdam*. Utrecht: Nederlands Instituut voor Sociaal Seksuologisch Onderzoek.

Wacquant, Loïc. 2004. *Body and Soul: Ethnographic Notebooks of an Apprentice Boxer*. New York: Oxford University Press.

———, ed. 2005. *Pierre Bourdieu and Democratic Politics*. Cambridge: Polity Press.

Waite, Linda J., Edward O. Laumann, and Aniruddha Das. 2009. "Sexual Activity, Later Age." In *Encyclopedia of the Life Course and Human Development* (3 vols.), ed. D. Carr, R. Crosnoe, M. E. Hughes, and A. Pienta, 3:362–66. Farmington Hills, MI: Gage.

Waller, Willard. 1937. "The Rating and Dating Complex." *American Sociological Review* 2:727–34.

Walsh, Katie. 2007. "'It Got Very Debauched, Very Dubai!' Heterosexual Intimacy amongst Single British Expatriates." *Social Cultural Geography* 8, no. 4:507–33.

Weinberg, Martin, and Colin J. Williams. 1975a. "Gay Baths and the Social Organization of Impersonal Sex." *Social Problems* 23:124–36.

———. 1975b. *Male Homosexuality*. New York: Oxford University Press.

———. 2005. "Fecal Matters: Habitus, Embodiments, and Deviance." *Social Problems* 52:315–36.

———. 2009. "Men Sexually Interested in Transwomen (MSTW): Gendered Embodiment and the Construction of Sexual Desire." *Journal of Sex Research* Jun 19:1–10.

Weinberg, Martin S., Colin J. Williams, and Douglas W. Pryor. 1994. *Dual Attraction: Understanding Bisexuality*. New York: Oxford University Press.

Weiss, Margot. 2011. *Techniques of Pleasure: BDSM and the Circuits of Sexuality*. Durham, NC: Duke University Press.

West, Candace, and Don H. Zimmerman. 1987. "Doing Gender." *Gender and Society* 1:125–51.

White, Edmund. 1980. *States of Desire*. New York: Dutton.

Whittier, David Knapp, and William Simon. 2001. "The Fuzzy Matrix of 'My Type' in Intrapsychic Sexual Scripting." *Sexualities* 4, no. 2:139–65.

Widick, Richard. 2003. "Flesh and the Free Market (On Taking Bourdieu to the Options Exchange)." *Theory and Society* 32:679–723.

Williams, Danny. 2002. "Circuit Bears and the Bear Circus." In *Bears on Bears: Interviews and Discussions*, 211–20. Los Angeles: Alyson.

Williams, Raymond. 1977. *Marxism and Literature*. London: Oxford University Press.

Willis, Katie, and Brenda Yeoh. 2002. "Gendering Transnational Communities: A Comparison of Singaporean and British Migrants in China." *Geoforum* 33, no. 4:553–65.

Willis, Paul. 1977. *Learning to Labour*. Aldershot: Gower.

Wilson, Timothy D., and Nancy Brekke. 1994. "Mental Contamination and Mental Correction: Unwanted Influences on Judgments and Evaluations." *Psychological Bulletin* 116:117–42.

Wilton, Leo 2009. "A Preliminary Investigation of Body Image and HIV Sexual Risk Behavior in Black Gay and Bisexual Men: Implications for HIV Prevention." *Journal of Gay and Lesbian Social Services* 21:309–25.

Wright, Les K. 1990. "The Sociology of the Urban Bear." *Drummer* 140:53–55.

———, ed. 1997a. *The Bear Book: Readings in the History and Evolution of a Gay Male Subculture*. New York: Harrington Park.

———. 1997b. "A Concise History of Self-Identifying Bears." In *The Bear Book: Readings in the History and Evolution of a Gay Male Subculture*, ed. Les K. Wright, 21–39. New York: Harrington Park.

———. 2002. "From Cult to Subculture to Couture: Evolving Bear Community." In *Bears on Bears: Interviews and Discussions*, 114–22. Los Angeles: Alyson.

Wrong, Dennis Hume. 1999. *The Oversocialized Conception of Man*. New Brunswick, NJ: Transaction.

Zhang Jiehai. 2009. *Zhonguonanrendiaocha* (The investigation on Chinese men). Nanjing: Jiangsu Literature and Art Publishing House.

Zheng, Tiantian. 2009. *Red Lights: The Lives of Sex Workers in Post-Socialist China*. Minneapolis: University of Minnesota Press.

# Author Index

Adam, B. D., 6, 7, 20, 29, 51, 52, 123–26, 137
Akers, A. Y., 51
Altman, D., 146
Arendt, H., 188n10
Armstrong, E., 7, 18, 46, 51, 54n4, 56n12, 85, 124
Ayala, G., 27

Bailey, B. L., 118, 181
Barthes, R., xi
Bataille, G., 114
Bearman, P. S., 123
Bech, H., 3, 124
Benjamin, J., 47, 55n9
Bernstein, B. B., 13
Bernstein, E., 185
Bersani, L., 98n12, 124, 134
Birken, L., 105
Bourdieu, P., xii, xiii, xviii, 2, 3, 4, 5, 11, 12, 13, 14, 16, 19, 20, 22, 27, 72, 73, 78, 81, 83, 84, 90, 91, 92, 95, 97, 98–99n14, 101–20, 121nn1–5, 122nn7–9, 123, 125, 146, 171–75, 179, 181, 182, 186
Boxer, A., 7
Breiger, R. L., 181
Brekhus, W., 32
Brekke, N., 183
Brubaker, R., 13, 97n6
Burke, E., 187n2
Buss, D. M., 35
Butler, J., 94

Caceres, C. F., 68
Canaday, M., 122n7

Carter, J. B., 122n7
Chancer, L., 185
Chauncey, G., 122n7
Chodorow, N., 55n9
Choi, K.-H., 27
Coan, D. L., 69n4
Cohler, B. J., 90
Connell, R. W., 88, 96n1
Constable, N., 148
Cooley, C. H., 44, 141
Cortinas, J. I., 68

Dale, S., 17, 21, 33, 34, 143, 149
Das, A., 8
Davis, M. D., 29, 45
D'Emilio, J., 7, 25, 74, 77
Desmond, M., 186
Desroches, F., 141
Dewey, J., 172, 180
Dilthey, W., 188n6
DiMaggio, P. J., 12
Dor, J., 55n9
Dugatkin, L. A., 176
Durkheim, E., 22, 182

Eisenberg, M. E., 51
Ellingston, S., 7, 26, 34
Emirbayer, M., 12
Eng, D., 148, 155, 167
England, P., 8
Epstein, S., 14, 55n9
Erwin, K., 144

Farrer, J., 7, 21, 27, 33, 34, 123, 124, 143, 146, 147, 148, 149, 153, 166, 167

Ferguson, P. P., 12
Fischer, C., 15, 37, 38, 41
Fitzgerald, F., 1, 7, 124, 134
Fligstein, N., 12
Foucault, M., 3, 102, 105, 111–15, 117, 119, 120, 121n2, 121n6, 121–22n7
Freud, S., xii, 20, 55n9, 96n2, 105, 121n6, 186

Gagnon, J. H., 8, 26, 102, 125, 183
Gamble, J., 143
George, M. C., 7, 14, 16, 20, 26–29, 37, 38, 55n7, 55n8, 71, 101, 120, 123, 124, 145, 146, 175, 184, 188n6
Gibson, J. J., 186
Giddens, A., 7, 11, 25, 81, 102, 120, 146
Gilligan, C., 88, 96n1, 98n9
Glaeser, A., 78
Gonzales, A. M., 145, 146, 147
Goode, W. J., 115
Gould, T., 8
Green, A. I., viii, xi, xiii, 1, 5, 7, 14, 15, 16, 17, 23n4, 25–30, 32, 33, 34, 36, 37–40, 43, 44, 47, 49–52, 54n2, 55n9, 56n15, 57–60, 62, 64, 69n2, 71, 72, 73, 76, 81, 82, 85, 91, 93, 97n5, 98n13, 123–26, 130, 134, 141, 142, 145, 146, 147, 165, 167, 188n8
Griffen, J. H., 186

Hakim, C., 21, 23n3, 48, 54n3, 145, 146
Halperin, D., xv, 7, 11, 25, 122n7
Hamilton, L., 7, 18, 51, 124
Hammack, P. L., 90
Hebdige, D., 83
Hennen, P., 7, 17, 18, 19, 28, 30, 32, 40, 53, 71, 74, 76, 80, 86, 96n1, 98n9, 98n11, 137
Herdt, G., 7
Heritage, J., ix
Ho, P. S. Y., 167
Ho, P. T.-T., 51
Hollister, J., 141
Hospers, H., 142
Humphreys, L., 32, 141
Husbands, W., 20, 123–26, 137

Illouz, E., 120

Jackson, S., 19, 62, 65
James, W., 186

Jamieson, L., 102
Jenkins, R., 83
Johnson, V., 12

Kalish, R., 7
Kant, I., 173, 187n2, 188n6
Kelly, J. A., 125
Kelsky, K., 167
Kennedy, E. L., 29, 45
Kimmel, M., 7
Kinsey, A. C., 20, 60, 110
Klossowski, P., 114
Knox, J., 142
Koffka, K., 182, 186
Köhler, W., 172, 180, 181, 182
Kok, G., 142
Kong, T., 146
Koshy, S., 146, 167

Lacan, J., 96n2, 113
Lamont, M., 97n6
Lan, P.-C., 144, 148
Lande, B., 186
Lang, G., 148
Larkins, S., 69n2
Laslett, B., 90
Laumann, E. O., 7, 8, 26, 34, 102, 125, 183
Levine, M., 1, 7, 41, 42, 50, 124, 134, 137
Levi-Strauss, C., 117, 180
Lindau, S. T., 8
Liu-Farrer, G., 148
Lizardo, O., vii, 12, 14
Locke, P., 89
Lu, H., 143

Mahay, J., 7, 26, 34
Martin, J., 142
Martin, J. L., vii, 5, 6, 7, 14, 16, 17, 18, 22, 26–29, 37, 38, 39, 55n7, 55n8, 56n11, 71, 72, 82, 120, 123, 124, 145, 146, 171, 173, 175, 176, 187n1
Marx, K., 111, 171, 172, 181
Maton, K., 104
Mauk, D., 69n2
Maxwell, J., 20, 123–27, 137
Maynes, M. J. 90
McClintock, E. A., 8
McIntosh, M., 8, 47
Mead, G. H., 44

Michael, R. T., 8, 26, 102, 125, 145, 146,
    167, 183
Michaels, S., 8, 26, 102, 125, 183
Molenaar, S., 142
Moody, J., 123
Muggleton, D., 83
Murray, J., 20, 51, 123–27, 137

Nagel, J., 147, 164

Orléan, A., 177

Packer, T., 69n4
Padgug, R., 7
Palk, A., 7, 26, 34
Pan, S., 146
Parsons, T., ix, 185
Paul, J. P., 27
Pierce, J. L., 90
Poon, M. K.-L., 51
Pratt, M. L., 147
Prieur, A., 124
Pronger, B., 142
Pryor, D. W., 57

Reback, C., 69n2
Rolison, G., 145, 146, 147
Rosch, E., 54n2
Rousseau, J.-J., 187n2
Rubin, G., 180
Rupp, L., 32, 39

Sanday, P., 7
Sartre, J.-P., 188n5
Schein, L., 144
Schilt, K., 186
Schrager, W., 69n4
Scott, S., 19, 62, 65
Seidman, S., 2
Silver, D., 6
Simmel, G., 181, 188n6
Simon, W., 55n9
Sklair, L., 164
Smart, J., 148
Sontag, S., 8
Stein, A., 14
Stoller, R., 47, 55n9
Stovel, K., 123

Stryker, S., 68
Sun, Z., 146
Suresha, R. J., 89
Sweeney, B., 7, 51, 124

Tanaka, M., 147
Taylor, V., 32
Tewksbury, R., 30, 31, 50, 124
Thoits, P., 51
Thomas, D. S. T., 56n10
Thomas, W. I., 56n10
Thornton, R. J., 125
Thornton, S., 83
Tsang, A. K. T., 167

Wacquant, L., 12, 13, 81, 97n4, 101, 102,
    104–8, 114, 117, 121n1, 121n2, 185, 186
Waite, L. J., 8
Waller, W., 22, 38, 29, 45, 50, 54n6, 177,
    179, 180
Walsh, K., 154, 165
Weber, M., 16
Weinberg, M., 1, 7, 18–19, 27, 28, 37, 42, 57,
    58, 69, 123, 124, 134
Weiss, M., 47
West, C., 79
White, E., 90
Whittier, D. K., 55n9
Widick, R., 12
Williams, C. J., 7, 18–19, 27, 37, 42, 57, 58,
    69, 123, 124, 134
Williams, D., 88
Williams, R., 84
Willis, K., 144
Willis, P., 13
Wilson, T. D., 183
Wilton, L. K., 27, 51
Woolf, V., 117
Wright, L. K., 79, 89, 96n3
Wrong, D. H., 55n9

Yeoh, B., 144
Youm, Y., 7, 26, 34

Zhang, J., 144, 151, 152
Zheng, T., 167
Zimmerman, D. H., 79

# Subject Index

active/passive binary, 17
adolescent pregnancy, 7; relation to low
  sexual status, 51
affect, 3, 49; affective characteristics, 3; as
  communicating sexual status, 132; as
  communicating a sexual type, 42, 49,
  137; reflexive relationship with, 3, 16;
  relation to sexual capital, 30, 49, 50,
  132; relation to structures of desire, 28,
  37, 137; variations in gendered affect of
  men, 136
age: as a basis of attractiveness, 38, 80, 131,
  140, 151, 185; as a determinant of sexual
  capital, 49, 56, 59, 138; as a factor in online dating/online profiles, 9–10, 132,
  133; gendered impact of age in finding a
  partner, 4, 8; relation to sexual circuits,
  21, 130, 139, 141; relation to structures
  of desire, 31, 37; sorting of social types
  based on, 136–37; as structuring erotic
  choices and sexual scripts, xiii, 7, 31, 33,
  143–44, 155; types of bears by age, 84
aggregation, amplification, and intensification: aggregation of actors, 73; in the
  clone community, 41–42; in college sorority life, 46–47; as exceeding individual desires as participants, 37, 38, 43;
  explanation of, 15, 41–43; as a field effect, 18, 42–43; in lesbian sexual fields
  of the 1940s and 1950s, 45–46; of nonsexual elements of partner desirability,
  43; of norms, 37; in relation to sexual
  capital, 18; in relation to structures of
  desire, 37–38, 44

attractiveness: aggregation and intensification of norms of, 18, 38, 42–43; attributions of, 64–68, 174, 182, 184; in the
  bear community, 84; Bourdieusian approach to, 175; compensation for a lack
  of, 185; endogeneity of, 177, 181; evolutionary basis for, 178; importance
  to partnering, 8, 55n7, 132; market approach to, 175; naturalist explanation
  of, 176–77; in online dating/online profiles, 133; physical bases for, 178; and
  pluralistic ignorance, 45; in the popularity tournament, 22, 54n6, 55n8,
  176–77, 179, 184; racialized standards
  of, 21, 152, 160–61, 162; reflexive stance
  toward, 134–35, 141; relation to circuits, 138–42; relation to sexual capital,
  48; relation to sexual status, 3, 132, 137;
  relation to structures of desire, 14–15,
  25, 31, 38, 44–46, 167; riddle of, 178;
  and sexual field theory, 15, 53, 184, 186;
  varying currencies of, 22, 139–41, 151,
  154, 188n8

*Bachelor's Ball, The* (Bourdieu), 107
bar: acquiring "sense of place" at, 92–93;
  distribution of sexual capital at, 50, 92;
  "doing gender" in, 79, 94, 159; feeling
  unwelcome at, 138–39; feeling welcome
  at, 40, 63, 88; high sexual status in, 132;
  low sexual status in, 132, 135, 140; relation to circuits, 28–29, 124, 127, 136–37;
  relation to collective erotic life, xiii, 5,
  9, 27; relation to sexual fields, 6, 54n2,

bar (*continued*)
131, 167; relation to sexual status order,
131; relation to sexual status structures,
56n10; relation to structures of desires,
14–15, 37–38; sexual signaling at, 78, 79,
140. *See also* Mabel's
bathhouse. *See* gay bathhouse
BDSM: construction of BDSM roles, 40,
90; as delivering sense of connection,
76; dominant and submissive roles in,
90; and gay leathermen, 40, 96n1; as
highly rationalized, 76; sexual capital in, 76, 90; as a sexual field, 89; socialization effect in, 40; training and
technique, 75, 76, 78, 90; use of "hanky
code," 78
bear community: beauty contests in,
88–89; as a challenge to the field of
struggle metaphor, 19, 84, 88, 91; collective "turning away from" leathermen, 79–80, 96n1, 96n3; democratic
power structure in, 17, 32; devaluation
of mainstream gay culture in, 86; formation of, 17, 73–80, 82, 96n3; inclusiveness and emotional warmth of, 40,
84, 85, 88, 89, 96n1; limited ranking of
"types" in, 84–85; oppositional relationship to other fields, 88, 136–37; sexual capital among, 80, 85, 141
bears: appearance of, 80, 84, 88; articulation of masculinity among, 79–80,
96n1, 97n4, 141; bear admirers, 86;
bear ideal, 89; bear websites, 10, 132; as
challenging instrumental sexuality, 78,
79, 96n1; explanation of, 96n1; in relation to leathermen, 78–79, 82; sexual
practices of, 17, 41, 80; socialization as,
40–41; types of, 84; use of sexual signaling, 79, 96n1, 96n3. *See also* bear
community
birth control, 7, 25
Bourdieu, Pierre: collecting process, 78;
critiques to orthodox interpretations
of, 83, 97n6, 171; as denying the autonomy of the sexual field, 102, 106, 109,
114–15, 119; development of field analytics, 114; emphasis on social class, 83;
on familialism, 112, 115; field of struggle, 72, 83, 90; importance of reflexivity
for, 104, 120; on libido, xii, 105–6; links
between sex, gender, family, and property, 116–17; misrecognition, 95, 98–
99n14, 121n4; notion of agency, 81; process of field formation, 81, 97n4, 105;
rejection of Michel Foucault, 113–14,
121n2; relevance to an analysis of subcultures, 83; relevance to sexual fields
framework, xiii, 2, 4–5, 11, 12, 14–17,
19, 22, 27, 123, 125, 146, 175; role of experts for, 103–4, 106, 114, 121n1, 121n3;
on the role of women, 117–18; sense of
place for, 91, 182; on sexuality in Kabylian society, 115, 121n5; study of matri-
mony and modernization, 107–8, 115;
on symbolic capital and the conservation of power, 13, 117, 119, 122n9; theory of gender, 115; tripartite model of
practice (field, capital, habitus), 12, 14,
83, 125; understanding of capital, 13,
105, 174–75; understanding of habitus,
13–14, 108, 174; understanding of the
field, 12, 13, 102–3, 146; view of psychoanalysis, 105, 109–10, 121n6, 122n8. See
also *Bachelor's Ball, The*; *Distinction*;
*Firing Back*; *Masculine Domination*;
*State Nobility, The*

capital: Bourdieusian understanding of,
12–13, 16, 83, 102, 117; as a core concept of fields theory, 12, 15, 27, 125, 174;
establishing the legitimacy of, 103; as
a field specific resource, 90, 93; importance for field significance, 34–35, 59,
64, 69n3, 155; as interconvertible, 13;
relation to ethnicity, 34, 155; relation to
partnering, 8, 34; relation to power and
domination, 112, 114, 116, 117, 119; relation to tiers of desirability, 59; temporal
relationship to fields, 72, 80; transmission of, 122n9; types of, 4; unequal distribution of, 8, 14. *See also* capital portfolio; sexual capital
capital portfolio, 34, 41, 145; as bifurcated
in two-sided fields, 34, 54n6, 59; historical changes to, 36. *See also* capital; sexual capital
"Castro, The" (in *Cities on a Hill*) (Fitzgerald), 1
China: cultural pluralization, globalization, and liberalization in, 146; fields

of interracial sexuality in, 144, 147; racial terms in, 149–50; standards of attractiveness in, 21. *See also* ethnosexual contact zone; Shanghai

circuits: actors moving between, 130, 142; composition of, 21; conceptual utility of, 20, 124, 125, 126, 141; definition/explanation of, 6, 20, 28, 123; descriptions of, 127–30; distinguishing between, 124, 141; formation of, 137; as potentially developing in microcultures, 142; relation to field theoretic approach, 52, 124; relation to sexual fields, 28, 126; relation to sexual sites, 21; social circuitry, 135; subjective consequences of, 130–41, 142

class reproduction, 13, 14, 106, 118, 119

clones: aggregation, amplification and intensification among, 41–42; currencies of sexual capital among, 50; explanation of, 41; self-presentation of, 42; sexual practices of, 42

collective sexual (erotic) life: as an aggregation of desires and attitudes, 38; as anchored to physical/virtual sites, 5, 27; as bringing together different actors, 6, 14; as a composite of sexual fields, 5, 124; effect of technology on, 9, 25; explanation of, 26, 123; impact on social actors, 9; as an independent social order, 7, 11, 26; levels of analysis of, 51–53; reentering, 8; in relation to circuits, 20, 123–24, 126, 141, 142; relation to erotic habitus, 37; relation to erotic world, 5; in relation to sexual fields framework, 15–17, 22, 51, 54; relevance to sociology, 18, 25; social architecture of, 7; types of, xiii

college life: campus rape/sexual assault and low sexual status, 51; hookup culture in, 7; popularity tournaments in, 22, 38–39; structure of desire within Greek campus life, 46

*Critique of Judgment* (Kant), 173

cultural production, 4, 14

dating: age-graded system of stratification, 8–9; dating logic, 180; dating market for Western women in Shanghai, 150, 152–54, 158–62, 166–67; dating networks, 6; desired capital when dating, 35, 43; gender differences in, 4, 35, 181; rating and dating system, 22, 38, 179; reentering the dating market, 4, 8; relation to circuits, 142; restricted dating pool. *See also* Internet dating

desexualization: contributing factors to, 148; definition of, 150; responses to, 154, 165; of Western women in China, 145, 150, 151, 153, 156, 165–66

deviance and social control framework, xiv–xv, 2

*Discourse on the Origin of Inequality* (Rousseau), 187n2

*Distinction* (Bourdieu), 109, 112, 115, 117, 173, 175

division of labor, 115, 120

*Elementary Forms of Religious Life, The* (Durkheim), 22, 182

embodiment: within BDSM, 76; definition of sexual embodiment, 62; embodied capital, 16, 56n14, 114; embodied dispositions, 16; embodied principles, 81; of habitus, 60, 62, 78; objectified embodiment, 62–63; processes of, 19, 58; reflexive embodiment, 62; sensate embodiment, 65–67; sense of misplacement as embodied, 95; sensory embodiment, 63–65; sexual desire and, 19, 142. *See also* Mabel's; trans women

erotic capital (Hakim): in contrast to sexual fields understanding of sexual/erotic capital, 23n3, 48, 54n3; portability versus cultural specificity of, 21, 146, 146. *See also* sexual capital

erotic choices, xiii, 146

erotic habitus: changing over time, 18, 81; as culturally specific, 160; explanation of, 27, 36; in Mabel's, 58; Michel Foucault and, 112; as operating below the level of conscious thought, 91, 95; relation to collective sexual life, 37, 56n15; relation to sexual fields, xi, 36–37, 55n9, 58, 60, 62, 67, 68, 167, 168; relation to structures of desire, 19, 37, 40; signaling between fields as an effect of, 73

erotic worlds: as bringing actors together, 5; development of, 2, 6, 7, 11,

erotic worlds (*continued*)
168; organization of, xiii, 125; relation to collective sexual life, 5; relation to sexual fields theory, xiii–xiv; as semi-autonomous, xiv, 6; as shaping sexual choices and behavior, xiv, 25; unique character of, 5

ethnicity/race: interracial sexual field, 145, 147, 153, 154, 166, 168; mismatch of sexual mores across, 160; racial adaptability, 165–66; racial castration, 148, 155; racial fetishization, 163; racialized perceptions/experiences of sexual fields, 138, 144; racialized sexual capital, 148; racial mobility, 144–45, 148, 163; racial patterns of sexual interaction, 21, 26, 31, 137–38, 166–68; racial terms in China, 149; relevance to structures of desire, 37, 38, 47, 133, 167–68; segregation of actors in/across fields based on, 137–38; specificity of symbols of capital across, 17, 49–50, 93. *See also* ethnosexual contact zone

ethnosexual contact zone: emergence of, 147; explanation of, 33, 147; patterned sociosexual relations in, 33–34, 166, 168; sexual mobility in, 145, 148, 164; as a stratified sexual field, 148, 168

evaluation schemes, 33, 56n10, 134, 140–41

exoticism, 2, 61, 163

*Explanation of Social Action, The* (Martin), 187n1

femininity: appended effeminacy, 93, 98n11; feminine self-presentation, 49, 64, 67, 68; feminization of labor, 109; males as effeminate, 30, 74, 78, 96n1, 136, 152, 160; racial mobility and, 148, 155; sexual valuation of, 19, 58, 59, 64–66, 68

feminism, 16, 88, 98n9, 118, 120

fetishism, 177; and BDSM, 76, 78, 80, 89; of commodities, 181; and leather masculinity, 94; racial, 162, 163

field effects: attraction/desirability as, 14, 18, 23n5, 26, 32, 39, 85, 176–82; considerations for analyzing, 183–86, 188n8, 188n11; examples of, 22, 25, 40, 68, 131, 165; naturalization of, 91, 95, 107; as social psychological work, 6. *See also* field

formation; fields; field theory; sexual fields; sexual fields theory

field formation: aggregation "up" to a new field, 73; contributing factors to, x, 72, 73, 81, 90; erotic energy accompanying, 76, 81, 97n7; example of, 75–76, 78–81; importance of analyzing, 114; rejection of existing field, 79–81, 96n2, 96n3, 97n4, 97n7; role of actors in, 97n3; temporal relationship with new forms of capital, 81. *See also* field effects; fields; field theory; sexual fields; sexual fields theory

fields: achieving field autonomy, 103, 125, 175; crossing between, 2, 148; dangers of fragmenting, 101; defining the boundaries of, 94, 104, 181; evolution over time, 91; explanation of, 125; field position, x, 3, 20, 21, 103, 133; functions of, x–xi; hierarchal relationship between, 19, 20, 72, 83, 85–86; as interconnected, 13; motivation within, vii, x, 125, 131; orthodoxy and heterodoxy in, 103–4; properties of, 12, 15, 27, 125; regulation of, 12, 102, 103, 122n10; relationship to subcultures, 83–84, 85; signaling within and between, 40, 73, 93; types of, 4. *See also* field effects; field formation; field theory; sexual fields; sexual fields theory

field theory: explanation of, 12; as an explanation of action, vii, viii, x, xii, 12, 13, 103, 171–74, 186; relation to sexuality in, 11, 14, 16, 17, 22, 26, 47, 72, 102, 106, 108–19, 171; as a theory of desire, xi, xii, 176–82. *See also* field effects; field formation; fields; sexual fields; sexual fields theory

*Firing Back* (Bourdieu), 111

force of meaning, 82

Foucault, Michel: biopolitics, 112, 114; capitalization of the sexual body, 112–13; deployment of sexuality, 111–12; on the emergence of "sex-itself" as an autonomous realm, 114, 120, 121n6; link between family and sexuality, 111–12; link between political hegemony and sexuality, 112; panoptic surveillance, 3; Pierre Bourdieu's relation to, 111, 113, 115, 117, 119, 121n2, 121–22n7

Freud, Sigmund, xii, 20, 96, 105, 121n6, 186
fronts: explanation of, 16; front/bodywork, xii, 58; relation to sexual status, 47; relation to structures of desire, 37. *See also* self-presentation

game, the: being out of, 9; competitiveness of, 85–86; connection to experts, 106; desire running counter to the rules of, 98n7, 125, 158–60, 169; investing one's self in, xii, 158, 179; knowledge needed to play, 2, 27–28, 94, 130; negative consequences for not following the rules of, 81, 85, 133–34; not playing but being judged by the rules of, 9, 125; player/observer in, 1; playing terrain of, 25; reentering, 165; rules of, 33, 80, 168
gay bathhouse, xiii, 5, 34, 35, 124, 127, 130, 134; level of sexual competition in, 30–31; sexual status order in, 138
*Gay Baths and the Social Organization of Impersonal Sex* (Weinberg and Williams), 1
*Gay Macho* (Levine), 1
gay village: in New York City, 2–3, 41; in Toronto, 56, 124, 126, 127, 130, 131, 139, 140
gender: complexity of, 68–69, 166, 184; doing gender, 64, 79, 97n4, 136; gender binary, xiv, 45; gendered mobility, 144–45, 148, 164; gendered perceptions and experiences of sexual fields, 4, 34, 38, 42, 93, 120, 144, 147, 150–57, 159–63; gender fluidity, 165; gender script, 41, 64; heteronormative constructions of, xiv, 42; Pierre Bourdieu on, 83, 102, 115–19; presentations of, 49, 59, 64, 65, 68; social status orders particular to, 17, 33, 58, 68
generalized other, 44
gestalt tradition: affective characteristics as gestalt, 49; focus of gestalt theory, 186; gestalt theorists, 172; understanding of an "object" in, 180

habitus: as changing, 81, 97n4; as a core concept of field theory, 12, 15, 16, 27, 83, 108, 125, 172; differences in, 93; inculcation of, 119–20, 186; in relation to practice, 13–14; in relation to the sexual field, 36–37, 174–75, 177; relationship to structures of desire, xi, 18, 38; understandings of, 13, 78, 117, 174. *See also* erotic habitus
heteronormativity, viii, xiv, 38, 42, 118
hexis, 16
HIV/AIDS, 51, 79, 126. *See also* sexually transmitted infections
horizontal differentiation, 33, 34, 52, 136, 137, 176, 186; definition of, 29–30, 33; example of, 29, 137, 29; within heterosexual fields, 34; within lesbian fields, 29; relation to field structure, 52, 136; relation to sexual status order, 20, 33

International Mr. Leather Contest, 88, 98n10; meaning of, 89
Internet: chat rooms on, 6, 53; communications of desirability on, 4, 10, 132–33, 136, 152, 153, 164, 166, 167; connecting different cities, 6, 10; field specialization created by, 10; making intersubjective self-assessments relative to others on, 126, 138; online communication of sexual status, 15, 31–32, 53, 133; popularity of, 7; in relation to circuits, 124, 126, 127, 129, 130, 141; as a virtual world, 5, 26. *See also* Internet dating
Internet dating, xiii, 6, 8, 10, 26, 27, 34, 35, 132
intersubjective assessments, 20, 28, 42, 44, 62, 86, 87, 126, 140
intersubjective validity, 172, 173
intrapsychic level of analysis, 37, 52, 53, 55n9

leathermen: circuits, 136, 137, 141; emergence of leathermen field, 19, 72, 73, 78, 82; ethic of healing with leatherman culture, 77; identity of, 75; importance of veteran status to, 74, 76–77; instrumental sexuality of, 76, 79, 96n1; masculinity among, 17, 74, 78, 80, 94, 96n1; relevance of hierarchies to, 89–90; sadomasochism in leatherman communities, 40, 75, 76, 89–90; sexual capital among, 76, 90, 92; sexual practices of, 17, 75; sexual signaling among, 79, 91, 93; socialization as, 40, 90; structure of desire, 30, 37, 40, 96n1 lesbians: butch/fem dichotomy among, 30, 45–46; lesbian sociality, 5, 29, 45–46, 98n9

libido: in classical psychoanalysis, xii, 20, 96n2, 105–6; libidinal libido, 106, 115, 119; Pierre Bourdieu's understanding of, 105–6

Mabel's: clientele, 58, 60, 61–62; commercial sex among patrons, 58, 59, 61, 63, 68; complex interaction of sex, gender, and sexuality at, 68–69; description of, 58–60; differences between bisexual and straight men at, 65, 66; distribution of erotic capital at, 60; erotic habitus of male patrons, 58, 62, 67, 68; as facilitating collective sexual life, 64, 67, 69; intersubjective rapport between patrons at, 19, 63; level of competition at, 59, 60; neighborhood context of, 57; processes of embodiment at, 19, 58, 62–67, 68; sexual capital among male patrons, 69n3; sexual capital among trans patrons, 59; sexual identification of male patrons, 61, 62, 68; sexual relations between patrons, 58, 61, 65, 66, 68; structures of desire at, 59; tiers of desirability at, 59, 61–62. *See also* self-presentation; trans women

market approach: in contrast to sexual fields theory, 71–72; limitations of, 71, 175; market analysis, 55n8; market metaphors of sexuality, 80, 175

marriage: arranged, 11; biracial/bicultural marriage, 166; as delayed, 7, 26; evaluation of, 9; extramarital relations, 9, 10, 143, 146, 147, 148, 156, 157, 161; gendered roles in, 152; homophilous tendencies of, 184; international marriage, 147, 169n1; marginalization in, 157; marriage partner, 5, 59, 63, 143, 148, 155; open marriage, 98n9; popular decline of, 117; relation to online dating, 9, 26, 34, 35; sexuality as autonomous from, 112, 146; trade-offs in, 183; transmission of patrimony through, 112, 116–17

*Masculine Domination* (Bourdieu), 112, 115, 117

masculinity: Asian, 152, 167; bear, 79–80,

96n1, 97n4, 141; clone, 41–42, 50; communication of, 49; construction of, 94, 95; contradictions within, 95; dislocated, 74, 75; hegemonic, 88, 96n1; hypermasculinity, 37, 50, 94; lack of, 33; leatherman, 17, 74, 78, 80, 94, 96n1; legitimate claim to, 78; masculinization, 21, 148, 150, 152, 155, 156–57, 165–66; naturalization of, 94; questionable, 107; rules of, 93, 94; types of, 37–38, 142

mental health, 51, 142

metasexual authority, 15, 16, 120, 121n6

microlevel of analysis, 19, 26, 30, 52, 53, 54n2, 126

misrecognition (Bourdieu), 95, 98n14, 110, 121n4

modernization, 115, 116

neoliberalism, 111

New York: Chelsea, 2, 3; Cherry Grove, 5; features of sexual fields in, 28; Greenwich Village, 41; Manhattan, 1, 3, 5, 47; urban gay center in, 2; West Village, 2, 3. *See also* gay village

nightclub: in China, 144, 151, 167; as a sexual site, 1, 5, 6, 8, 27, 53; sexual status order at, 31, 131; variation in patronage at, 28, 136–37

*Observations on the Feeling of the Beautiful and the Sublime* (Kant), 187n2

panoptic surveillance, 3, 134

partnering: effect of age on, 8; effect of ethnicity on, 21, 26, 31, 47, 137–38, 148, 166–68; effect of gender on, 8, 34–36, 152, 155–56; hookup, xiii, 7, 46, 58, 60, 141; importance of sexual fields to, xiv, 6, 15–16, 36, 47; infidelity, 8, 9, 10, 143, 146, 147, 148, 156, 157, 161; local, 9, 21, 155, 158, 159, 162, 163, 166; long-/short-term commitment, 8, 9, 11, 26, 35, 47, 75, 131, 144, 147, 154, 156, 157, 165, 167, 185, 188n7; monogamous, 5, 7, 8, 9, 26, 54n1, 161; popularity and, 39; possibilities for, 4, 7, 85, 142, 159; pursuit of, 1, 2, 4, 5, 27, 125; relation to circuits, 131–32, 135–42; relation to sexual stratification system, 7, 31, 61, 62, 66; relevance of social/sexual status, 8, 22, 25,

51, 55n7, 175; technology easing access to, 9–10, 11, 26; types of capital relevant to, 32, 34–36, 43, 85. *See also* dating; marriage; selection of sexual partner; sexual relations

patriarchy, 116, 118

patrimony, 104, 112, 116, 117, 118

phenomenology, x, 20, 22, 126, 130, 177, 179, 183, 184, 186

*Philosophical Enquiry into the Origin of Our Ideas of the Sublime and the Beautiful, A* (Burke), 187n2

popularity tournaments: effect on structures of desire, 18, 39, 55n8; endogenous/exogenous popularity effects, 177, 179, 181, 184; explanation of, 17, 38–39; influence of status discordance in, 39; and institutionalization, 179; as leading to a hierarchal structure, 177; perceiving relative status in, 39, 179; popularity itself as attractive, 22, 177; rating and dating system, 22, 38, 179

power: Bourdieusian (capital), 16, 17, 105; conservation of, 104, 117; conversion of capital and, 13, 110, 118–19; differences in, 34; disruption in power relations, 81; as erotic, 17; field effects as having, 95; field resources as having, 4; Foucauldian (subjectification), 16, 117; legitimation of, 98n14, 103, 109; manifestation of, 78; power of consensus, 84; power-knowledge, 16, 109; quest for, 97; relation to sexual capital, 48, 158; relation of sexual desire to, 16, 17, 47, 48, 55n9, 72, 106; symbolic, 4, 107; Weberian (coercion), 16

practice (Bourdieu), xiii, 3, 12–14, 47, 54n1, 64, 123, 125, 126

psychology: approaches to sexuality in, viii, ix, 12, 54n5, 55n9, 56n14, 119–20; concept of libido in, 105, 106; influence on feminist theory, 120; Pierre Bourdieu's views on, 20, 105–6, 109–11, 113, 115, 122n7; relation to sociology, 105

queer theory, viii, xiv, xv, 16

race. *See* ethnicity/race

rational action theory, ix, 12, 110, 146, 183

reflexivity: importance to sociology, 104;

for Pierre Bourdieu, 104–5, 120; with regard to one's within field theory, 186

religion: relation to sexual preference structures, 10; waning influence of, 7

romantic narrative, 87, 98n9

San Francisco: Leather Pride Week in, 98; Silicon Valley, 5; Tenderloin district, 5, 57; urban gay center in, 2. *See also* Mabel's

scripts: cultural, viii, xi; gendered, 41–42, 64, 68; mobilization of, 64; rule following, 12; sexual, xiii, xv, 68, 188

selection of sexual partner: double standard of aging and, 8; effect of ethnicity/race on, 21, 26, 31, 47, 137–38, 148, 166–68; effect of sexual status on, 8, 22, 25, 51, 55n7, 175; as gendered, 8, 34–36, 152, 155–56; relation to sexual stratification system, 7, 31, 61, 62, 66; relevance of economic/cultural capital for, 32, 34–36, 43, 85; as varying by sexual orientation, 10, 38, 65, 66, 67. *See also* dating; marriage; partnering; sexual relations

self-presentation: as constructed, 94; examples of, 42, 92, 93; explanation of, viii; gendered, 59, 64, 65, 68, 94, 96n1, 98n11; norms of, 138, 142; typologization based on, 137. *See also* fronts

sex: as biological, xiii, xiv, 19, 120; as psychological, 120. *See also* gender

sexology, 16, 20, 109, 111–13, 115, 119

sexual arena, 5, 6, 14, 50, 86, 146, 177, 184. *See also* social arena

sexual body, 112

sexual capital: actors' assessments of, 20, 29, 31, 32, 39, 51, 56n10, 91, 125, 134, 140; as an aggregation of individual desires, 18, 48; as the basis for sexual strategies, 31, 40, 51, 85, 146, 155, 157, 166; currencies of, 34–35, 50, 53, 86, 90, 91, 142; definition of, 15–16, 48, 145, 146; as determined by affect, 33, 47, 49, 140; as determined by age, 138, 140; as determined by physical appearance, 33, 49, 138, 140; as determined by sociocultural style, 49–50; distribution of, 16, 30–31, 50–51, 124, 151; as field dependent, 21, 29, 48–49, 145, 146; function/

sexual capital (*continued*)
    effects of, 28, 146; individual desires'
    discordance with, 39, 48; as intercon-
    vertible to other forms of capital, 13,
    16, 48, 59, 110, 119; investing in, 146,
    154, 167; as part of a field of struggle,
    16; as property of a field, 16, 48, 49, 165;
    as property of an individual, 16, 48, 49,
    165; as racialized, 140, 148, 161; rela-
    tion to circuits, 126, 130, 140–41; rela-
    tion to configuration of sexual sites, 31,
    167; relation to field formation, 72, 76,
    77, 78, 81, 97n7; relation to sexual fields
    theory, 16, 19, 26, 27, 48, 72, 184; rela-
    tion to status in a sexual social struc-
    ture, 21, 28, 40, 48, 137; as saturated
    with culturally constructed meaning,
    56n14, 168–69. *See also* capital; capital
    portfolio; erotic capital
sexual decisionmaking, 165, 167, 171, 175,
    177, 182–85
sexual desire: cultural and historical rep-
    resentations transposed on, 47, 166–68;
    first-order, 179; perceived desirability,
    17, 18, 39, 42, 47, 51, 62, 151; second-or-
    der, 179
sexual fields: as accommodating preexist-
    ing desires, 22, 36, 39, 43, 55n9, 72, 77;
    as affecting self-perception of actors, 6,
    9, 33; compared to other fields, 4; com-
    plexities of, 18, 34; crossing between, 3,
    48, 148; as decoupled from institutions
    of social control, 4, 10; different links to
    power, 17; distinguishing between, 28,
    29, 48, 94, 124, 141, 145, 168–69; effects
    of, 6, 14, 18, 22, 36, 39–40, 55n9, 64, 95;
    effects on nonactive field players, 9, 28,
    44; as embodied, 16; evolution of, 18,
    19, 36, 50, 60, 91, 175; explanation of,
    vii, xi, xiii, 27, 123; as a field of force, 5,
    14–15, 19, 28, 73, 76, 77, 78, 80, 82; as a
    field of struggle, 4, 5, 14–15, 19, 28, 32,
    82–83, 86, 87, 89, 90; as founded in de-
    sire, xii; gravitational pull of, 6, 19, 28,
    172; high level of specialization of, xiii,
    xiv, 5, 10–11, 14, 25, 87, 105, 135; inter-
    subjective assessment of position in, 20,
    28, 42, 44, 51, 58, 62, 82, 86, 87, 126, 140;
    as materialized in physical/virtual sites,
6, 27, 33, 68, 69, 123; parameters of, 3,
    6, 31–32, 38, 58, 59, 60; propensity for
    typologization within, 29, 32, 50, 54n6,
    84, 135, 137; questioning the hierarchal
    nature of, 19, 72, 82, 84–86, 88; recog-
    nition of, 44; relation to circuits, 20, 28,
    124; relation to different types of capi-
    tal, 16, 34–35, 48–49; relation to sexual
    niches, 27; rewards of, 13, 15, 48; self-
    selection into, 36; as shaped by social/
    geographic context, 9, 21–22, 28, 33, 34,
    43, 74–75, 135, 148, 165; as shaping at-
    traction/desire, 15, 18, 19, 22, 23n5, 38–
    42, 46, 72, 76, 77; social organization
    of, vii, 7, 25, 30–32, 47, 89, 125, 145, 176;
    structural configurations of, 12, 125;
    three senses of, 72; as two sided, 34,
    46, 54n6, 59. *See also* field formation;
    fields; horizontal differentiation; verti-
    cal stratification
sexual fields theory: approach taken by, xv,
    17–18; in contrast to market metaphors,
    71; contributions/advantages of, xv,
    11, 14, 15, 20, 22, 48, 54, 76; core con-
    cepts of, 14–17, 26–28; emphasis on the
    social/collective level, xiv, 14, 15, 16, 26;
    future directions for research in, 90–
    91; importance of attending to histori-
    cal contexts, 74–75; levels of analysis,
    51–53, 54n2; as linking social structures
    in sexual fields to individual sexual
    scripts, xiii; in relation to Bourdieusian
    field theory, 4, 5, 12, 14, 22, 125; in rela-
    tion to queer theory, xv, 16; in relation
    to social constructivism, xiv, xv; as a
    tool for conceptualizing society/social
    life, vii, xiii
sexual hierarchy, 7, 30, 31, 33, 72, 82, 83,
    168, 177
sexuality: as an autonomous field, 10, 20,
    25, 43, 102, 105, 106, 108, 112, 114, 119,
    121, 146, 175; expert discourse about,
    16, 109, 112, 113, 120; governance/reg-
    ulation of, xiv, 7, 53, 106, 111, 120, 122;
    legitimate exercise of, xv, 99, 106, 110,
    112, 116, 117, 120, 146
sexuality studies, vii
sexually transmitted infections: concern
    about, 7; relation to low sexual status,

51; relation to sexual fields, 52, 53. *See also* HIV/AIDS

sexual marginalization: of gay men, 142; when moving across fields, 148; of white women in Shanghai, 145, 150–51, 154, 156, 163–65

sexual mobility, 144, 145, 148, 164

sexual niches, 27, 130, 136

sexual norms: of attractiveness, 18, 43; Bourdieusian view of, 117; familial hegemony over, 116; influence of law on, 122; influence of networks on, 125; liberalization of, 7, 108, 111; of marital fidelity, 8; relation to circuits, 142; relation to desire, ix; relevance of field theory to, x

sexual preference structures, xiv, 8, 11, 35

sexual relations: casual, 8, 9, 61, 68, 143, 146, 165, 184; commercial, 58, 63, 68; recreational, 68. *See also* dating; Mabel's; partnering; selection of sexual partner

sexual revolution, 7, 102, 111, 118

sexual risk taking, 10, 51, 126, 131. *See also* HIV/AIDS; sexually transmitted infections

sexual sites: analyzing, 54n2; crossing between, 3; horizontal segregation of players across, 136–37; relation to circuits, 21, 28, 123, 124, 126; relation to collective sexual life, 5, 26, 27, 50, 135; relation to economic/sexual capital, 35; relation to sexual fields, vii, 27, 29, 72, 123; relation to structures of desire, 38; sexual status order particular to, 29, 34, 50; vertical stratification within, 137–38

sexual socialization: as assimilation, 39, 45, 51; as imitation, viii, 39, 40; as internalization, 38, 39, 40, 67, 78, 94

sexual status: achievement of, 30, 47, 103; as context specific, 48–49, 50, 53, 125, 130, 145; effects of high sexual status, 15, 21, 28, 31, 39, 47, 51, 133, 138; effects of low sexual status, 18, 21, 28, 31, 46, 51, 133, 166; geographic mobility and, 21, 164–65; recognition of, 6, 33, 39, 44, 134; relevance of capital portfolios to, 17, 34, 146, 147; status discordance, 39;

48; status distinctions/markers and, 15, 44, 84, 87, 132–33

sexual status order: association with sexual sites, 3, 29, 31, 50, 54, 138–40; formulation of position within, 6, 26, 31, 33, 39, 44, 56n10, 125, 134; functions of, 7, 15, 44–45, 54n1; inescapability of, 125, 134; interactional basis of, 30, 39, 48, 55n6, 126, 131, 141; objective/subjective elements of, 18, 69; relation to structures of desire, 37, 41, 43, 44; variability of, 31–32, 53, 125

sexual strategy: Bourdieu's study of, 107; gender fluidity/masculinization as a, 161, 165, 166; geographic mobilization as a, 165; moral reorientation as a, 154–55, 156–57, 164; racial adaptability as a, 163, 166; relation to perceived field position, 31, 33, 50, 53, 54, 135, 146, 164; relation to socially structured space, 167–68; resignation as a, 164; resistance as a, 160, 164

sexual stratification system: approaches to, 4, 53–54, 55n9, 112, 124, 146; awareness of position within, 2; explanation of, 2, 3, 15, 16, 51, 124, 147. *See also* sexual hierarchy

sexual system, xiv

sexual types: definition of, 29, 137; discerning between, 34, 135; examples of, 33, 84, 136, 159, 162; identification with, 33, 45; labeling of, 18, 33; as not mutually exclusive, 33, 137; as organizing/segregating actors into social groups, 29–30, 32, 36, 135–37, 141; propensity for typologization, 32, 135; ranking of, 84; relation to sexual capital, 50

Shanghai: as an advantaged playing field for Western men, 21, 143–44, 147; boom in overseas investment/trade/tourism, 143; expatriate sexual field, 160, 162, 164; gendered perceptions/experiences of sexual fields in, 144, 148, 159, 167–68; heterosexual field in, 21, 158–59; marginalization of Western women in, 21, 145, 150, 153; racialized perceptions/experiences of sexual fields in, 144, 148, 166–68, 169; relations between Western and Asian men/women

Shanghai (*continued*)
in, 17, 33, 151, 152, 167; reputation
of, 143; sense of sexual threat among
Western women in, 156–57; as a sexual purgatory for Western women, 144;
sexual strategies of Western women in,
150, 154–55, 157, 159, 161, 163, 164–66,
168; Western women's contradictory racial mobility in, 144; Western women's
views of Asian men in, 151–52, 160–61,
163; Western women's views of Asian
women in, 151, 153, 162. *See also* China;
ethnicity/race; ethnosexual contact
zone; West, the
social arena, x, 3, 12. *See also* sexual
arena
social constructivism, xiv, xv
social learning theory, viii, 12, 55n9
social networks, 6, 20, 21, 26–28, 48, 123,
125, 141–42, 144
social status, 31, 55n6, 113, 144
social stratification, 19, 34, 43
sociology: approaches to sexuality within,
viii, xiii, xv, 23n4, 141, 146; carnal sociology, 185; contribution of sexual fields
theory to, 11, 12, 14–15 18, 22, 23, 51,
165, 171; importance of sociological reflexivity, 20, 104; importance of studying sexual stratification for, 15, 53–54;
study of deviant sexuality within, xiv;
as theorizing the sexual with market
metaphors, 71
*State Nobility, The* (Bourdieu), 115, 117
Stonewall riots, 41, 42, 79
structures of desire: apprehending sexual
status order, 18, 43, 44; definition of,
14–15, 27; examples of, 2–3, 10, 14–15,
32, 37, 41, 45–46; functions of, 14, 15,
28, 38, 43, 44, 47; as governing fictions,
44, 46; as a learning process, viii, 47;
materialization of, 37, 54n2; as molding
social actors, 43; as narrowly defined,
11, 31, 138, 148; as an ordering of sexual
behavior, vii, 47; as an ordering of sexual desire, 27, 37, 43, 44, 45, 72; as relational, 41; relation to erotic habitus, 38;
relation to sexual capital, 28, 48; in relation to sexual fields theory, 15, 26; relation to two-sided fields, 29, 32; rele-

vance to different types of capital, 43;
as site specific, 14, 31, 48
structuring structures, 174
subcultures: analysis of, xiii, xiv, xv, 29; application of Bourdieusian to, 83; differences between fields and, 83, 85; relevance of sexual fields theory to, xiii;
within a field, 26, 137
sublimation, xii

tearooms, 32, 141
theory of social action, vii, viii, ix, 172,
187n1
tiers of desirability: at the bottom, 48; at
Mabel's, 60, 67, 68; positioning one's
self within, 6; recalibration of, 60; relation to circuits, 126, 135; relation to sexual field, 59, 82; sexual actors stratified
between/within, 29, 30; at the top, 31;
as well-defined, 31
Toronto: gay sexual district in, 40, 130, 131,
140; LGBTQ community in, 21; study
of sexual health in, 21; Toronto Pride,
123, 126; Yorkville, 31
Toronto Pride Survey: findings based on
age, 130; findings based on ethnicity, 130; identification of circuits, 124,
127–30, 139, 140, 141; methodology,
126–27
trans women: desirability of Asian
trans women, 59, 64; ease of sexual
interaction with, 63; flattering attention from, 62–63; front/bodywork by,
58–59, 64–65, 68; interactions with
each other, 57, 59; men's interactions
with, 19, 57–58, 60, 61; men's relation
to penises of, 65–66; in relation to ciswomen ("real" women), 59, 61–62, 63,
64, 66; sexual capital among, 59, 60;
tiers of desirability among, 59. *See also*
Mabel's

vectors, 172, 173, 176, 177, 185, 187n2
vertical stratification: example of, 30, 136,
176; explanation of, 30, 32–33, 137; factors influencing, 30, 31, 32; features
of, 32–33; relationship to sexual fields,
29; relationship to structures of desire,
30, 52

violence: leathermen's experiences of, 75–77; physical violence, 107; sexual violence, 51, 60; soft violence, 107; symbolic violence, 105, 107, 116

West, the: emasculation of Asian men in, 148, 167; emergence of gay male enclaves in, 7; erotic worlds unique to, 6; features of sexuality in, 11, 146; Internet linking cities in, 6; norms in, 151; plurality of desire in, xiii; rituals of courtship of, 118, 154, 158; sexual mores, 158–59, 164; Western philosophy, 172; Western privilege, 166